Ed Stetzer is a cultural navigator helping us walk faithfully in the midst of this cultural storm.

MATT CHANDLER
Lead pastor, The Village Church; author of *The Explicit Gospel*

Once again, Ed has analyzed a troublesome trend in our culture and given us solid advice on how to respond to it in a Christlike manner. If you've ever wondered how we can share the love of Jesus in the midst of all the shouting and division, you need to read this book immediately.

RICK WARREN
Senior pastor, Saddleback Church; author of *The Purpose Driven Life*

From political campaigns to nightly news, from clickbait headlines to social media, we exist in such a perpetual state of outrage that escape seems impossible. But with thorough research, compelling anecdotes, and clarity of both vision and communication, Ed Stetzer offers a way out that is not only possible but–for the Christian–imperative.

KAREN SWALLOW PRIOR
Author of *On Reading Well: Finding the Good Life through Great Books* and *Fierce Convictions: The Extraordinary Life of Hannah More–Poet, Reformer, Abolitionist*

Sometimes it seems that everyone is angry today. Division and strife are everywhere. In *Christians in the Age of Outrage*, Ed Stetzer lays out the problems in the culture and in the church, but then gives us a God-honoring path to bring our best even when the world is at its worst.

BRYAN LORITTS
Author of *Insider Outsider: My Journey as a Stranger in White Evangelicalism and My Hope for Us All*

It's an angry world right now, and we need a grace-filled and gospel-driven response. My friend Ed Stetzer shows us how to walk through the minefields of disagreement in winsome and God-honoring ways.

SAMUEL RODRIGUEZ
President of the National Hispanic Christian Leadership Conference

CHRISTIANS IN THE AGE OF OUTRAGE

Christians
in the Age *of*
Outrage

HOW TO BRING OUR BEST
WHEN THE WORLD IS AT ITS WORST

ED STETZER

The nonfiction imprint of
Tyndale House Publishers, Inc.

Visit Tyndale online at www.tyndale.com.

Visit Tyndale Momentum online at www.tyndalemomentum.com.

Visit Ed Stetzer's website at edstetzer.com.

Christians in the Age of Outrage: How to Bring Our Best When the World Is at Its Worst

Published in association with the literary agency of Mark Sweeney and Associates, Naples, FL 34113.

For information about special discounts for bulk purchases, please contact Tyndale House Publishers at csresponse@tyndale.com, or call 1-800-323-9400.

Library of Congress Cataloging-in-Publication Data
Names: Stetzer, Ed, author.
Title: Christians in the age of outrage : how to bring our best when the world is at its worst / Ed Stetzer.
Description: Carol Stream, Illinois : Tyndale House Publishers, Inc., 2018. | Includes bibliographical references.
Identifiers: LCCN 2018024370 | ISBN 9781496433619 (hc) | ISBN 9781496433626 (sc)
Subjects: LCSH: Christianity and culture. | Anger–Religious aspects–Christianity. | Violence–Religious aspects–Christianity.
Classification: LCC BR115.C8 S734 2018 | DDC 261.0973–dc23 LC record available at https://lccn.loc.gov/2018024370

Printed in the United States of America

24	23	22	21	20	19	18
7	6	5	4	3	2	1

To Rick Warren, who taught me
much about engaging culture well

Contents

Welcome to the Age of Outrage

"YOU'RE A LIAR."

"No, *you* are."

Billy is a jerk. Billy and I grew up on the same street in Levittown, New York, and I remember this thought flying through my head just before he and I got into another one of our countless fights. I've edited out the expletives–it was New York, after all–but every fight always ended the same: with each of us yelling at the other and storming off. We were friends because we were neighbors, but mostly we fought. As kids, that's how most arguments go. Yelling. Fighting. Insults. Running away.

Eventually I lost touch with Billy. If I saw him today, we might still fight, but I imagine there would be fewer expletives and tears. After all, we've both grown up. But when I look around at the way our world deals with conflict today, I realize culture has not.

Suddenly the go-to move of politicians and journalists has become "You're a liar," followed by the rejoinder "No, *you* are." We're bombarded with this level of discourse every day.

And it's filtered down (or maybe it filtered up) throughout the culture. Facebook is a cesspool of conspiracy theories, straw-man arguments, and schoolyard bullying. We have reached the point where the comment sections of major newspapers are a greater testament to the depravity of man than all the theology of the

Reformers put together. Many publishers have removed comments from below their online articles so the vitriol will end.

These arguments have a cumulative effect, with each successive interaction ratcheting up the outrage. Even those rare instances of well-intentioned and reasonable discussion eventually fall victim to misunderstanding and offense. In these cases, I often remember Godwin's Law: "As an online discussion grows longer, the probability of a comparison involving Hitler approaches one."[1] In other words, people eventually start comparing others to Hitler. And just like that, we are off to the races of anger, insults, and division.

Outrage from Christians

Lest we get on our high horses about all those bad, angry people out there, we need to recognize that outrage often comes from Christians. During his fifteen minutes of fame, Joshua Feuerstein started the 2015 Starbucks Red Cup controversy. Soon people were saying that Christians were upset, though I saw only one person–Joshua Feuerstein–truly outraged. He posted a Facebook message saying, "Starbucks REMOVED CHRISTMAS from their cups because they hate Jesus."[2] He also tagged media to attract attention. Without fail, the outrage cycle began.

Of course, Starbucks denied the accusation, assured worried Christians everywhere they were welcome to say "Merry Christmas" to their hearts' content, and insisted that the company did not hate Christmas. Can you imagine the conversation in the Starbucks boardroom? Did they say, "Those Christians are fair-minded, gracious, and thoughtful"? I am guessing not.

The reality was that Feuerstein tried to use Christian outrage to raise his platform. The news and opinion website Vox explained,

> Feuerstein's new Starbucks outrage video might be the
> biggest of his social media career. It's a rant stemming
> from a conservative Christian belief that there is a "war

on Christmas," and that each year during the holidays, Christians are persecuted by companies.[3]

Of course, it would be interesting (and maybe even outrageous) if it were true. But Vox goes on to say,

> Feuerstein's most blatant untruth, and the reason for all the current furor about the 2015 red cup, is the implication that Starbucks at one time printed the word "Christmas" on its holiday cups and is now being stifled or stifling itself from doing so. In the past six years, Starbucks, which doesn't identify itself as a Christian company, has *never* put the words "Merry Christmas" on its holiday cups—instead, it's used wintry and vaguely holiday-esque imagery and language, including ornaments that say things like "joy" or "hope," snowmen, and holly.[4]

So literally we can show that what Feuerstein said is not true. But outrage overwhelms truth. I saw some people defending Feuerstein by pointing out that there were other things that Starbucks did, or that there were bigger issues at play. (I'd ground my daughters for responding to facts with such misdirection.) But the outrage of the culture overwhelms the truth of the moment. And when it does, it hurts our witness.

You'd think that someone had broken into churches and desecrated the altars if you looked at some Facebook feeds. And of course, the news reports said everyone was outraged, but I think it was Feuerstein and a few friends. And that's really all it was. Starbucks never put *Jesus* or *Christmas* on their cups. They once had snowmen and some trees before going to plain red. So Starbucks hates Jesus because they now have cups without snowflakes?

These kinds of controversies are so frustrating! This was a foolish fight on a nonsensical issue. When outraged Christians feed media outlets with stories that make Christians look foolish, that hurts the gospel. It adds to the perception that Christians are rage-addicted snowflakes and, more important, distracts Christians from their mission. That's what fake controversies and unwarranted anger do.

No, Starbucks did not hate Jesus, but some folks sure seem to enjoy embarrassing his followers. And by the way, Starbucks employees were never told they could not say Merry Christmas. But that's not their job anyway–that's our job. It's the Christian's job to tell people about Jesus, not the barista who may be Jewish, secular, or whatever.

Don't get outraged at things that don't matter.

Outrage toward Christians

Yet outrage can just as easily be directed toward Christians by a hostile world intent on shaming and attacking rather than engaging.

In early 2018, the online publication *Pitchfork* turned out this clickbaiting headline: "Coachella Co-Owner's Latest Charitable Filing Shows Deep Anti-LGBTQ Ties."[5] Coachella is a music festival that is connected to AEG, an entertainment company owned by Philip Anschutz, who is an evangelical Christian. The story listed five of the "deep anti-LGBTQ" organizations: The Navigators, Dare 2 Share Ministries, the Center for Urban Renewal and Education, Movieguide Awards, and Young Life. The biggest gift among these was to Young Life ($185,000; June 21 and November 15, 2016), which was pilloried for their policy that "anyone 'sexually active outside of a heterosexual marriage relationship' shouldn't work or volunteer for the organization."[6]

In other words, Young Life holds the traditional view of marriage that has been a foundational component of Christian theology for centuries and is held today by most evangelical (as well as Roman Catholic, Orthodox, and other) organizations. Even so, the publication made no attempts at dialogue, gave no empathy or consideration as to why these views are important or nuanced. Just blanket insults aimed at provoking division.

Outrage has no time for dialogue, and it won't be distracted by nuance or even truth.

Get the pitchforks, *Pitchfork*.

Why This Outrageous Book?

This is a book about outrage. It's an acknowledgment that our world, or at least our part of it, seems awash in anger, division, and hostility. Outrage is all around, so we have to decide how to walk through this. We are living in a day—and this is indeed our moment—when we need to live like Christ, as gospel Christians in the midst of shouting, anger, and hatred. And it's going to get worse.

To be sure, there is a lot in this world that is outrage inducing. Terrorism, sex trafficking and exploitation, systemic racism, illegal immigration, child poverty, opioid addiction . . . and the list goes on. These issues deserve a measure of outrage, don't they? They certainly deserve our anger.

And this is part of the problem. What do we do when the anger becomes too much? When our righteous indignation at injustice morphs into something completely different? How do we know when righteous anger has made the turn into unbridled outrage? These questions do not have easy answers, but they deserve our consideration if we want to be faithful disciples of Christ.

This book is roughly composed of three sections. In the first, I outline what I think are the two primary catalysts for our outrage. It is crucial to grasp the *what* and *why* of our indignation if we Christians are going to have victory over it in our own lives and are to engage effectively in this world. In this respect, we need to understand not only what causes outrage in this culture but how Christians have contributed to, if not led the way in, perpetuating it.

The first cause of our outrage stems from the increasing polarization of American society, in terms of both religion and politics. The second cause lies in the unprecedented advance of technology that has completely altered almost every facet of our daily lives in less than a generation. (Nobody had an iPhone on June 28,

2007, but the world was inalterably changed the next day, when the iPhone was unveiled. Now, no one–my daughters tell me, *no one*–can live without a smartphone.)

After examining the causes of outrage, this book considers four lies that reinforce and deepen our world's anger. These include not only lies that this world tells us, but more important, the lies that we as believers tell ourselves. As we'll see, some believers react to cultural shifts with intense fury, but for too long, the majority of Christians have shrunk back. Either out of fear or shame at the way some Christians engage poorly with their opponents, these believers have adopted silence and retreat as their default state.

In the book's third section, I propose ways that Christians can counteract the outrage in their lives and this world by being intentional about developing a Christ-centered worldview, living as God's ambassadors, loving others in a winsome way, and engaging thoughtfully with others, both online and face-to-face. In other words, your online life needs to be submitted to Christ just as your IRL experience should be. (For those who don't know, IRL is what the cool kids say when they mean "in real life.") But the fact is, online life is real life as well–just with better-looking versions of ourselves as our profile pics. We will talk about how to live for Christ in all contexts.

Christians in the Age of Outrage was written in consultation with a national survey of evangelicals and non-evangelicals by the Billy Graham Center Institute, in partnership with LifeWay Research. Relevant findings from the survey appear at the beginning of each chapter to help give context to the issues and challenges I address. For transparency and clarity, I have included the relevant questions and data for each chapter's opening points in the appendix that begins on page 283.

For the study, LifeWay Research surveyed approximately three thousand Americans in three groupings: Americans with evangelical beliefs, Americans who self-identify as evangelical, and non-evangelical Americans.[7] Unless specified otherwise, references to evangelicals in this study include only those individuals who are evangelical by belief. To determine if a respondent fit the profile of an evangelical by belief, LifeWay Research asked about their level of agreement with four separate statements:

1. The Bible is the highest authority for what I believe.
2. It is very important for me personally to encourage non-Christians to trust Jesus Christ as their Savior.
3. Jesus Christ's death on the cross is the only sacrifice that could remove the penalty of my sin.
4. Only those who trust in Jesus Christ alone as their Savior receive God's free gift of eternal salvation.

Respondents had to cite strong agreement with all four statements to be categorized as being evangelical by belief.

Instead of Outrage, Engage

This book is intended to help Christians move from contributing to the age of outrage to effectively engaging it with the gospel. I'm convinced that this is, indeed, one of the greatest challenges of our day. Now to be fair, our challenges are a lot less threatening than those faced in previous centuries—there are no stakes upon which we might be impaled. But the stakes are still high. They impact how and if we can engage this moment well for the cause of Christ and his Kingdom.

I don't hold any punches in calling Christians to think critically on how we have contributed to the problem. At the same time, Christians are not defined by the crazy and caustic representatives we see on cable news. All over the world, the majority of Christians are already bringing their best in building the Kingdom of God. While we need to face head-on the areas where we need to grow, we must also reject the self-loathing all too common among American Christians.

This book is not just a complaint about outrage (being outraged about outrage seems ironic, eh?). It's not just a description of the outrage we face today. It's also a prescription for how then we might live in a way that advances Christ's message by listening respectfully as well as speaking out.

We see the importance of this give-and-take in the story of Caleb Kaltenbach.

Kaltenbach found himself in the spotlight when his tweet about finding a Bible in Costco's fiction section went viral. Leading with the headline "Costco–The Bible Is Fiction," Fox News promoted the idea that Kaltenbach had uncovered a conspiracy against Christians and the Bible. Kaltenbach was even quoted as characterizing the store's decision to group the Bible with fiction as "bizarre."[8]

Within minutes, the story was picked up by the *Drudge Report*, and Christians quickly worked themselves into an outraged lather over the perceived insult.

How dare Costco!

This is a slap in the face to all Christians!

Boycott!

Suddenly a labeling error that listed Bibles as fiction had become a covert theological statement on the very nature of Scripture. What likely happens hundreds of times in bookstores every day had become an insidious spark that unleashed Christian outrage against Costco.

This despite the fact that a company spokesman insisted the CEO of Costco was a devout Catholic.

This despite attempts to quell the outrage with *reasonable* explanations of a simple mistake.

This despite Christian leaders reminding followers to exercise discernment and grace.

When the "Christian outrage machine" kicks into full gear, it becomes a runaway train. It seems the world has nothing on those who profess Christ when it comes to outrage.

When I noticed that Caleb Kaltenbach follows me on Twitter, I reached out to him about what had happened. It turned out that he is one of those reasonable, levelheaded Christians trying to fight against the outrage. As I learned more about his story, I realized Kaltenbach is actually a picture of the non-outraged Christian.

But hey, don't let that slow down the outrage train.

As he recounted the events that led to his tweet, Kaltenbach insisted that he thought the label was an interesting if not amusing mistake. He posted a photo of the Costco Bible, never imagining that he would be approached by the press for an interview or that it would balloon into a full-scale onslaught of Christian outrage. He wasn't angry, offended, stunned, shocked, upset, or concerned for the faith of impressionable Christian children everywhere. In the news interview, Kaltenbach tried to convey this mentality as best he could while at the same time taking the opportunity to point people to Jesus. He even said, "I do not think that Costco did this intentionally. I don't believe there's an evil mastermind genius working at Costco to undermine the authority of Scripture."[9]

Unfortunately, a narrative of outrage is too tempting to pass up, and the story quickly got away from Kaltenbach. In the wake of the story, he tried to make his intentions clear:

> It was never my intention to crusade against Costco or
> their CEO (who is a devout Catholic). I'm not on the cul-
> tural warfare path by any means. I believe that if this story
> gets summed up by label stickers then the opportunity
> was missed and a shadow has been cast over the Gospel.
> If however, we can have good conversation and get some
> people thinking about God, then there just might be a party
> in heaven soon (Lk. 15:7).[10]

Kaltenbach did his best to seize the opportunity to engage both sides of the outrage with the gospel and to challenge their assumptions about others. Some people listened, but others merely shouted him down. Costco apologized for the clerical error, but few if any Christians reciprocated by expressing regret for their reaction or even perceived they'd done anything wrong. To them, outrage worked.

But the story doesn't end here. Kaltenbach navigated the fields of outrage effectively, in part, because he had experience faithfully confronting a wave of hostility. He was raised by a same-sex couple, the two lesbian women he knew as his mothers. Then he met Jesus, and his entire worldview changed. After he sorted through what his new faith meant for his view of human sexuality, his parents eventually disowned him. In his book *Messy Grace: How a Pastor with Gay Parents Learned to Love Others without Sacrificing Conviction*, Kaltenbach winsomely outlines why Christians have struggled to demonstrate grace to the LGBTQ community even as we hold fast to orthodox teachings on homosexuality.

Kaltenbach has faced some outrage for his views, as you might imagine. So I asked him why he is on a mission to promote dialogue between the two sides. He explained, "I've read the end of the story. The last chapter of Revelation says, *God wins.* Because God is in control and will redeem all things, I can be calm, bold, and gracious as I share the gospel."

Kaltenbach has seen the outrage from both Christians and non-Christians. He's been shot at from both sides of the outrage battle . . . but he's walked the field in the middle, between the mainstream cultural highway and the increasingly distant side road where we live. He's sought to show and share the love of Jesus.

And both women who raised him now follow Jesus. I imagine Kaltenbach, those two women, and Jesus would want us to be winsome as we walk out our faith as well.

That's where we are going from here: We will look at the moment we are in and the mission we are on in the age of outrage.

Let's jump in.

PART 1

Why the Age of Outrage?

Everyone can be destructive and negative. It's easy to stand on the sidelines and shout out what's wrong with a situation and why everyone and everything is bad or wrong.

And pithy words are easy to come up with. I saw someone's post on Facebook after a school shooting. It was a cartoonlike graphic with these captions:

"Dear God, why do you allow such violence in school?"
—A concerned student

"Dear concerned student, I'm not allowed in school."—God

Actually, for the record, God is everywhere. And so are stupid T-shirts. But it is easier to be angry and pithy than to be Christlike and on mission. Such outraged approaches are self-destructive. Some of them are even contrary to what God calls us to as leaders of his church. We need to be constructive, offering Christians a vision for how to navigate outrage and be more effective in showing and sharing the love of Christ.

And speaking of schools, God is indeed at work in some surprising ways there. For example, Katie Beiler is a literacy liaison for Pequea Valley School District in Lancaster County, Pennsylvania. She visits families in their homes to encourage parents to read aloud and develop other habits to build their preschoolers' vocabulary and social skills. Beiler's aim is to ready young children for kindergarten—something that has been a problem in her district. Pequea Valley has been experiencing a rise in poverty, and in 2017 only 64.8 percent of third graders passed Pennsylvania's standardized English language arts test.[1] Beiler plays an essential role in ensuring that Pequea Valley preschoolers are exposed to books and language before they enter the school system.

What is unique about Katie Beiler's role is that she is employed by Grace Point Church, not Pequea Valley School District. In order to keep the balance of separation between church and state, Beiler uses a nonreligious curriculum, reports to a district official, and has a Pequea Valley identification tag. However, she also gives monthly updates to Grace Point's pastor. Currently, Pequea Valley has a $45,000 grant that applies to Beiler's position, which helps offset the cost to Grace Point Church, but when the grant ends the church will shoulder the entire $70,000 annual cost. This program is so important to Beiler and to the entire church community because they want to be, in the words of lead pastor Tim Rogers, "a transforming presence in the town square."[2]

Yet that's just not how it's done in most places. Far too often we make snarky references on Facebook rather than engage in Christlike ways, as Grace Point Church has done. But before we get to where we want to be, we have to acknowledge where we are now.

Good thinking requires good diagnosis. It requires a discussion of what is wrong, how we got here, and what blind spots and behavior are feeding the problem. So part 1 of this book is necessary to lay the groundwork for the rest of the book.

Let's get out the stethoscope before we start prescribing the treatment. *But* let's not confuse diagnosis with the cure.

CHAPTER 1

Outrage Cause #1:
A Cultural Forking

- Of evangelicals with an opinion, 82 percent believe that since the 2016 presidential election, groups within the Christian church have become increasingly polarized on issues of politics.

- Of evangelicals with an opinion, 73 percent believe the 2016 presidential election revealed political divides within the Christian church that have existed for a long time.

WHEN I CAME TO WHEATON COLLEGE, I began to serve as the Billy Graham Distinguished Chair. (The chair is distinguished, not the chair holder, I assure you.)

That role, and the role at the Billy Graham Center at Wheaton, came with a key responsibility. Eventually, I was given a card that I was told I needed to carry on my person. On campus, traveling to conferences, and even on family vacation, I needed to make sure this card was always on me.

This was all part of something called "The Washington Project," a secret phrase we would use to refer to what we would do after Mr. Graham passed. (Hint: I'm not good at keeping secrets.)

But this was a serious responsibility, and I took it as such. It got to the point that I was thinking about having the card tattooed to the back of my hand.

Printed on the card were step-by-step directions to follow when Billy Graham died: the people I needed to call, the e-mails I needed to write, and the flights I needed to book. We knew that when this news finally broke, there would be a frenzy of activity. Arrangements would need to be made, interviews given, and articles published. This wasn't hype; we understood that the opportunity to celebrate the life of Billy Graham was going to be a major platform to continue the work to which he devoted his life: preaching the gospel to the world. As it turned out, his funeral was, in a sense, his last crusade, and millions tuned in.

But why? Why such an ordered procedure? Why such intensity to make sure the process happened immediately? Why such a big deal?

Because it was Billy Graham.

Non-Christians and even younger Christians today may have difficulty understanding the impact and importance of Billy Graham. After all, thousands of preachers today have their own followings, YouTube videos, and podcasts. Ask ten Christians who their favorite Christian preacher or leader is, and you will likely get ten different answers. During the second half of the twentieth century, however, the vast majority of Christians gave the same answer: Billy Graham.

When obituary after obituary called Graham "America's pastor," it wasn't an exaggeration. To many Americans, including presidents, Pulitzer Prize–winning journalists, and award-winning actors, Graham *was* their only connection to Christianity. He *was* their pastor.

Graham seemingly walked effortlessly across the cultural divisions that proved insurmountable to so many other leaders. From Karl Barth to Carl Henry, from Martin Luther King Jr. to Richard Nixon, from Johnny Cash to Queen Elizabeth, Graham won friends among communities and traditions, and in doing so, he proved to be one of the most unifying forces in American life.

To grasp the scale, consider that in Gallup's yearly poll listing the ten most admired men, Graham appeared sixty-one times between 1948 and 2017. For comparison, among other men the one who came closest was Ronald Reagan, who appeared thirty-one times. Queen Elizabeth came closest overall; she has appeared forty-nine times in the list of the ten most admired women. Among people who are not national leaders, Oprah Winfrey has appeared thirty times and Bill Gates has been on the list eighteen times. Consider how staggering that is. As much as the world loves Oprah or Bill Gates today, Graham had more than double the appearances of Oprah and was on the list three times as often as Gates.[1]

Consider also that in a recent research project we conducted at the Billy Graham Center, we asked evangelical pastors, "What two nationally known pastors have been most influential in the way you do ministry at your church?" Though Graham had been out of the spotlight for nearly two decades, he was still ninth among all pastors. He jumped to second when we asked the same pastors who the most influential pastor on their ministry in the 1990s was. More than just shaping the public perception of Christianity, Graham was (and continues to be) considered by many Christians as an example to follow, not only in their evangelistic projects but in their entire ministries.[2]

For almost seventy years, Graham had been the living embodiment of the West's religious openness. Even those who did not believe recognized in Graham a model of Christian virtue and ethics. He won begrudging respect from those we might classify as his cultural or theological opponents—a situation that seems almost impossible today.

One of the major causes for the age of outrage is that this religious and cultural consensus has evaporated. Graham's death in February 2018 was not the beginning of this change but serves as an appropriate bookend to a past age. Out of the spotlight for many years, Graham's declining presence in American life parallels the decline of the consensus he forged throughout his life. Thus, the incessant need of many Christians to find "the next Billy Graham" speaks to a recognition that we have lost a unifying force within a culture that was already splintering.

When Nominals Become Nones

Baseball great Yogi Berra used to say, "When you come to a fork in the road, take it."

America did. So did Canada, the United Kingdom, and Australia. The majority of people in these nations were once vaguely Christian, but for years, those with loosely held religious beliefs have been dropping them, and as a result, the entire English-speaking Western world is becoming more secular.

Focusing on the United States for a moment may help, though similar trends are taking place across the English-speaking Western world. Most Americans, who identify as loosely Christian, are becoming less so–they are more frequently choosing "none of the above" rather than "Christian" when surveyed about their beliefs. In fact, each year about an additional one percent of Americans no longer identify as Christian.[3]

Put another way, the nominals are becoming the nones. And as they become nones, their mind-set is more aligned with secular-minded people and they have less affinity with the avowedly religious. At the same time, the percentage of the devout has remained relatively stable.[4]

The effect of this trend is that American culture is incrementally polarizing along religious lines. People are either becoming more secular or staying devout, though the biggest group is becoming more secular. This is where we meet the fork in the road: How do we engage with our faith in a culture now polarized along faith lines rather than being at least nominally Christian?

It is useful to think about culture as a river, flowing in the direction of our collective beliefs and values. Within this river, there were once three primary streams, each of which included about a quarter of the population (the other quarter being self-identified non-Christians). These three groups are

Cultural Christians: People who self-identify as Christian because they are not something else and were born in a historically Christian country. They are Christians, in their minds, because that is part of their heritage.

Congregational Christians: People at church on Christmas Eve, and maybe for the occasional wedding or funeral. Although they may not have a vibrant faith, they retain some connection to a local congregation, probably going back on Easter, for example. As a result, over the last few decades, most churches have tried to reach these people.

Convictional Christians: People who identify as Christians and are decidedly more religious. They more likely go to church regularly, live values that align with Christianity, and choose their spouses based on their faith. (According to the General Social Survey[5] and some analysis I have explained more thoroughly in *USA Today,*[6] the percentage of people in this group has remained relatively steady for the last few decades.)

While historically there have been divergences and reunions in our cultural river, the overall consensus among Americans (like most of the West) was shaped by a common Judeo-Christian belief system. Even though there was significant disparity when it came to the importance they attached to religion, all three streams shared an underlying commitment to (sometimes vaguely held) Christian beliefs and values. In essence, each group moved in the same direction. While there was a fourth stream defined by other religious traditions and/or secularism, those beliefs were outside the mainstream.

Today we are witnessing a shift in this model. About 25 percent of Americans (higher in other English-speaking countries) identify as non-Christians, either because they are another religion (Jewish, Hindu, etc.) or because they are secular (atheist, agnostic, or just "none of the above"–we call that last category the "nones.") That stream continues to expand.

At the same time, the percentage of Convictional Christians in the US population has remained generally stable. What *have* changed are the number and beliefs of Cultural and Congregational Christians. As a result of the collapse of mainline Protestantism and the growth of secularism, Convictional Christianity has incrementally moved outside the American cultural mainstream. In fact, as I explained in the *Washington Post,*[7] as the numbers of Cultural and

Congregational Christians decrease, the worldview and values of these Americans have shifted toward the secular stream and away from that of Convictional Christians.

However, the percentage who say they regularly attend church has remained relatively steady, and regular church attendance is often a marker of Convictional Christians. The graph on the following page shows regular church attendance for Protestants, which include mainline Protestant, evangelical, and historically African American churches. As you can see, attendance actually went up in 2016. (I know, I know, that's not what the doomsday stat books say, but it still is true.) And yes, some people exaggerate their church attendance. But the numbers tell us that the percentage of religious people who call themselves Christians has remained relatively steady.

So Convictional Christianity and regular church participation by its members have not substantially declined. That fact was confirmed by the release of a recent Pew Research report, which led to the Religion News Service article "Pew Study: More Americans Reject Religion, but Believers Firm in Faith"[8] and the *Christianity Today* article "Pew: Evangelicals Stay Strong as Christianity Crumbles in America."[9] That's not to say all is well, but clearly a substantial number of people still live out their self-identified Christian faith in the United States.[10]

However—and this is key—Convictional Christianity has incrementally split from the mainstream of Western culture. This has provoked anger among some Christians. Since their values and practices shaped culture for so long, they had the impression that they owned the culture in some sense. These Christians want their country back, and by that they mean they want their cultural power back. This anger can lead to hostility against those they believe have taken it, fear that this trend will continue and lead to their marginalization, and confusion as to what to do about it.

President Trump's election is a reminder that cultural Christianity remains a potent force in American politics, as he rallied many self-identified Christians who felt marginalized in this new cultural moment. Even so, those now swimming in the stream of secular thought are tempted to flex their new cultural power, though they do not yet have a clear-cut leader. In other words, people are divided and motivated to pick fights, and they consistently talk past one another. This is what happens when a culture comes to a fork in the road.

Outrage.

Among Americans:
All Protestants and non-denominationals who regularly attend church

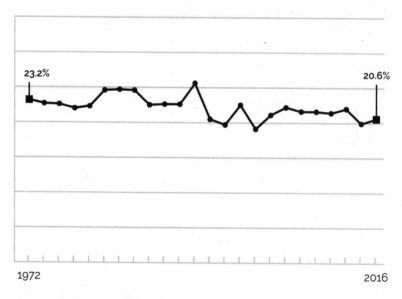

23.2%

20.6%

1972

2016

Daniel Price / Ed Stetzer (Billy Graham Center, Wheaton College) based on data within GSS materials.

Smith, Tom W., Peter Marsden, Michael Hout, and Jibum Kim. *General Social Surveys, 1972–2016* [machine-readable data file] /Principal Investigator, Tom W. Smith; Co-Principal Investigator, Peter V. Marsden; Co-Principal Investigator, Michael Hout; Sponsored by National Science Foundation. --NORC ed.-- Chicago: NORC at the University of Chicago [producer]; Storrs, CT: The Roper Center for Public Opinion Research, University of Connecticut [distributor], 2015.

1 data file (57,061 logical records) + 1 codebook (3,567p.). -- (National Data Program for the Social Sciences, No. 22).

Consider how this cultural forking has fueled the age of outrage. At its core, cultural division breeds anger by polarizing communities and teaching us to yell past one another rather than engage. There is always the temptation to view cultural power as a zero-sum game in which the only way to engage is to fight and the only outcome is a win-lose situation. In these cases, Christians have traditionally struggled with reducing their spiritual identity to merely one among many. Worse still, Christians can allow political and cultural identities, rather than Kingdom mission, to drive their engagement.

The Dark Side of Teams

A few decades ago, my wife, Donna, and I arrived in Buffalo, New York, to plant a church, our very first pastorate. Filled with the optimism and confidence of youth, we dug into the community and were greeted with open arms. There was one problem: I am not nor have I ever been a football fan. I'd be hard pressed to explain the difference between an offside and a touchdown. (I'm kidding. A touchdown is when you score from the foul line, right?) If you know anything about Buffalo, you understand that cheering for the Bills is a way of life. Once a member of the Bills mafia, always a member (just promise not to tell my new Chicago Bears neighbors about it).

One thing that sticks in my mind these many years later is how this common identity around a football team was so powerful for a young couple starting out in ministry. Football was part of how the community embraced us and how Donna and I bonded with them. We quickly learned the language (I can talk the "K-Gun" offense with the best of them) and became active members of this weird fan base that seems to transcend the political and cultural divisions raging throughout the country.

The experience reinforces just how powerful teams and group identity can be in creating community and fostering productivity and innovation. Through working on teams, individuals learn how their sacrifice and cooperation make great achievement possible.

There is something powerfully alluring about teamwork,

particularly the sense of belonging and the confidence around a goal that stems from shared convictions. We all have an innate desire to belong to a team that will give us both identity and purpose. In many ways, this is positive, providing us with support and encouragement.

Yet lost in our idolization of teams and teamwork is the recognition that the drive to belong and to forge community has a dark side as well. There is an inherent danger that the bonds created by a shared belonging and identity can often compel individuals to behavior and attitudes that would otherwise be unthinkable.

Herein lies the danger: Teams have a tendency to cultivate devotion to both their collective objective and to one another at the expense of other teams. In other words, our sense of "sameness" or solidarity around a common identity and mission inevitably conflicts with other groups. In something trivial like sports, this is obvious: In order for your team to win, the other team needs to lose.

MIT professor Harold Isaacs was one of the first who explored this mentality of group identity in politics, arguing that underlying almost all political change was the engagement between competing group identities.[11]

More than even demonizing other people, the creation of groups can lead us to excuse the behavior of those in our own camp. In one study out of the United Kingdom, researchers observed how university students responded to smelling sweaty T-shirts, some of which displayed their university's logo and others which carried the logo of a different university. In two studies that measured both self-reported disgust and observable metrics of disgust, the researchers noticed that the students were noticeably less put off by the smell of those T-shirts they thought had been worn by students from their own university.[12] Students showed a willingness to put up with their sweaty classmates because they were on their team, yet those students showed reluctance to extend the same grace toward outsiders. In other words, whether we view people as being on our team has a direct bearing on how we perceive and interact with them, regardless of whether their behavior is the same as those in other groups.

From teamwork to tribalism

This issue of *polarization* (when communities sharply disagree about values, beliefs, and opinions) has recently jumped into hyperdrive–particularly along partisan lines. A 2017 Pew Research study said tribalism has increased significantly in the United States since 1994. In a survey of American attitudes across ten measures, Pew tracked responses according to political metrics, along with other divisive indicators such as race, education, age, and gender. What it found was that where other indicators stayed the same, the average gap between the views of Republicans and Democrats on fundamental issues increased from 15 to 36 percentage points between 1994 and 2017. For instance, in 1994, 32 percent of Democrats and 30 percent of Republicans said that immigrants' hard work and talents strengthen our country. By 2017, the share of people from both parties who agreed with that statement had increased. However, the share of Democrats holding that view had jumped to 84 percent, while only 42 percent of Republicans now said that immigrants strengthen, rather than burden, our country.[13] A parallel 2017 study at Pew revealed that not only is society becoming more polarized, but that an "overwhelming majority (86%) of Americans say conflicts between Democrats and Republicans are either strong or very strong."[14] The level of polarization/tribalism in America, specifically around political identification, has reached such a point that we have begun to tangibly feel these divisions.

Sadly, Christians of varying religious traditions, ethnicities, and socioeconomic backgrounds have often followed their non-Christian friends deep into these political divisions. Thus, even as the country slowly entrenches itself along political, cultural, and economic lines, professing Christians are often on the front lines of these divisions.

This is not being countercultural with the message of Jesus; rather, this form of tribalism conforms to the pattern of this world and does not fight for the basic truth that should unite all Christians. These secondary issues have conflated the spiritual and the natural in a way that weakens our witness and embroils us in deep conflict that distracts from and distorts the gospel of Jesus.

Unflinching devotion to a tribe not only pushes us to fight against issues that are not connected to the gospel and don't advance the mission of God, but it also affects how we view others who disagree with us. They become opponents we have to beat rather than lost people made in the image of God whom we are to love and extend God's grace to. Our true fight is not against those who are hurting in the world; it is against the sinful and demonic forces of darkness.

When we become primarily identified with any tribe outside the body of Christ, especially when we are identified to the point where others are repelled by us, we've traded our Kingdom-based identity for a world-based identity. It's burning a bridge. It's building a wall. The most damaging example of Christians at their worst is when someone claims a Kingdom-based identity but pursues some world-based end. Trying to use Christianity to achieve political, economic, or social objectives only increases the outrage directed toward us.

Fighting for a place at the cultural table

Yale Law professor Amy Chua warns that the combination of polarization and insularity is increasingly defining American political and cultural interaction: "Whites and blacks, Latinos and Asians, men and women, Christians, Jews, and Muslims, straight people and gay people, liberals and conservatives—all feel their groups are being attacked, bullied, persecuted, discriminated against."[15] I think that Chua puts her finger on the problem: While each group may act in different ways, their friction and conflict with other groups is motivated by an underlying fear. Even though groups may scoff at the idea that others feel persecuted, there is little doubt that in their own way and for their own reasons, each has a significant fear of the other.

While some camps may be fearful because they have a long history of being persecuted, others are afraid because they see culture changing rapidly and are concerned where they will be when the music stops. There is a reordering of society right now as the dynamics between groups are changing.

Think about some of the hot-button issues that dominated recent elections.

Manufacturing. In the 2016 presidential election, Donald Trump won, in part, by flipping three Rust Belt states–Michigan, Pennsylvania, and Wisconsin–that had not gone Republican since Reagan. In the wake of the election, countless articles have chronicled how manufacturing changes–increased automation, factory relocation, and declining wages–pushed working-class voters to change parties.[16] They saw in Trump someone who recognized their cultural and economic anxieties. That was a massive shift. For most of the twentieth century, American manufacturing built the middle class, and suddenly a large portion of this demographic was afraid about their future.

Immigration. Americans have always been very welcoming to immigrants–except when they're afraid because of the economic or national security implications. Fear drives a lot of this. Many Christians are angry because they feel as if they've lost Christian America and their home field advantage.

Sexuality. When we consider the history of civil rights in America, the rate at which attitudes toward LGBTQ issues have changed is astounding. The percentage of Americans who favor same-sex marriage grew from 35 percent in 2001 to 62 percent in 2017.[17] At the same time, the rapid acceptance of same-sex relationships means that most defenders of LGBTQ rights have fresh memories of times when they were denied basic liberties and protections.

Every group begins from a posture of losing *their* rights, *their* voice, and *their* cultural influence, whether they have had it for generations, have recently attained it, or still aspire to it. The uncertainty inevitably breeds fear, distrust, and anger as each group vies for a seat at the cultural table. Even though Christianity has largely occupied a position of cultural dominance in America, major cultural shifts have provoked a similar fear that it, too, may be left behind. Thus, much of the outrage over the cultural shift from a Judeo-Christian worldview has been a product of our anxieties at the sheer pace of the change.

Talking Past One Another

If you're looking for more evidence of how polarization is dividing the United States and other Western nations, consider how people of differing religious or political outlooks gather information and evaluate the motives and actions of those outside their own groups.

Echo chambers: getting stuck in a bubble

During the 2012 presidential election, pollsters made clear that the outcome in Ohio was going to come down to the wire and that winning the state was crucial to Obama's reelection. Yet I saw far too many confident assertions from conservative media sources that Obama was going to lose Ohio in a landslide. Late in the campaign, I knew from a broad survey of polls (not to mention the historical precedent that sitting presidents rarely lose swing states by a large percentage) that Obama would almost certainly carry the state. The day after the election, I tweeted: "Obama reelected. For those shocked this wasn't a Romney landslide, I'd broaden your news viewing beyond @foxnews." I wasn't making a political statement; it was simply obvious that the polls were going for Barack Obama–except on Fox News.

Let me say, when the first major media outlet announced late on election night that Obama had carried Ohio, many people who followed Fox and other conservative outlets were angry.

I saw this as further evidence that nowhere is America's polarization more apparent than in the ways we consume and engage media–in other words, in how we get our news and express our opinions about the news online. As Americans have been able to customize their news, we have witnessed the creation of "media silos." In today's world of catchy phrases, sociologists and political theorists have countless ways to describe the effect: bias bubbles, belief filters, echo chambers, and dampening dungeons (okay, I made that last one up). The net effect is the same: Whenever we allow our political identity to shape the way we engage the world and others, we invariably close off outside sources that we do not consider part of *our team*. It is an "us versus them" mentality that can spiral out of control.

Researchers from Italy's IMT School for Advanced Studies Lucca and the Kellogg School of Management at Northwestern University studied online users' consumption of social media and its potency to shape their worldviews and beliefs. They found that not only are online users attracted to forming information silos,[18] but that these sources can quickly breed division between people who previously had similar perspectives. Despite fervent hopes among defenders of the Internet that its openness to every viewpoint would broaden people's minds, researchers have actually found the opposite. Far from expanding the conversation, people are constructing their own silos by seeking out information that simply reinforces their existing views and bias. As a result, the moderates are becoming extreme rather than the extremes becoming moderate.[19]

The effect of obtaining our information from these information silos is the sense that we are living in different worlds from those with opposing beliefs, completely cutting ourselves off from those who do not think, look, and talk like us. Tribalism not only divides people, it also impacts how they translate data and research into their lives. As a result, our world becomes an echo chamber of ideas that leaves us dangerously entrenched in beliefs, habits, and perspectives that are often caricatures of reality.

Yet there is good news: When we understand that many Western nations are incrementally moving toward greater political polarization, we recognize a significant opportunity for Christians. As

the world divides along strict party lines, the church can overcome and transcend these inferior identifiers. After all, the insular
group identities of the left and right will not prove as captivating
or appealing as a community built around faith.

Navigating the promise—and pitfalls—of compromise

In her biography of her late husband, Keith Green, a legend in
Christian contemporary music, Melody Green chose one of his
most iconic songs for the title: *No Compromise*. The song embodied
much of Green's life story and driving spiritual devotion. As Melody
wrote of her immediate reflection upon the song, "It seemed to cap-
ture the heart of what Keith wanted to say—how important it is that
believers quit compromising with the world and start living radically committed lives."[20] Frustrated by Christians who he believed
diminished the gospel by making allowances for sin, Keith Green
called us to a faith that was radical in singular devotion to Christ
and that brokered no compromise with this world.

Even today, the passion and intensity in Green's stand against
compromise resonate with believers. Yet it's one thing to avoid
compromise when it comes to upholding orthodox Christianity;
it's quite another to view compromise, dialogue, and moderation
as weaknesses, moral failure, and grounds for exclusion in the
political realm.

This is one reason the 2016 election was so agonizing for
Christians who believed they faced a no-win situation. On one
side, many thought the Republican candidate's moral character
should have disqualified him from public office; on the other side,
a number of Christian voters were dismayed by a Democrat who
advocated one of the most radical positions on abortion rights in
American history. If you were a believer who cared deeply for the
unborn yet refused to support a candidate of dubious moral quality, where could you go? Some Christians begged Democrats to
make some compromise on abortion to signal that there was a
place within their party for pro-lifers.

Nothing.

Then, in the wake of their loss to Donald Trump, House Minority Leader Nancy Pelosi assured us that there was room in the Democratic Party for pro-lifers; Bernie Sanders even went so far as to endorse a pro-life candidate in Nebraska. Planned Parenthood president Cecile Richards promptly chastised both politicians for even this minor sign of accommodation.[21]

In a *New York Times* editorial, David Brooks outlined how this all-or-nothing mentality was damaging not only the Democratic Party, but the country.[22] This column was greeted by such ferocity of outrage that you would think Brooks had called for the execution of the Democratic Party in Times Square. Fond of chastising Christians for their support of Republicans simply because of their pro-life position, the left has proven equally unable to compromise its own dogma to provide a place for them within the Democratic Party. Even the mention of moderation is enough to bring out the pitchforks and torches.

While refusing to compromise in politics can lead to further polarization, Christians cannot afford to concede when it comes to issues of righteousness and justice. The #MeToo movement is an illustration of a time when all sectors of society must band together. This movement has been a tidal wave picking up momentum, and this reckoning has been a long time in the making and sorely needed. Unfortunately, it also highlights how Christians have sometimes seemed to value our institutions and communities above the gospel. We are still grappling with the consequences of #MeToo and how to properly channel the movement's concerns and objectives. But one truth it has laid bare is how often the right decision is sacrificed for the easy one in an effort to protect the organization over the individual.

Churches in particular are just now awakening to the reality that we have been deficient in handling cases of abuse. Too often elder boards, pastoral staff, and denominational leaders have minimized or discredited instances of sexual abuse and misconduct.

When we allow thoughts of *What will this do to our business/*

school/church if it gets out? to restrict our pursuit of righteousness, we have compromised. When the church protects the powerful at the expense of the victim, we have compromised. And in the end, these compromises add up and convince the world that the church is not a community for the broken in search of healing but just another human institution that puts expediency above righteousness and justice.

Valuing expediency over expertise

One evening a few years ago, I had an experience that every pastor dreads. I had just finished preaching when I noticed an older gentleman waiting patiently to talk with me. Now 99 percent of these interactions are harmless if not actually encouraging. People often want to tell the preacher they appreciated some point, connect on some mutual friend, or say the preacher is in their prayers.

It's that one percent of the time when things go off the rails, and preachers have a sixth sense for when it's about to happen. Let me tell you, alarm bells were ringing as this man approached. With a determined stride and unblinking eyes, he was clearly bent on speaking his piece even if the Rapture tried to interrupt. With little preamble, he jumped right in to tell me why some research I had cited in my sermon was wrong. I listened intently as he explained that through his own observations and what he'd pieced together on the Internet, I had made a grievous error he needed to set straight. After he finished, I patiently explained to him that I had overseen the study in question as the head of LifeWay Research.

Undeterred, the man doubled down. He may not have had any studies to cite—and his research was limited to a few blogs and Wikipedia—but that in no way diminished his confidence. In the end, I thanked him, and we parted ways. But I was struck by the contrast. How could someone I knew to be completely wrong be so irrationally confident? The man not only was self-assured in his wrongness, he actually *initiated* the conversation!

This, however, is hardly unique. Every week, preachers around the United States, who have spent hours poring over God's Word, invariably field an assortment of individuals armed with little more than the confidence of their convictions. This highlights something important in our culture: Many people are willing to create their own reality to affirm their rightness, ignoring facts, logic, and others' objections. One distinctive of today's outrage is how we often value confidence and aggression more than truth in our public interactions. During a time of 24/7 cable news and social media, it is the controversial but confident shouting personalities who garner followings, even if what they say is demonstrably false. We live in a time when one can often be wrong but seldom, if ever, in doubt. Over time, this attitude devalues truth, erects barriers to substantive engagement with others, and ratchets up the volume of disagreement.

An underlying problem that gives rise to this behavior is how cultural attitudes toward expertise and authority have shifted. The very democratic spirit that ensures every person has equal value in the political process can, when applied to the issue of authority and expertise, be destructive. In some cases, like the one I encountered after my sermon, it is frustrating but mostly harmless.

Now, I am not saying that I am always right. And people can, do, and should question my stats. Neither am I suggesting that experts are always right. (For example, I believe the impossible–a Savior was born of a virgin at the edges of the Roman Empire two thousand years ago–and that contradicts the conclusions of scholars like Bart Ehrman and Richard Dawkins.) But something is happening in our culture, and we need to understand it, lest we fall prey to it.

In his book *The Death of Expertise*, Tom Nichols argues that the underlying problem isn't so much a rejection of knowledge as a visceral or angry reaction to any claims to expertise. Regardless of the qualifications of experts, such as a lifetime of study or experience in a field, people are increasingly antagonistic to them but often willing to trust what they find on conspiracy websites. Nichols writes, "Americans now believe that having equal rights in a political system also means that each person's opinion about anything must be accepted as equal to anyone else's. This is the credo of a fair number of people despite being obvious nonsense. It is a flat assertion of actual equality that is always illogical, sometimes funny, and often dangerous."[23]Armed with no experience and some sketchy information culled from the corners of the Internet, more and more individuals are brash, confident, demanding, and frequently dead wrong. This predictably produces conflict and outrage in a world in which self-reflection is a sign of weakness and confidence is truth-making. There is little incentive for patient and nuanced discussion. For that reason, I think we need to discipline—yes, to disciple—our minds (and the minds of our friends) to think more critically.

Christians have a well-documented poor track record in this area. Now, this is not new. Christians have, for a long time, had an anti-intellectual streak. I'm not the first person to think that; Mark Noll, a professor at Notre Dame, has long cautioned evangelicals against a virulent strain of anti-intellectualism that emboldens the worst tendencies of our movement. In *The Scandal of the Evangelical Mind*, Noll famously warned, "The scandal of the evangelical mind is that there is not much of an evangelical mind."[24] Even as Noll applauded evangelicals for our virtues of charity, evangelistic zeal, and community building, he warned of significant long-term risk for damage when we neglect our intellectual life.

It hurts our witness by making us, at times, look stupid. And few people want to be part of a faith that they see as a group of easily fooled, angry people.

Demanding silence in the face of disagreement

In 2017, Princeton Seminary awarded the Abraham Kuyper Prize for Excellence in Reformed Theology and Public Life to Tim Keller, the founding pastor of Redeemer Presbyterian Church in New York City and a bestselling author. Princeton was once a bastion of orthodox Protestantism whose lecturers included Charles Hodge, B. B. Warfield, and J. Gresham Machen, and the Kuyper Award was one of the few remaining vestiges of this heritage. A Dutch statesman and theologian, Kuyper had given his famous "Lectures on Calvinism" at Princeton in 1898, and that work continues to be one of the most influential pieces of public theology today.

Although Keller won the award in recognition for his work as both a well-respected theologian and an urban pastor, controversy erupted immediately after the announcement. No one would question Keller's influence—in 2018 *Forbes* included him on its list of the world's top fifty leaders.[25] Yet some students and faculty objected to Keller on the basis that he did not support the ordination of women or LGBTQ causes. The university abruptly changed course and revoked the honor. In an example of Christ's humility and graciousness, Keller suggested Princeton not give him the award but still hold his lecture to foster dialogue, discussion, and greater intellectual exploration. The university agreed, and Keller's lecture was a huge success.

The event reinforces an emerging problem in our culture where the mere existence of disagreement is likely to spark outrage with the predictable effect of silencing dialogue. Suddenly everyone begins to respond as if stepping on eggshells. When disagreement is equated with persecution or hatred, the intensity of our divisions ratchets up, and moderate voices are cowed into silence out of fear of being similarly branded. Labels such as *homophobic, sexist, racist,* and *anti-Christian* are thrown around in an attempt to shut down any engagement before it even begins. There can be no actual exchange of ideas or dialogue in this environment.

It is becoming increasingly clear that Christians who hold to historic orthodoxy are no longer welcome in certain circles. In her article "The Wrong Kind of Christian," Tish Warren recounted how she had mistakenly believed that she had earned a place at the wider cultural table.

The subtitle of the article explained, "I thought a winsome faith would win Christians a place at Vanderbilt's table. I was wrong." Her orthodox views and work with InterVarsity's student chapter on campus became sticking points with her classmates. She wrote,

I thought I was an acceptable kind of evangelical.

I'm not a fundamentalist. My friends and I enjoy art, alcohol, and cultural engagement.

We avoid spiritual clichés and buzzwords. We value authenticity, study, racial reconciliation, and social and environmental justice.

Being a Christian made me somewhat weird in my urban, progressive context, but despite some clear differences, I held a lot in common with unbelieving friends. We could disagree about truth, spirituality, and morality, and remain on the best of terms. The failures of the church often made me more uncomfortable than those in the broader culture.

Then, two years ago, the student organization I worked for at Vanderbilt University got kicked off campus for being the wrong kind of Christians.[26]

There are some situations you can't winsome your way through. Eventually the group was deregistered by the university, which essentially killed any access the campus ministry had to minister to the student body. Even as Warren and others tried to fight back, the reality was that their version of (orthodox) Christianity was no longer welcome.

You see, the lanes are moving apart. And people who are moving in a more secular direction are now part of the mainstream. As Warren explained, they see the Christian belief system as discriminatory. And who likes discriminators? They are akin to racists. So the cycle continues and the outrage grows—but Warren took a different path. Rather than complaining or criticizing the university, Warren wrote blog posts and articles to help clarify why InterVarsity asked its student leaders to affirm its doctrinal statements. Even as she urged Vanderbilt to live up to its stated claim of welcoming pluralism, she expressed the group's love of the university and desire to remain a voice on campus.

Like Warren, Keller defended Christians' right to hold fast to their beliefs and explained the danger in trying to silence them. In his lecture at Princeton, Keller noted the importance of transcending insular group mentalities that breed fear and suspicion. "You can't disagree with somebody by just beating them from the outside," he said. "You have to come into their framework. You critique them from inside their own framework; you don't critique them for not having your framework."[27]

Keller got to the root of the problem. As the world has fragmented into independent groups with their own worldviews and moral frameworks, these factions invariably judge others by their own standards. When others don't live up to their judgments, they have a visceral reaction to them rather than trying to understand their positions. More important for the believer is that when we respond to outrage with outrage, we ruin our witness. When we desire to beat the other into submission with claims of intolerance, offense, or bigotry rather than trying to engage our opponents in dialogue, we cannot be ambassadors of Christ's love.

We need to recognize that what we often see as a scriptural issue, the world around us sees as a justice issue. Their framework of belief around any opposition to LGBTQ beliefs is similar to how most people feel about racism. I'm outraged by racism and hope you are as well. However, I am not outraged by following the teaching of Scripture when it comes to sexuality. Therein lies the problem—we and the rest of the world see things from a different starting place. When we see someone discriminated against because of their race, Christians should have a visceral, gut response of justifiable anger and righteous indignation. That is the same response many people have when Christians do not support same-sex marriage. We start from our understanding of Scripture; they do not start from that same place.

The problem comes when we believe that the reason others hate us must be *because* they disagree with us. This is why we respond to intellectual disagreement with emotional reflex. We truly believe we are so right that the other person must disagree with us based on moral hatred rather than simply intellectual dissent.

The Fork in the River

Let's go back to the river illustration, because by understanding where we have come from and where we are, we can gain a better appreciation of where we are going. As these trends continue, it appears likely that the cultural divide between Convictional Christians and other groups will actually widen.

Remember, the number of Convictional Christians appears to be holding steady, but the number of Cultural and Congregational Christians is shrinking by about one percent per year. And that rate may be accelerating. In other words, those streams are moving away from Convictional Christian belief and practice. I've seen it myself.

You see, like many in the Northeast, I grew up a little bit Catholic. Actually, most of my family did. We were Catholics on Christmas and Easter; the rest of the time, Saint Bernard's Catholic Church was the church we did *not* go to on Sundays. Most of our neighbors went as well because, like us, they were "Chreasters" (people who go on Christmas and Easter, and yes, that's a thing).

As I look at my family now, I see that most of us are not where we started. As is often the case, people don't tend to stay a little bit religious. Over time, they become more or less engaged. As such, most of my family are not involved in church or matters of faith today. They have moved away from the nominal Catholic experience. But some of us—a minority, to be clear—have moved the other way, becoming more involved in church and matters of faith. (I go to church way too much . . . let's just get that out there.)

That's what happens today. Nominal people tend not to stay nominal. And why would they? Unless there is cultural pressure and guilt (hello, Irish Catholics on Long Island, where I grew up!), there is no reason to keep following traditions that don't have meaning. Yet for some of us, our faith has changed and deepened.

My family is a microcosm of our culture and its shifting faith practices. We've come to a fork in the river.

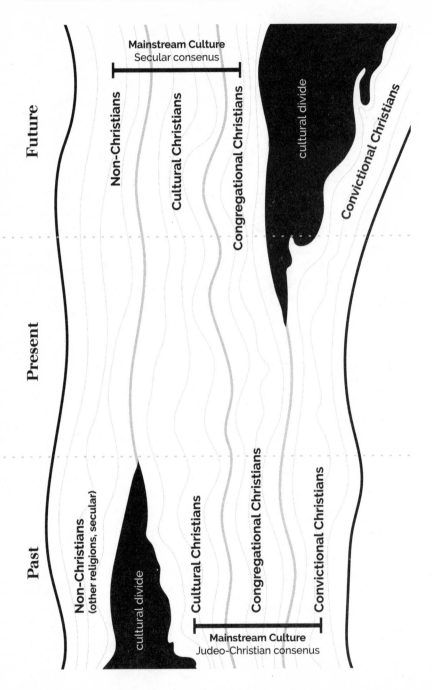

Christians can try to make their stand by turning back the clock. We can try to reclaim a cultural norm that is dying if not already dead. Or we can grasp the central truth of the moment in which we live, understanding the challenges and opportunities Christians face in this new culture. We have to consider both the moment we are in and the mission we are on.

CHAPTER 2

Outrage Cause #2:
The Technology Discipleship Gap

- Evangelicals are more likely than non-evangelicals (49 percent to 38 percent) to connect with people like themselves on social media, leading to the formation of possible echo chambers.

- Evangelicals (73 percent) and non-evangelicals (67 percent) overwhelmingly agree that interactions on social media have increased the divisive political climate in America.

IN 2015, THE CITY OF FLINT, MICHIGAN, became the focus of national attention when it issued a warning that elderly residents and children should avoid using city water due to lead contamination.[1]

While the mere mention of lead is enough to put the fear of God into many today, there was a time when it was everywhere. Lead helped house paint dry faster, and for generations lead pipes were the most common means of getting drinking water to people. Beginning in the 1920s, lead was added to gasoline to help boost octane levels, which improved the power and efficiency of cars. My 1971 Volkswagen Bug, and many other older cars, were designed to run on leaded gas.[2] The widespread use of lead in gasoline, according to Philip J. Landrigan in a *Bulletin of the World Health Organization* report, had catastrophic effects: "By contaminating air, dust, soil, drinking water and food crops, it has caused harmfully high human blood lead levels around the world, especially in children."[3]

Think of it: Less than a century ago, Americans woke up in rooms painted with lead, drank water tainted by lead, and drove cars running on leaded gasoline. We had no clue what we were doing to ourselves. I assure you, as a kid growing up in New York, I probably consumed a lot of lead.

Today, lead serves as a cautionary tale of the uncritical pursuit of progress. It's a warning that we need to understand the risks and threats associated with new habits and tools before we allow them unfettered access to our lives, our households, and our communities.

Just as we think back with dismay on how widely lead was used for much of the twentieth century, I believe future generations may look back with regret on our current unbridled embrace of all things technological. We have undergone a digital revolution, and this has predictably fueled our culture of outrage in ways we often do not appreciate. The technology and online habits of both Christians and non-Christians often reflect disturbing behavior and thoughts that are damaging us and our communities.

In *Irresistible: The Rise of Addictive Technology and the Business of Keeping Us Hooked*, Adam Alter cautions against uncritically welcoming technology into our homes and routines. In a *New York Times* interview, Alter states:

> In the past, we thought of addiction as mostly related to chemical substances: heroin, cocaine, nicotine. Today, we have this phenomenon of behavioral addictions where, one tech industry leader told me, people are spending nearly three hours a day tethered to their cellphones. Where teenage boys sometimes spend weeks alone in their rooms playing video games. Where Snapchat will boast that its youthful users open their app more than 18 times a day.[4]

Quoting the ethicist Tristan Harris, Alter noted that the problem isn't willpower but that "there are a thousand people on the other side of the screen whose job it is to break down the self-regulation you have."[5] There are, quite literally, people on the other side of the glass who are working to make you addicted.

We live in a world that is bombarded by technological developments, and our habits are being developed long before we stop to think whether these advancements and practices are helpful. In a study charting well-being among American adolescents (measured by self-esteem, life satisfaction, and happiness), psychologists discovered a significant decline beginning after 2012.[6]

In exploring the underlying causes, researchers observed that increased use of smartphones by teenagers is likely a contributor to the trend. They found that teenagers who spent more time engaged in screen activities (i.e., social media, the Internet, texting, and gaming) registered lower levels of psychological well-being. On the other hand, teenagers who limited smartphone use and regularly engaged in nonscreen activities such as in-person social interactions, sports or exercise, homework, and church activities had higher psychological well-being. In essence, technology use is having a noticeable and negative effect on our kids.[7] Now I'm not suggesting we should return to the days of landlines or carrier pigeons, but it's worth considering how our technology is shaping us.

Christians often have the same bad habits as everyone else, practices that damage not only their well-being and relationships, but also their spiritual vitality and witness. Despite these dangers, when was the last time your church taught on social media or proper media consumption? Substantive, disciple-making teaching on how Christians can develop godly technology habits? Aside from youth pastors warning of cyberbullying, when have messages touched on the way technology is shaping our lives or how our online behavior relates to our faith? I have heard plenty of sermons that address the problem of pornography, but I can count on one hand the number of times a pastor or Sunday school teacher discussed a more comprehensive online discipleship.

Christians have seen the emerging digital marketplace, and rather than thinking critically about its nature and effects, they have dived in. Innovation for the glory of God, we tell ourselves, even though we know that innovation for the expansion of the platform is often closer to the truth. Discipleship may not even cross our minds.

We are not in Kansas anymore. While the world struggles with the where, who, and why of moral education and formation, the church should be Christians' source of teaching on forming life-giving habits. The Christian community is built around the concept of discipleship, but many churches have not thought about how to teach proper discipleship practices in this digital world. We need to realize that the older models and methods do not always work, and begin thinking differently if we want to reach and disciple our youth and adults so they are equipped to engage with our digital world.

I believe much of the hostility perpetrated *by* Christians has its root in this discipleship gap, a glaring need that the church must address if it hopes to stem the tide of hostility. In this chapter, I examine specific trends related to the current technological revolution that are contributing to this outrage. My hope is that by bringing these habits to the foreground–and illustrating how Christians have fallen prey to them as well–we can begin to consider how to better disciple others for effective mission in our digital world.

Clicks over Content:
Outrage Drives Content Production

In the fall of 2016, as the US presidential campaign headed into the final stretch, this headline caught my attention: "Christian Speaker Beth Moore Stands in the Gap for Hillary Clinton."[8] The election was pitting evangelical voter against evangelical voter, but few religious leaders outside the most partisan had jumped in with full-throated endorsements for one candidate or the other. That October, a 2005 behind-the-scenes videotape from the TV show *Access Hollywood* surfaced in which candidate Trump used vulgar, offensive terms to describe his own demeaning and abusive behavior toward women. Soon after the tape surfaced, Moore, a renowned evangelical Bible study leader, expressed her disgust through several tweets. (I did as well. Actually, I think every right-minded person was upset, including those who voted for now-president Trump.)

Moore is a gifted Christian author and speaker who has taught the Bible to millions of women through her speaking, books, and

Bible study curriculum. I've collaborated with Moore on projects in the past and each time walked away impressed by her commitment to the gospel and to discipling God's people. While I shared Moore's disgust in the wake of the videotape, I was genuinely surprised when I read the headline that she would go political.

So I clicked.

Turns out, no, Beth Moore was not supporting Clinton, nor had she even addressed the election explicitly. The entire article was based on tweets in which Moore expressed her outrage at how this kind of objectification of women was deemed acceptable by Christian leaders. Bravely adding her voice to those who spoke out against the abuse of women even before the #MeToo movement existed, Moore used her platform to draw our attention to the inconsistency between the gospel and the objectification of women.

Moore did not say she was supporting another candidate. She did say this:

> Wake up, Sleepers, to what women have dealt with all along in environments of gross entitlement & power. Are we sickened? Yes. Surprised? NO.[9]

> Try to absorb how acceptable the disesteem and objectifying of women has been when some Christian leaders don't think it's that big a deal.[10]

> I'm one among many women sexually abused, misused, stared down, heckled, talked naughty to. Like we liked it. We didn't. We're tired of it.[11]

> "Keep your mouth shut or something worse will happen." Yes. I'm familiar with the concept. Sometimes it's terrifyingly true. Still, we speak.[12]

I agree with every single word. And every person who voted for Donald Trump should agree with every single word.

Yet Breitbart News reported Moore's comments with a headline explicitly stating she had stood in the gap in support of Democratic candidate Hillary Clinton. If my children twisted another person's words in this way, I'd ground them for lying.

But, you know, outrage gets clicks.

These kinds of headlines, known as clickbait, are increasingly common today, even by reputable news organizations that should know better. That's because they are an effective way of driving Internet traffic, which in turn pays the bills. The increasing value of clicks reveals how much journalism and news have changed.

Jack Murtha, a fellow with the *Columbia Journalism Review*, noted that the online magazine *Slant* pays its writers, who submit three articles per week, only $100 a month as a base salary. However, they receive an additional five dollars for every 500 clicks.[13] In this world, why wouldn't you chase the most controversial stories and write the most sensational headlines? An obsession with page views will undoubtedly change how and why media content is produced, along with its truthfulness and quality.

Christians, unfortunately, have also learned there is a ready audience for conflict. Compare the number of views, shares, and comments between controversial and more constructive posts. It is staggering, disheartening, and unbelievably tempting. Too often the focus is not on who can exhort others but who can make the craziest statement.

"Guess which pastor is a racist!"

"The cover-up at this major ministry will shock you!"

"The Jesus your pastor won't tell you about!"

Of course, pastors concerned with low attendance or lethargy in worship have long understood that controversial attacks against other Christians can energize their sermons. Sensationalism has been a favorite tactic of attention seekers for generations, but today catchy headlines promise a lot and deliver nothing to millions. Even those who start out with honest intentions to build up the church eventually recognize that controversy generates traffic. For ministry leaders called to faithfully engage the church in both prophetic and pastoral tones, it's not always easy to discern what drives us. It takes careful thought, a level of self-awareness, and the humility to admit a mistake if necessary.

The depressing truth about clickbaiting is that it is just as effective with Christians as with the rest of the world.

Dr. Jekyll and Mr. Hyde

Have you ever met someone you really liked in real life only to be disappointed with their online behavior? They may be kind and thoughtful face-to-face, but their online profile is a wreckage of conspiratorial memes, political rants in ALL CAPS, and way too many kitten videos.

What happened?

The introduction of greater online capabilities and access has introduced a new problem to our common social relationships: How do our online and real-life behavior match up? Sometimes we don't appreciate that a discrepancy between the two can be disastrous.

It reminds me of Robert Louis Stevenson's *The Strange Case of Dr. Jekyll and Mr. Hyde.* Published in 1886, the book tells the story of how a lawyer, Gabriel Utterson, investigates the identity of a murderer named Edward Hyde and his strange relationship to Utterson's friend, the well-respected physician Dr. Henry Jekyll. Unbeknownst to Utterson, Jekyll had been so troubled by his own evil urges that he developed a potion that allows his dark side to remain dormant until he drinks it. When he does, Jekyll turns into his monstrous alter ego, Edward Hyde, who leaves his house at night to terrorize London. The story is a disturbing tale about private and public morality and how their dissociation can be destructive to our souls.

Psychologists have noticed this trend between people's private and online personas. One helpful study on the reasons for people's different behavior depending on whether they are off- or online was published in 2004 by John Suler, professor of psychology at Rider University in New Jersey.[14] His article explores six factors he believes lead to an "online disinhibition effect," a term used to describe why people often act differently in their online interactions than they do in person. In some instances, the difference in behavior is so severe that persons are detached from reality when interacting online, saying things that demonstrate their online lives are wholly separate from their offline world.

Many people mistakenly believe they project their true self online, often in anonymity or at least under the illusion of invisibility. Suler rejects the idea that the aggressive part of a person is the true self; instead, he says both people's personal nonaggressive interaction and their online aggressive interaction make up the totality of their personhood.[15]

Christians, too, have a raging Hyde within them that often comes out through their computers or mobile devices. We can quickly devolve into behavior that is anything but humble, loving, and sacrificial. Instead, it is often prideful, domineering, and pushy.

I'm reminded of a Christian theologian whose books had a major impact on my own thinking. I have heard him lecture on several occasions and even had an opportunity to sit down and talk with him. In each venue, he was a powerful combination of insight and kindness. I always listed him as a model for young Christians entering the pastorate or academia to aspire toward because of both the quality of his work and his heart for others.

A few years later I came across his social media profile. It was like seeing *Invasion of the Body Snatchers.* I couldn't understand how the man I respected could demean others and display so little of the warmth I had experienced when reading his books and meeting him in person.

He was a Twitter jackwagon.

Christians need to grasp the hypocrisy of engaging online in a way that would be wholly intolerable if we were face-to-face with others. To disassociate our online conduct from any real-life consequences fails to grasp that in our digital age, people are always watching. As a result, the consistency of our witness is perhaps never more important than when we speak online. We may think no one cares, but what we post there causes others to think twice about whether we are being genuine in our other interactions. Which one is the real you? Are you the Dr. Jekyll Christian (thoughtful and respectful) or the Mr. Hyde Christian (snarky and dismissive)? The truth, as in Robert Louis Stevenson's story, is that it's impossible to separate one from the other.

The Rise of Fake News

In announcing that the phrase *fake news* was the 2017 Word of the Year, *Collins Dictionary* noted that its usage had increased 365 percent from 2016. Trying to avoid the politically charged nature of the idea, Collins defined fake news as "false, often sensational, information disseminated under the guise of news reporting."[16] In essence, it is news that is purposefully false but designed to trick us into believing it is true.

Perhaps just as destructive is how people use fake news to delegitimize real news perceived as damaging to "us" or to "our side." When a Dutch journalist confronted the newly minted US ambassador to the Netherlands, Pete Hoekstra, about disparaging comments he had made in the past about that country, Hoekstra claimed the accusation was fake news. When later confronted with video of his comments, Hoekstra was forced to apologize.[17]

In either case, the development of fake news is a major concern when it comes to the way we engage with world events, the political process, and other communities. How do you converse with others when you don't trust their news source and/or they don't trust yours? Such distrust leads to people screaming at each other with little means of settling disagreements.

This upsurge in fake news and claims of fake news often leaves

Christians either reacting or surrendering to the culture. Though I had never addressed this problem before, beginning in 2017 I had to begin teaching and writing about how Christians need to respond to, and ultimately repent of, their involvement with fake news.

Whenever I write an article about a subsection of Christians or political leaders some Christians may support, I am invariably greeted by an avalanche of angry readers yelling, "Fake news!" At the same time, research into the promotion of fake news during the 2016 US presidential election cycle shows that Christians were effectively targeted by Russian bots. Fake Christian accounts like the "Army of Jesus" blended disturbing images with purported spiritual messages about the election and proved remarkably effective.[18] Many Christians liked and shared these posts, revealing that we may not be as discerning as we believe.

I actually got a note from Twitter that I had interacted with such fake news Twitter bots. As a Twitter user, I autofollow everyone back, but I recall one of the Russian bots frequently sending me tweets. Twitter was concerned, I guess, that I had gotten caught up in the fake news reality. It seems that many were.

The Outrage Cycle: How Outrage Builds

One of the most startling and disconcerting features of our age is how outrage tends to build, slowly mounting into wave and counter-wave and counter-counter-wave that consume everything in their path. What starts off as an innocent mistake or a meaningless joke can quickly be turned into a national debate about profound moral, theological, and cultural problems. Often, this cycle creates massive collateral damage in the lives of those who sparked the initial debate.

There is a glitch in the system. Rather than outrage burning and then dying down, it seems to flare up bigger and faster. But it does not always build in the same manner. There are three distinct forms of online outrage, each of which can be equally destructive in its own way.

Outrage cycle #1: mob justice

In *So You've Been Publicly Shamed*, Jon Ronson recounts stories of how outrage builds to a crescendo of anger that ultimately reaps unprecedented destruction and shame. Ronson explains how a group of young academics created a fake online profile to mimic him. When Ronson asked them to take the account down, they refused. In anger and desperation to stop what he saw as a version of identity theft, Ronson videotaped an interview between himself and the young men during which they refused his request to delete the profile.

He was entirely unprepared for the results when he posted the video on YouTube.

To Ronson's pleasant surprise, the masses on the Internet sided with him, and he delightfully watched as comments on the video criticized the young men. But his joy quickly turned to ashes as the comments and anger ramped way up. Unwittingly, Ronson had unleashed an outrage culture upon these men that was now entirely out of his hands.

This is the trouble with mob outrage. Once it ignites, it is unstoppable, and each successive wave seems to validate and justify the next level. It's not so different from mobs in real life, which often begin after people watch a fight break out between two people. These bystanders often think, *As long as* I'm *not the one to throw the first punch, it's okay to join in.* This herd mentality systematically justifies our anger and deepens its expression. What starts as "you're wrong" quickly becomes "I hate you and hope you die." Even when participants think they are exacting justice, the scale and ferocity of their anger can quickly spiral out of control.

Outrage cycle #2: counter-outrage

During Hurricane Harvey, an online report claimed that megachurch and prosperity gospel pastor Joel Osteen had closed the doors of his church, refusing to help disaster victims. As the waters rose, the story said, Osteen's Lakewood Church directed people to other shelters rather than open their 16,800-seat arena. Predictably, this produced a torrent of outrage against Osteen. Christians who saw his ministry as heretical gleefully joined in the fury.

While I am among those who aren't on the same theological page as Osteen, I published an article pointing out that the original report was misleading, that the outrage was unwarranted, and that Christians needed to stop piling on. As I said at the time, I wasn't so much defending Osteen as I was proclaiming the need for us to defend the truth and to resist the temptation to join mobs of outrage against those we simply don't like. "The irony for some in this moment is clear," I said. "They hate Osteen because they believe he distorts the truth—and then they do the same when they critique him with false information."[19]

In other words, some Christians hated Joel Osteen more than they loved the truth. When the reports first surfaced, these people believed the worst because they already despised him. (I should add, I've seen such vitriol directed at me over untrue accusations—a hundred tweets an hour at one point. Truth did not matter, only vitriol did.)

What I was unprepared for from my readers was the response of those who used the anger at Osteen as a justification to rage against the outrage. To some, the criticism of Osteen was an example of a secret agenda against Christians in general or against Osteen specifically. In their minds, my article had vindicated their suspicion that people were out for the pastor, so they unleashed equal amounts of anger and conspiracy-laden rants against the "other side."

What the Osteen story reveals is that inevitably a counter-outrage arises to fight against the first outrage. One group unleashes against an individual or group for a perceived infraction, and a second group rises up in defense by counterpunching just as hard or harder. Even in cases where we could say that one side is fighting for a better cause, the intensity of their outrage eventually disqualifies any points they were trying to make. In the end, it becomes two groups yelling at each other about how the other is missing the point.

The unbridled anger itself often seems to justify a similar level of intensity. This reveals a troubling underlying problem in our culture: Even in cases where we know outrage is wrong and we need to combat it, we are ill-equipped to meet outrage except by matching its viciousness. We see people screaming at something they hate, and our response is to scream back. This response is self-defeating, provoking others to double down on their initial outrage by turning their anger against us.

Outrage cycle #3: Milkshake Duck outrage

You can safely put *Milkshake Duck* into the column of terms I never thought I'd use. Yet it is a perfect encapsulation of how outrage builds. The term comes from Australian cartoonist Ben Ward, who tweeted, "The whole internet loves Milkshake Duck, a lovely duck that drinks milkshakes! *5 seconds later* We regret to inform you the duck is racist."[20]

Ward perfectly captures the spirit of outrage in which even the most charming stories eventually turn into tragedies. It has reached the point that when a good story emerges, a countdown timer seems to start ticking until the moment when something emerges that tarnishes its perfect image in our minds. Think Ken Bone from the 2016 presidential debates or "Gary from Chicago" at the 2017 Academy Awards. The higher the initial charm, the more potent the subsequent outrage at the person's discovered flaw.[21]

An alarming example of this occurred in December 2017 when a young Tennessee boy named Keaton Jones was catapulted to national attention because of his story of being bullied at school. Through tears on a video recorded by his mother, Keaton recounted how other students had made fun of his clothes and hair to the point that he was afraid to have lunch at school.

The story quickly went viral with national news outlets picking it up and social media platforms rebroadcasting the video. Hundreds of thousands of people responded with encouragement to Keaton, empathizing with his pain. Across the ideological, cultural, and religious divide, respondents cited their own experiences of bullying and isolation, revealing an underlying experience that united rather than divided. It seemed we had stumbled upon the redemptive power of our rapid-reaction culture.

But it was a mirage.

Within a few days, allegations against his family emerged, ranging from questions about allegedly racist Facebook posts by Keaton's mother to the credibility of a GoFundMe.com page. With alarming speed, the tide of encouragement for Keaton turned to a tsunami of outrage. People vented their sense of betrayal over these discoveries, replacing the earlier solidarity with condemnation.[22]

The cycle of outrage arises when people feel they have in some way *wasted* their compassion upon unworthy events or people. This brand of outrage can particularly devastate someone because of the sheer drop a person experiences when, after being an object of love, he or she is suddenly scorned. The same people who voiced admiration or support suddenly call for that individual's head on a pike. At its heart, this phenomenon reveals that often even the expressions of kindness and support on the Internet are conditional on the sense that these objects of our compassion deserve it.

While each of the three cycles is different, they all end in anger and division. They illustrate that even when good intentions or the desire to support a worthy cause create an outpouring of online support, the creation of an outrage cycle to swing the debate the other way may not be far behind.

Outrageous Antics of Christians Online

Before moving on, I want to outline the *kinds* of Christians who can hurt our witness through their online behavior. Not all these categories are equally destructive, but they all carry inherent risk that needs to be understood. Though I can think of many Christian leaders who fall into each of these groups (and have been tempted to join in several of these tactics myself), my objective is not to call out examples of specific Christian leaders. In fact, people throughout the church—pastors and laypeople, theologians and students, elders and greeters—fall into these patterns. Our eyes will be drawn to find categories for the people who annoy us, but I'd encourage you to think through these examples in two ways. First, what category do those whom you are allowing to influence you fall into? Second, where do you fit?

THE VENGEFUL OUTCAST

Every tradition has them. The ex-Catholic, ex-evangelical, ex-Reformed, and so on. They line up to tell the world everything wrong with their old camp, spilling the beans and dishing on the secret handshakes. For some reason, because they went to vacation Bible school for a dozen years, they assume they understand the ins and outs of an entire theological community. The sad truth is that these vengeful outcasts often become our proxies for engaging with other communities. Why would I need to talk to Catholics about what they believe when an ex-Catholic will give me a (totally unbiased) account of their faith? Thank goodness I don't have to engage those homophobic evangelicals; I have half a dozen converts to mainline Protestantism on speed dial.

THE CHICKEN LITTLE

To these Christians, everything is always the worst. Whether it's society, the church, or politics, they are always pointing out the negative. Whenever a community they don't like voices a concern, they dismiss it as inconsequential. Whenever a leader they have criticized takes a step in the right direction, they point out that it's not enough. It seems they aren't out to build bridges but to demand unconditional surrender. They have confused being prophetic with being Chicken Little.

THE CONTROVERSY HUNTER

Just as with clickbait, these Christians are hunting for the slightest heresy, the slightest scandal, and the slightest misstep to pounce on. Little thought is given to whether what they are saying is true, constructive, or good; the point is to generate as much attention as possible. They know that the question they constantly ask themselves—*What will get me likes or views?*—depends on how much outrage they can provoke.

THE PROVERB MACHINE

Perhaps fearing the possibility of provoking the mob, some Christians try to sit on the sidelines. Endlessly tweeting Bible verses and quotes from their favorite pastors, they're more like Christian fortune cookies than people interested in engaging others. They appear to be retreating in confusion or fear. While this usually does not hurt others, I'm not convinced it helps, either.

THE CULTURE CRUSADER

Christians often get a black eye from rising up to defend our culture at the expense of the gospel. These cultural defenders tend to struggle with conflating their community or tradition with their faith. The result is that when they get into debates over social and cultural issues such as marginal tax rates, they bring a passion that should be reserved for the gospel.

THE HERETIC RETREAD

Are you interested in the heresies of church history but don't have time to do the research? Want to flirt with Marcionism or Arianism but need a guy wearing a cool vest or a woman in a fedora to reduce it down to catchphrases in a video set to soft rock music? Don't worry, the Internet is full of leaders ready to sell you on how the church has gotten Jesus or the Bible completely wrong for two thousand years and how they've now put it all together. The truth is, the historic Christian faith has endured for centuries, and God is calling us all to the hard and often obscure work of personal sanctification and community mission.

THE PASSIVE-AGGRESSIVE SUBTWEETER

There is a law that for every forum for conflict and disagreement, passive-aggressive people will find some way to bend it to their will. The rise of the "subtweet" is evidence of this. By not directly referencing the object of their outrage, Twitter users somehow think they have avoided the fight. These kinds of indirect engagements arise from pride without the empathy to actually engage the person with whom the subtweeters disagree. They want credit for defending or criticizing another without the work or accountability that goes into direct exchanges.

THE POLITICAL OBSESSIVE

Do you have that one friend who can make everything about politics? Republican or Democrat, it doesn't really matter. Nowadays the Internet often feels like a room filled with "that guy." Their Facebook pages are packed with political commentary, and they are always among the first to post their interpretations of some major event. Whether they take the progressive or conservative viewpoint, they write as if each event is *everything* to them. More troubling, sometimes they interweave their political beliefs with theology as a means to prove that disagreeing with them is disagreeing with God.

This list of online profiles is hardly exhaustive, but it does include common characters I meet in the church and online on a regular basis. The way they engage others through technology may feel good, and they may believe they are contributing to the Kingdom, but in the end, they just feed the outrage.

Everyone will have their temptations, and the allure of the Internet is that it sometimes feeds these tendencies by making us think our engagement doesn't really matter or, worse, that these tendencies will win attention. In response, we need to be willing to think critically about who is influencing us and how we engage with others. Are we contributing to or fighting against the age of outrage?

The New Roman Roads:
Outrage Machine or Kingdom Tool?

As the Roman Empire expanded more than two thousand years ago, one of the first things the military did was build roads, bridges, and milestone markers. We take such public infrastructure for granted today, but it is difficult to overstate how this innovation of well-constructed, measured, and protected roads transformed Western civilization. Standardized transportation drastically accelerated the pace at which people, trade, and information could move. It also facilitated the rapid cultural blending process by which Rome exported their language, culture, and religion throughout their new empire.

At the center of the Roman forum, Caesar Augustus constructed the Milliarium Aureum (or Golden Milestone) as a monument to Roman culture and authority and the empire's place as the center of the civilized world. The expression "all roads lead to Rome" originated here, since all the empire's highways were said to radiate from the Milliarium Aureum.[23]

An unintended consequence of this network was the unprecedented expansion of Christianity. Not only did roads enable missionaries to travel faster, but because the roads were guarded by troops from the Roman army, early Christians were protected from the common dangers of travel that for centuries had restricted rapid movement. Likewise, the cultural blending these roads created helped the gospel assimilate quickly from city to city and across multiple languages. Throughout his missionary journeys, Paul not only walked seamlessly between cultural regions, he also recruited traveling companions from various cultures.

First-century Christians expanded the gospel to the far reaches of the known world using the network of roads constructed by the Roman Empire; today we use the digital highway to advance the gospel. Instant communication, previously only dreamed of in science fiction, is now commonplace. Every week I am able to equip ministry leaders through my online leadership seminars, collaborate with others on writing projects, and send out massive amounts of content to every corner of the globe. No longer does the extreme isolation of remote communities present an insurmountable obstacle to ministry.

At the same time, the freedom and accessibility of these digital platforms have elevated voices within the church that had been marginalized or ignored in previous generations. Suddenly, a Wichita pastor has the capacity, with the right retweets by other people, to gain a national platform among his peers. His voice can influence what people read, how they think, and where they go. Low-income communities can rise up and ask for help with the same voice and on the same platform the president uses. This opportunity has been used for much good and care of the voiceless and the neglected. We must not lose sight of the fact that we live in a golden age for producing and sharing ministry information.

Yet technology can just as easily be adapted to destructive purposes. The same roads that facilitated Christianity's growth were also a powerful tool in its persecution. Rome frequently lined its roads with crucified criminals belonging to sects and ideologies that the empire perceived as threats. As Christianity grew, the roads that facilitated the expansion of the gospel became a weapon to stem its advance.

Our modern technology has a similar potential for destruction, sadly often at the hands of Christians themselves. The easy accessibility of resources (along with the ability to keep them secret) has predictably led to the increase of sinful addictions within our homes. The rise of social media has provoked a new age of outrage, a season in which collective biases and tribalism can be unleashed upon others with little regard for the fact that the faces behind the avatars are image bearers of God. The diffusion of voices has predictably led us to a crisis of authority so that the loudest and craziest voices of the evangelical movement are often perceived as its leaders.

The key point is that technology is neither inherently good nor bad. Rather, like the Roman roads, it is a tool that God has provided and that is becoming more powerful with each generation. It can advance the work of the gospel: facilitating church plants, getting aid to the needy, encouraging the downtrodden, and equipping the saints for ministry. It can also become, as with the tower of Babel, a source of pride that tempts us to place our trust in human ingenuity.

It is a mistake to believe that we or God need these tools in order to be successful in building the Kingdom. It is an even graver error to forget that these tools are influencing our discipleship in ways we may not fully appreciate. The challenge for believers is to understand when our technology habits are leading us into greater anxiety, fear, anger, and pride, and to be willing to course correct as necessary. Let me again be clear: This does not mean we must reject technology. We simply need to harness these tools rather than allow them to master us. We need to be willing to see ourselves in examples of outrage, recognize that this is not the calling of a believer, and lay down these patterns of self- and community destruction for the sake of the gospel.

Maybe one story will help to illustrate the path we will walk in this book. A friend on social media shared with me about his interactions with his brother-in-law. He explained,

> I am conservative, and my brother-in-law is very left socialist. He is quite aggressive on Facebook, so I started replying— trying to refute his arguments. Some of his Facebook friends (whom I did not know) casually said I had some points. This made him angry. He told me my next post was demeaning, and he unfriended me. That is when I realized my priorities were all wrong. The next time I saw him in person, I sincerely apologized. Since then I refuse to talk politics even when he baits me. I am trying to build our friendship so our discussions of spiritual things, which are now sort of shallow, can grow into something more meaningful.

My friend saw that he might be right about some of the issues but understood that having a relationship was more important than scoring points. I learned this same lesson early in my marriage–the person is more important than the point. Then as I grew as a person, I saw that was true not only in my marriage; it was true in all my relationships.

You can insist you are right all the time, or you can have friends. But you can't do both. It seems that many people have decided, intentionally or unintentionally, that they want only friends who agree with them. (And they are muted or unfriended by many others.) There is a better way.

PART 2

Outrageous Lies
and
Enduring Truths

Like most public speakers, I often receive notes, e-mails, texts, tweets, and personal comments about various aspects of my preaching, teaching, and speaking. Most often they're complimentary, kind, and helpful. Other times, they are . . . well, not.

People comment on the color of my shoes, how I comb my hair, and whether or not I should be wearing jeans when I preach. I don't receive a lot of questions about the content of my sermons, but I regularly get in-depth answers to questions I didn't know I had asked.

Over the years God has helped me find the humor in these stories, and now I usually appreciate the underlying desire of people to connect with me. Rarely do any observations surprise me anymore.

Until recently.

One viewer sent me an e-mail with his thoughts:

> I watched your sermon online. I played it again because
> I was struck by the number of times you adjusted your
> glasses while preaching. The second time through,
> I counted 74 times you adjusted your glasses in just the
> first 36 minutes of the sermon. At that point, you took
> them off. So I stopped counting.

But he wasn't done. Next, he broke out the calculator.

> This was an average of once every 30 seconds. Keep in
> mind that this is an incomplete count because I could not
> see you when there was text on the screen. I tell you this
> in Christian love because I know you are interested in
> anything that may distract listeners from hearing what
> you are preaching and teaching. So I hope you will accept
> this, knowing that I want your ministry to be as effective
> for Christ as possible.[1]

This e-mail was clearly a sincere attempt to be helpful with no ill intent, but it caught me off guard. Anyone who uses glasses understands they slip, particularly when you're speaking in public and the combination of lights and stress causes you to sweat. At first, I wanted to laugh off the e-mail as another example of someone with too much time on his hands, but when I considered his numbers, I was actually surprised. Did I really adjust my glasses *that* often?

After reviewing the "tape" myself, I realized he was right. I quickly jumped online and ordered a product that promised to stop glasses from slipping, "as seen on *Shark Tank*." I don't know if it worked or if I'm simply more aware of my glasses slipping, but my online friend hasn't sent me any more e-mails.

The truth is that until I received his well-intentioned critique, my glasses *were* slipping and I didn't even know it. My attempts to push them back up were absentminded and haphazard at best. Because I wasn't aware of how distracting this could be, I wasn't intentional about understanding *why* the problem existed or what I could do about it. And so my glasses just kept slipping, and I kept adjusting them.

Slip, adjust.

Slip, adjust.

Slip, adjust.

This is not the way glasses are designed to work. You can have the best prescription and the most stylish frames, but if they don't stay on your face in front of your eyes, they aren't working as intended. I hadn't even noticed; instead, I just pushed them back up. Of course, that short-term solution didn't last long.

More often than not, our temporary fixes to problems become so second nature that we do them without thinking through their cause. In our present-day outrage culture, the reality is that the glasses of many Christians are slipping. Whether it's the polarization in our culture, the creep of new technology, or simply the ferocity and volume of the shouting voices around us, the gospel lens through which we see the world needs to be adjusted. And it needs to be more than a temporary fix. Indeed, we need to rethink why and how we engage with our culture.

The lens through which we see our society should be the gospel of Jesus Christ. He created the world to be good, true, and beautiful, but it was broken in the Fall. Because of sin, the world is lost. God sent his Son, Jesus, as our perfect Savior to save us from sin and brokenness, and to bring us back to God.

Because the gospel is the proper lens and the right prescription, this book is not about putting on a new lens through which to see the world. Rather, it is about recognizing that we've allowed our gospel lenses to slip and then adjusting them so we see the world properly.

We have examined cultural polarization and advancing technology, two of the underlying causes of the age of outrage. Before we consider how Christians should engage this new and hostile world, we need to clear off the junk that clouds or distorts our thinking.

In this second section, then, I want to examine four lies that distort our vision. If we want to make progress in discipleship and engage an outraged world with the gospel, we need to call them out.

CHAPTER 3

Lie #1: "Christians Are the Worst!"

- Of non-evangelicals who changed their opinion about evangelicals since the 2016 election, six said their opinion worsened for every one who said it improved.

FEW CAN DOUBT THAT public perception of Christianity, Christians, and evangelicals has taken a big hit in the last few years. To be fair, Christians have done a lot to contribute to this decline. From unloving posts on social media to unwise political comments by their leaders, Christians have certainly earned some of the frustration. Indeed, this book is written in large part to encourage the church to think critically about how we can move away from this behavior, and toward fruitful gospel ministry. At the same time, however, the narrative has far exceeded reality.

Christians need to own our responsibility in creating a negative cultural environment, but over time a lie has emerged, one that we need to reject just as passionately as we accept that we've contributed to the current climate. If we do not, we risk ignoring how Christians can be targets of the age of outrage as well as perpetrators and contributors.

Though there is much pseudo-history about the origins of America, it is true that we are a country founded largely on Judeo-Christian principles. Those standards of ethical and moral behavior have conditioned many in our culture to expect certain conduct from Christian adherents, including honesty, kindness, and avoidance of what are culturally understood to be vices. When believers–whether true disciples or simply followers in name only–don't live up to those generally accepted standards, society and social media users yell, "Hypocrite!" (Online, it's usually spelled in all caps).

As we discussed in chapter 1, many Americans label themselves as Christians only out of family tradition or because of the seeming advantages of adhering to the same faith as the majority of their neighbors. Such people are not equipped spiritually to live a faithful Christian life, and so they behave as other secular people do. These non- or nominal Christians often respond with outrage because they don't have the spiritual gifts and biblical tools to exhibit Christian love. Without the indwelling Spirit, they inevitably devolve to expressions of outrage.

No Different from the Rest of Society?

Religion writers and academics have recently argued that as compared to the rest of the population, Christians often have the more negative impact on their communities. An article from the Religion News Service that was published in the *Washington Post* opened with this blaring statement: "Conservative Protestants in red states aren't the only one seeing high divorce rates–so are their neighbors." The reporter, Sarah Pulliam Bailey, discussed the study behind this finding:

> Researchers found that simply living in an area with a large concentration of conservative Protestants increases the chances of divorce, even for those who are not themselves conservative Protestants.
>
> According to researchers who took into account race, income and other factors, marriage and fertility trends that are common among conservative Protestants–younger marriage, more kids, less higher education–affect all people in areas most populated

by conservative Protestants, no matter their personal
religious affiliation.[1]

Americans expect conservative Christians to be more faithful
in marriage and to be a positive influence on their neighbors. Yet
according to this study of divorce rates and religion in the *American
Journal of Sociology*, the opposite is true.

Outrageous.

Researchers Jennifer Glass from the University of Texas and
Philip Levchak from the University of Iowa looked at divorce rates
in every county in the United States. They found that those with
the highest number of conservative Christians also had the highest divorce rates. Even when controlling for factors such as poverty and education, the researchers found a positive correlation
between religion and divorce rates.[2]

Other studies have also found that something about conservative evangelical faith in the United States seems to make people
vulnerable to divorce. It's a finding that puzzles both researchers
and church leaders. After all, conservative Christians value marriage and family highly. They vow to get married and stay married
"till death do us part."

So you'd expect places like the Bible Belt, where evangelicalism
is the dominant faith, to have low divorce rates. But that's seemingly not the case. For instance, Oklahoma and Arkansas are two
of the most evangelical states in the country, according to the Pew
Religious Landscape Survey. More than half the people (53 percent) in those two states say they are evangelicals. That's twice the
national average. But both states have high divorce rates.

Oklahoma had the highest divorce rate in the nation in 2016;
Arkansas and Florida weren't far behind. Other Bible Belt states
like Kentucky, Tennessee, and Alabama also have higher than
average divorce rates. Then there's Mississippi, where the divorce
rate nearly matches the marriage rate.

Meanwhile, states like Illinois and Massachusetts, where there
are few evangelicals, have some of the lowest divorce rates in the

CHRISTIANS IN THE AGE OF OUTRAGE

nation. As the researchers put it, "something about the cultural and organizational practices of conservative Protestants works against their aspiration to promote stable lifelong marriages."[3]

Critics of evangelicals are less kind. Michelle Goldberg, writing for *The Nation*, writes, "It looks as if right-wing Christianity itself undermines modern marriage."[4]

Well, but hold on . . .

What Is the Real (Statistical) Deal?

It is statistically true that communities with more evangelicals have higher divorce rates. But something can be statistically true and misleading at the same time, because faith is not the only factor affecting divorce. And we know from other studies that evangelicals and other Christians who go to church regularly have low divorce rates.

Here are some additional facts: Residents of the Bible Belt are more likely to get married than people in other areas of the country. The marriage rate in Arkansas is nearly twice that of Massachusetts.[5] More marriages mean more potential divorces. Folks in the Bible Belt also tend to marry at earlier ages than people in other parts of the country.[6] They also are generally less well off economically—two more factors known to lead to higher divorce rates, says Charles Stokes, an assistant professor of sociology at Samford University. He concluded, "Early-marrying couples face a double dilemma of learning to live together (and perhaps raise children together) while also struggling to get by."[7]

Statistics from the US Centers for Disease Control and Prevention support Stokes. Men and women who marry young—before the age of twenty—are less likely to stay married for twenty years. So are people whose parents were divorced. Those with college degrees are more likely to stay married than those with only high school diplomas.[8]

The CDC also found that faith plays a role. Women who were raised in "other religions" are most likely to stay married for twenty years (65 percent), followed by those raised Catholic (53 percent), and Protestant (50 percent). Nones–those who claim no religious affiliation–are the least likely (43 percent) to stay married for at least twenty years.[9]

Nones are also a bad influence on other marriages, according to the "Red State, Blue State, and Divorce" study. Researchers found the number of nones or unaffiliated people in a community affected divorce rates. The so-called "unaffiliated effect" is "three times larger"[10] than the evangelical effect on divorce. In other words, if you replaced all the evangelicals in the Bible Belt with nones, divorce rates would skyrocket.

Therefore, not only do divorce rates correlate with faith, they also correlate with other factors. Many of the conclusions about Christians and divorce may be statistically accurate but woefully incomplete and thus wholly misleading. Such misunderstandings can lead to outrage at those whom secularists and nominal Christians see as hypocritical believers.

Nones in Disguise Generate Outrage

The rise of nones is regularly cited as one of the most significant religious and cultural developments of the past generation in the Western world.[11] This increase has been cited by observers of religion as exhibit A of America's declining religiosity, with those identifying as religiously unaffiliated growing from 16 percent to 23 percent between 2007 and 2014.[12] So who are the nones, and what do they mean for the church and for our study of outrage?

In *American Grace*, Robert Putnam and David Campbell helpfully point out that only a minority of nones identify as atheist or agnostic. In fact, many still express some belief in God, the afterlife, and morality even as they reject traditional religious affiliation and participation.[13] Essentially, they are that "spiritual but not religious" person you meet at your local coffee shop.

In explaining the rise of nones in American religion, Putnam and Campbell point to the changing landscape in moral attitudes among Americans. We can trace the evolution of public opinion away from traditional Christian ethics, particularly concerning gender, sexuality, and drugs, beginning in the 1990s. As these moral opinions shifted, Putnam and Campbell contend, those who were not spiritually or confessionally active had little reason to self-identify as Christian any longer.

I believe the most significant contributor to the outrage expressed toward and by Christians is caused by those nones who are holding on to their Christian affiliation. Many self-identifying conservative Christians are actually nones in disguise. They may have some conservative Christian positions, but they have no Christian foundation. They identify as Christians out of cultural convenience rather than because of a conversion experience and biblical worldview. These nones in disguise, or what most would call nominal Christians, are not truly Christians at all, so for the most part, they do not act like true believers.

In some ways, these nominal believers are worse off than true nones because they are trying to live like Christians without any of the support that comes from Christian communities. When researchers look at marriage and divorce data for Christians, they usually group nominal and convictional Christians together. But these two groups are, as we've seen, different in significant ways. Grouping Christians together for the purposes of polling may be easy and make it appear that there is still a high percentage of Christians in the country, but the majority of people who claim to be Christian do not have a Christian worldview. Rather, they have a secular worldview with a few dashes of Christianity sprinkled in.

A similar problem has existed for generations among historians and theologians fighting over the definition of *evangelical.* This difficulty was exacerbated when evangelicals burst onto the political stage in the 1970s. Sociologists and political theorists alike scrambled to understand this group and to measure who they were and what they wanted. Led by George Gallup, pollsters throughout the seventies and eighties tried several ways of differentiating between evangelicals. Finally, they settled on asking respondents if they self-identify as "a born-again, or evangelical, Christian."[14] This essentially redefined a movement previously distinguished by its belief, activism, and institutions in light of self-identification.

Interest in who evangelicals were, what they thought, and what influenced their voting decisions intensified during the 2016 US presidential election. The importance of this group was verified when postelection polling indicated that 81 percent of white evangelicals voted for Donald Trump.[15] It was a staggering number, not because evangelicals favored the Republican candidate over the Democrat (the closest Democrats came to reversing that trend was when Jimmy Carter was on the ticket). No, what caught so many off guard was the sheer size of the majority. Trump, a real-estate magnate from New York with a troubled marital past and a string of moral and ethical challenges, won more evangelical support than any other twenty-first century Republican presidential candidate.

Since the election, the 81 percent statistic has served as a rallying cry for those who believe evangelicalism, if not American Christianity more broadly, is in the midst of an identity crisis. Suddenly, leading theologians, pastors, musicians, and missionaries were contemplating walking away from the evangelical movement or label. Evangelicalism, which had begun as a renewal movement emphasizing a prophetic social piety and activism resulting from a transformative conversion experience, had seemingly become politicized.

When it seemed like the confusion couldn't get worse, allegations of sexual assault surfaced in 2017 against the Republican candidate for the US Senate seat in Alabama. Headlines predicted Roy Moore was likely to win the seat due to the strength of his evangelical support. More concerning, a poll released as the campaign reached the final stretch indicated evangelicals were *more likely* to support Moore after the allegations broke.[16] This fed into a snowballing narrative that evangelicals were selling their souls for a seat at the political table. Whether for a tax break, a bathroom bill, or hopes for a Supreme Court justice, evangelicals were digging in along political lines regardless of the standard bearer. But in both cases, practicing evangelicals and inactive, in-name-only evangelicals were included in the same category, and that makes a difference.

Several studies show that religious identity has little bearing on the ethical or theological views or behaviors of those who self-identify as Christians. In other words, the beliefs and practices of most people who call themselves Christians do not look like what we'd expect from people who are actual disciples of Christ.

A 2017 study from LifeWay Research confirmed the discrepancy between the number of Americans who say they are evangelical and those who hold a Christian worldview. While 29 percent of Americans self-identified as "born-again Christians" and 24 percent self-identified as "evangelical Christians," only 15 percent strongly agreed with core evangelical beliefs. In fact, researchers found a stark difference in the demographics and political attitudes of those with evangelical beliefs as compared with those who merely self-identify as evangelicals.[17] This discrepancy likely reflects the fact that evangelical Christianity has become a stand-in for a cultural or nominal Christianity in America. The irony here, as Baylor professor and author Thomas Kidd points out, is that evangelicalism was founded in part to "*combat* nominal Christianity, meaning a Christianity that is more a cultural label than a vital, active faith."[18] Yet somewhere in the past generations, evangelicalism has incrementally come to symbolize the cultural Christianity it once fought.

Being a Convictional Christian Makes a Difference

Nominal Christianity is a problem for the church because it conflates professing Christians who have a worldview defined and shaped by the gospel with those who are merely culturally Christians. Self-identifying as a Christian in a culture whose default religious identification is Christianity is easy.

When we look again at divorce rates, we see that regular church attendance does make a difference. Brad Wright, a sociologist at the University of Connecticut, studied marriage and church attendance data from the General Social Survey (GSS). In his book *Christians Are Hate-Filled Hypocrites . . . and Other Lies You've Been Told*, Wright cites GSS data that shows that about four in ten (42 percent) Christians and members of other faith traditions say they are divorced. By contrast, about 50 percent of nones say they are divorced. However, Wright found a significant split in divorce rates between evangelicals who attend church weekly (38 percent) and those who rarely or never go to church (60 percent).[19]

There's a similar difference in those who cohabitate. About 2 percent of evangelicals who go to church weekly say they are living with someone outside of marriage. That number, says Wright, jumps to 7 percent for evangelicals who never go to church and 8 percent for nones.[20]

Wright also found a link between domestic violence rates and church attendance. According to the National Survey of Families and Households, about 6 percent of Christian men who do not attend services regularly admitted "hitting, shoving, or throwing something at their partner in the previous year."[21] That's about the same rate as nones.

But 2 percent of Christian men who attend church regularly had committed an act of domestic violence. Christian women showed the same difference, with about 8 percent of non-attendees saying they'd committed a violent act, as opposed to 3 percent of weekly attendees.[22]

So counting active evangelicals with inactive Christians is both misleading and unhelpful. Nominal evangelicals are, at least statistically, not great representatives of Christ.

Nominalism Impacts Everything

A major cause of outrage against Christians is the hypocrisy of nominal Christians who simply cannot live out the fullness of their purported worldview. In this respect, *nominalism has just enough Christianity to be dangerous.* We can see this danger in two respects.

First, nominal Christianity is dangerous to those who attempt it because they quickly find out that trying to run the race of the Christian life without genuine faith is not only exhausting, it's impossible.

Every year, hundreds of thousands of runners participate in about a thousand marathon races across the country. They buy the right gear, sign up for a race, and line up with the other participants. But when the starting gun sounds, some fall apart in the first stages of the race. They neglected to train. They thought they could show up and run a marathon with no conditioning, no experience, and no preparation. But what matters in a race are the weeks or months of training and hundreds of miles that provide the knowledge and strength to run the race.

Nominal Christians are like marathon runners who signed up for the race, got their official number, and bought the fancy running gear–but never went out and did the actual training ahead of time. They can't run the race because they have not prepared. They haven't developed the habits of faith–like prayer, Bible study, and worship–that would transform them into true disciples. They are not part of a community that can sustain and inform their worldview. They have the T-shirt but not the ability to complete the race. So they run in vain.

Worse than running without preparation is trying to run the race of the Christian life *without the Holy Spirit.* As Christians, and as evangelicals in particular, we believe conversion is not merely the result of words we say or a change in self-identification. We are not Christians because we *say* we are. What makes us Christians is the indwelling of God's Spirit, who comes to those who "repent and believe" (Mark 1:15). This Spirit makes all the difference in running the race. Jonathan Edwards said this:

> If there be such a thing as conversion, 'tis the most
> important thing in the world; and they are happy that have
> been the subjects of it and they most miserable that have
> not. . . . If there really be such a thing as conversion, then

you that are unconverted can't reasonably have any rest
in the condition that you are in.[23]

Edwards points out that a fundamental and massive difference
exists between the convictional Christian, who has experienced
the indwelling of the Spirit, and those who are only nominally
Christian. The Spirit who "raised Jesus from the dead" now
"dwells in" those who belong to God through faith (Romans 8:11).
Nominal Christians, on the other hand, try to live out the moral
life of Christianity, yet remain spiritually dead because the Spirit
of God does not live in them.

The second danger of nominal Christianity is that it creates a
false set of expectations within the community, which assumes that
nominal and convictional Christians live according to the tenets of
their faith. Ross Douthat, a *New York Times* columnist, put it this
way: "The social goods associated with faith flow almost exclu-
sively from religious participation, not from affiliation or nominal
belief. And where practice ceases or diminishes, in what you might
call America's 'Christian penumbra,' the remaining residue of religion can be socially damaging instead."[24] This is perhaps where
nominal Christianity is the most destructive. While nominalism
may begin from a conservative worldview that mimics Christian
positions, it lacks the spiritual worldview that informs the why and
how of these views. Nominal Christians are a distorted reflection of
Christianity because they try to have the religiosity without Christ.

Nominal Christians often are shaped by a conservative worldview, but they may not express those opinions in Christ-honoring
ways. For example, Christians can and should debate political
issues. As one of many possible applications, we can debate levels of immigration, how to best address border security, and how
to deal with undocumented immigrants who live in our country.
But when we speak of immigrants in disparaging and unchristian
ways, or when we spew vitriol toward people made in the image of
God because they hold opposing views, we sound more like talk-
radio commentators than people with a gospel-shaped worldview.

Not *of* Us

First John gives an eloquent description of what faith looks like in the life of the believer. Christians should be "living in the light, as God is in the light" (1:7, NLT); should confess sin, confident that God is "faithful and just to forgive" (1:9); and should "live their lives as Jesus did" (2:6, NLT). The countercultural life of a believer is defined by both a right view of the triune God—as the Creator, Savior, and indwelling Sustainer—and right actions lived in light of God's redemptive work. In many ways, John's letter serves as a mission statement for the church on how to live in yet not of the world.

John addressed nominalism in his day and ours when he wrote about those who had departed from the believing community:

> These people left our churches, but they never really
> belonged with us; otherwise they would have stayed with
> us. When they left, it proved that they did not belong with
> us. But you are not like that, for the Holy One has given
> you his Spirit, and all of you know the truth.
> 1 JOHN 2:19-20, NLT

This fascinating passage offers several crucial insights into how Christians should respond to nominalism in the age of outrage.

First, participation in the believing community is the true mark of someone belonging to the Christian faith. While these fake Christians in the New Testament had been in the church, their lack of genuine faith eventually led them to exit the community. While church attendance does not make one a Christian, the idea that one could live the Christian life without the church is foolish. John Stott put it more bluntly in the way only an Englishman can:

> We are not only committed to Christ, we are also
> committed to the body of Christ. At least I hope so. I trust
> that none of my readers is that grotesque anomaly, an
> un-churched Christian. The New Testament knows

nothing of such a person. For the church lies at the
very center of the eternal purpose of God. It is not a
divine afterthought. It is not an accident of history.
On the contrary, the church is God's new community.[25]

Second, God is sovereign over the winnowing process (see
Matthew 3:11-12), promising that he does it for our benefit. I have
been the pastor on Sunday mornings when I've noticed, as the
music started, that there were fewer seats filled than the previous
week. I have spoken at conferences where attendance has been
noticeably down. I have attended revival services that previously
packed stadiums but now struggled to fill small amphitheaters.
The sting of declining numbers is hard to accept even if we know
that those who left had never really bought into the Christian life.
There is inevitably the temptation to try to sustain the numbers, to
change our methods and even our message to accommodate those
who are leaving.

Into this temptation, God tells us that *he* is responsible for
those going out, making plain the division between those with a
Christian worldview and those who have simply mixed in with the
crowd. Nominal Christians are not always easy to spot; they thrive
on blending in and going with the flow—although they are often
exposed when they respond in outrage. Now that the cultural flow
is starting to shift in a more secular direction, God is revealing to
us the true state of the church and the state of the mission field in
which we find ourselves.

"No True Scotsman": The Limits of Nominalism

Even as we recognize that the public's perception of our faith has
soured in part because of nominal Christianity, we need to avoid
making a mistake of our own: condemning any fellow believer
who takes a position that doesn't match up with ours. There is
a temptation among Christians to point at every example of outrage caused or facilitated by professing Christians and proclaim

that "they're not really Christians!" Whenever we see a professing Christian politician cast a questionable vote or when we read an offensive blog post from a pastor, we can be tempted to simply retort that the person is not truly a believer. *True* Christians would never vote that way, think those thoughts, or behave in that fashion. Within this framework, we are able to dismiss every poorly behaving social media user with "Christ follower" in their profile. They are simply *not one of us.* If they were actually one of us, they wouldn't be that outraged, dismissive, ignorant, or unloving.

In *How to Think Straight,* the British philosopher Antony Flew called this the "No-true-Scotsman Move." At its heart, this fallacy is the unwillingness to accept any counterexamples to the way we categorize people, dismissing them as irrelevant instead. Flew introduced the idea with a great illustration:

> Imagine some aggressively nationalistic Scotsman settled down one Sunday morning with his customary copy of that shock-horror tabloid *The News of the World.* He reads the story under the headline, "Sidcup Sex Maniac Strikes Again." Our reader is, as he confidently expected, agreeably shocked: "No Scot would do such a thing!" Yet the very next Sunday he finds in that same favorite source a report of the even more scandalous ongoings of Mr. Angus MacSporran in Aberdeen. This clearly constitutes a perfect counterexample, one which definitively falsifies the universal proposition originally put forward. . . . Allowing that this is indeed such a counterexample, he ought to withdraw, retreating perhaps to a rather weaker claim about most or some Scotsmen. But even an imaginary Scot is, like the rest of us, human; and none of us always does what we ought to do. So instead he amends his statement to: "No true Scotsman would do such a thing!"[26]

Flew went on to note that this move is effective because it shifts the ground of discussion without the participants realizing it.

When we're angered by the actions of other professing Christians, we can discount them by simply declaring that their behavior or beliefs are evidence that the offenders were not *truly* Christian.

No true Christian would vote for Donald Trump.
No true Christian would vote for Hillary Clinton.
No true Christian would oppose immigration.
No true Christian would oppose same-sex marriage.
No true Christian would shop at Whole Foods.

When we look at the reasons that people voted for or against candidates in the last US presidential election, we find that people are not as one-dimensional as some have claimed.

When the Billy Graham Center Institute asked evangelicals what issue was *the most important* in deciding how they cast their vote in the 2016 election, there was significant diversity. (See graph on page 72.) No single issue garnered more than a fifth of the vote; most often cited was the economy (17 percent), followed by health care (11 percent) and immigration (10 percent). This doesn't even take into consideration the myriad of ways evangelicals might explain *why* this single issue was the most critical to winning their vote. Undoubtedly, many would point to a mixture of theological and political reasons to explain their decision.

In any case, the lack of anything close to a majority should give us pause when making claims about what a true Christian can and cannot do outside of clear biblical warrant. Christians today frequently cite biblical authority for both denigrating those with whom we disagree and avoiding substantive reflection as to why other Christians might think or act differently than we do. This doesn't mean we cannot criticize others when we believe something has displaced the gospel within their worldview. Rather, it should cause us to reflect on why others saw an issue as so important and central to Kingdom ministry.

Making sweeping generalizations and dismissing broad sections of professing believers without careful reflection and

In the 2016 presidential election, which reason was most important to you in deciding how to cast your vote? (select one)

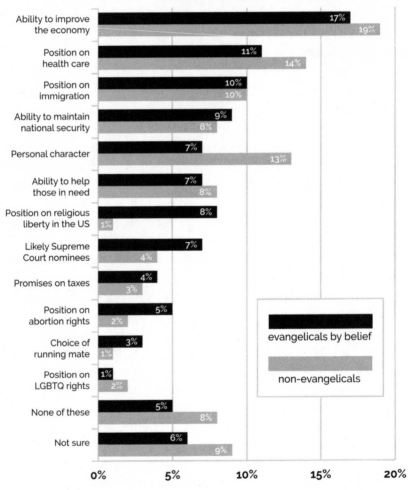

Reason	evangelicals by belief	non-evangelicals
Ability to improve the economy	17%	19%
Position on health care	11%	14%
Position on immigration	10%	10%
Ability to maintain national security	9%	8%
Personal character	7%	13%
Ability to help those in need	7%	8%
Position on religious liberty in the US	8%	1%
Likely Supreme Court nominees	7%	4%
Promises on taxes	4%	3%
Position on abortion rights	5%	2%
Choice of running mate	3%	1%
Position on LGBTQ rights	1%	2%
None of these	5%	8%
Not sure	6%	9%

From 2018 research study conducted by the Billy Graham Center Institute, in partnership with LifeWay Research engagement breeds contempt on both sides, effectively excommunicating whole sections of the body. Rather than extending grace in failure or taking off our cultural blinders, we simply pronounce others outside the fold.

When we treat fellow Christians in this way, we also give tacit support to society's view that "Christians are the worst!" As believers, however, we recognize that we are not above mistakes and failure. We are sinful people who, while redeemed and indwelt, are still hampered by our flesh. Do Christians get divorced at rates higher than their secular neighbors? No, but that doesn't mean Christian marriages are perfect or that people of faith don't sometimes get divorced.

Christians cannot blame nominal believers as a way to avoid dealing with the very real and destructive contributions we have made to the age of outrage. On the other hand, we must reject the cultural narrative that says Christians are responsible for every self-identifying Christian with nothing but a nominal faith.

If Christians accept this narrative from the wider culture, we risk being smothered by every crazy and attention-starved person who claims to speak for Christianity. The truth is that despite some of the headlines, the majority of *Convictional Christians* are living out their faith in imperfect yet compelling ways. However, because the media often covers only the loudest moments and controversies, we miss the quiet work of the people who have been transformed by their faith and are striving to show and share the love of Jesus within their communities.

CHAPTER 4

Lie #2:
"My Outrage Is Righteous Anger"

- Evangelicals (78 percent) and non-evangelicals (74 percent) express high levels of concern about the lack of civility in the public discussion of social issues.

IN THE LAST CHAPTER, we considered a lie that our culture often directs at us: Christians are hypocrites! While that presumption is faulty and needs to be challenged, I am even more concerned by the lies that we believers tend to tell ourselves. Why? Because these untruths not only damage our witness, they lead us to places of outrage in our own thinking and behavior. One of the chief examples of these kinds of lies is when we try to disguise our outrage as righteous anger. "My outrage is righteous."

Having spent a fair bit of time with people online, I have heard most of the responses Christians give when told to cool their outrage:

> We need to get angry!
> Jesus was angry with the Pharisees for their
>   self-righteousness!
> God was angry with those who oppressed the poor!

The age of outrage has succeeded in trapping Christians by wrapping itself in one *very* appealing lie. The center of this lie is a bait and switch, trying to pass off outrage as righteous anger.

We try to disguise our worldly anger behind appeals to theological or ethical justification. We need to be angry, the logic goes, because of all the sin in the world. This is what makes this lie so powerful. Yes, there is a lot in this world to anger us, and Scripture *does* call us to be angry about many things. We should be angry over sin in ourselves and in the world. We should be angry about injustice. We should be particularly angry at how quickly we can grow inoculated, numb, or apathetic to injustices. In fact, we can actually *contribute* to the outrage when *we fail to get angry* about the things that anger God.

So while this lie originates from a truthful premise, the lie develops when we conveniently ignore the fact that not all anger is the same. Righteous anger, for instance, must be—wait for it— righteous. This means that God is looking for a certain character to our anger. Scripture consistently warns us about the proclivity of anger to turn into sin when we are reckless, unthinking, and self- ish. In essence, the Christian faith does call us to righteous anger, but it is a lie to conflate this with outrage. Outrage is nothing but a cheap imitation of righteous anger. It is a production of our flesh that may at times give the appearance of godliness without the substance to back it up.

Christians give in to this lie when we unthinkingly unleash outrage in the name of righteous anger. When we do so, we reveal to the world that we are playing by their rules rather than being guided by the Spirit of God. So how do we differentiate between righteous anger and outrage? In order to root out this lie, let us first define righteous anger in light of Scripture. We can then better see just how ugly outrage is and how we can pursue righteous anger without falling prey to unbridled fury.

What Is Righteous Anger?

Any theology of anger must begin by recognizing that God gets angry. Contrary to what some modern hipster pastors have claimed,

God does become angry—angry at sin, angry at injustice, angry at rebellion.

Scripture speaks about God pouring out his wrath on evildoers. Why? Because he is so perfectly holy, any manifestation of sin and evil is a direct affront to him (Ezekiel 7:8; Isaiah 63:1-6; and Revelation 14:9-11). His anger is intertwined with his holiness and judgment. J. I. Packer defines righteous anger as "the right reaction of moral perfection in the Creator towards moral perversity in the creature."[1]

In other words, because God is perfect in his holiness, his anger is always righteous. Biblical scholar John Murray writes that God's righteous wrath flows from "the holy revulsion of God's being against that which is the contradiction of his holiness."[2] And this is a good thing! If God remained so impassive that every act of evil, oppression, or injustice was essentially ignored, we would find his response defective.

However, we need to pump the brakes when it comes to our own anger. While God's perfect and holy nature ensures that his anger is always righteous, humans are flawed and biased. Even when we are certain that our anger is righteous, our flesh may distort our vision and blind us to the truth. This is why Paul cautions in Ephesians 4:26, "Be angry and do not sin." Thus, although there are times when righteous anger is the necessary response to this world, Scripture calls us to exert significant control over why, how, and how long we are angry (Proverbs 29:11; Ephesians 4:26-31; and James 1:19-20).

If the age of outrage has taught us anything, it's that we Christians are *exceptionally bad stewards of our anger.* Thus, while Christians can and should be righteously angry, we need to be far more vigilant. With this in mind, let me offer three characteristics of righteous anger.

1. **Righteous anger is directed toward things that anger God.**
   In one of the opening chapters of Mark, the Gospel writer includes a compelling story about Jesus' anger (3:1-6). While

most people point to the story of Jesus turning out the money changers from the Temple as an example of his anger, I think this story in Mark 3 subtly but powerfully captures the truth of Jesus' righteous anger in a compelling fashion. This passage explains that Jesus entered the synagogue and saw a man with a withered hand. It seems as if a trap had been set for Jesus, as Mark tells us that people were watching to see if Jesus would heal on the Sabbath. Recognizing this trap because, duh, he's Jesus, he asked the obvious question: "Is it lawful on the Sabbath to do good or to do harm, to save life or to kill?" (verse 4). The question turned the tables on those who were trying to trap Jesus. Now they were forced to choose between Jesus healing the man or upholding their interpretation of the law. Predictably, no one wanted to make this choice.

In response, Mark tells us that Jesus "looked around at them with anger, grieved at their hardness of heart" (verse 5). Notice the emphasis is not so much on the fact that Jesus was angry but on the source of his anger. Not only had the onlookers manipulated a suffering man to try to entrap Jesus, they had used the Sabbath as an excuse to accuse Jesus of wrongdoing. In one action, they had used God's law and the suffering of others to advance their own ambition. In response, Jesus perfectly captured how righteous anger stands at the cross section of the holiness of God *and* the oppression of the suffering.

Righteous anger is prompted by the same things that anger God, including injustice, corruption, immorality, and oppression of the poor and needy, as well as the defamation of his glory (false teaching, hypocrisy, and the like).

2. **Righteous anger mirrors the way God is angry.** While most people view "the God of the Old Testament" as all about fire and brimstone and Jesus as loving and kind, this reveals a fairly high level of ignorance of Scripture. Take,

for instance, Exodus 34:5-7. Here we have the pinnacle of the Old Testament description of God as *the Lord describes himself to Moses*:

> The LORD descended in the cloud and stood with him there, and proclaimed the name of the LORD. The LORD passed before him and proclaimed, "The LORD, the LORD, a God merciful and gracious, slow to anger, and abounding in steadfast love and faithfulness, keeping steadfast love for thousands, forgiving iniquity and transgression and sin, but who will by no means clear the guilty, visiting the iniquity of the fathers on the children and the children's children, to the third and the fourth generation."

Consider this: How does God think of himself? What language does he use to describe himself to his people? Not "all-powerful" or "holy," although those elements are certainly there. Rather, he says he is "abounding in steadfast love and faithfulness."

God's righteous indignation flows from his love and faithfulness; likewise, if your anger is not consistently and sacrificially tempered by steadfast love and forgiveness, it is not righteous anger. In order to *earn* the responsibility of displaying God's righteous anger to the world, you first need to demonstrate that you can be a faithful vessel of his steadfast love and forgiveness. Anyone can be angry. The Scriptures teach us to be angry in the way that God is angry by leading us to his holiness first.

3. **Righteous anger submits to God's role as ultimate judge.** When it comes to how we reflect God's righteous anger, we need to be cognizant of the vast gulf between God and ourselves. Even though we may feel moral certitude on an issue,

we are limited and prone to misunderstanding. While we can rely upon God's Word and the indwelling of his Spirit to assess and respond to injustice, oppression, and rebellion, we are not the ultimate judge who will bring retribution.

When God says, "Vengeance is mine, I will repay" (Romans 12:19), he doesn't qualify that with "but only if you don't *really* want to dish out some of the sweet justice yourself." Often God's call for us is to endure, to wait patiently, and to accept loss and persecution because we know that God as the ultimate judge will bring justice.

Reading through the imprecatory psalms (a collection of psalms in which the author prays for God's judgment upon his enemies), one is struck by the anger that seethes off the pages. In Psalm 69, for example, David burns with anger against his enemies, calling for God's justice and judgment. Lost in the jarringly harsh tone is the reality that David is setting his anger before the Lord, waiting for him to accomplish his will. Even though David is "afflicted and in pain" (verse 29), he understands that his anger is subject to God, who will bring real judgment.

What Is Outrage?

As we've seen, when Scripture depicts righteous anger, it sets the bar high. Outrage exhibits few if any of the short- or long-term characteristics Scripture associates with righteous anger. Righteous anger is aimed at the glory of God, but outrage is an angry reaction to personal injury or insult. Where righteous anger is purposeful and designed to advance specific objectives and ends, outrage exhibits little critical thought as to its underlying focus, motivations, expressions, or ends.

Outrage is motivated by a desire to punish or destroy rather than reconcile and refine. It is frequently accompanied by hubris and a confidence in its judgment, categorically rejecting any nuance. Outrage is fast and decisive rather than reflective, choosing to exhibit God's retribution rather than reflect his persistent, steadfast love.

Sadly, there is a ready supply of examples of outrage in our culture. From them, we can derive six broad characteristics.

1. **Outrage is *disproportionate.*** Outrage often unleashes on people in smothering waves of anger. There is little or no thought to the level of intensity; all offenses are treated the same. Even when anger begins in response to a real offense, it quickly snowballs. One of the principles of a just war is that combatants must think in terms of proportionality. This discipline is completely lost on many social media warriors and cable news talking heads.

2. **Outrage is *selfish.*** We often vent and rage against others because in the end, it feels good. We believe our anger puts others in their place. Whether it's a politician we despise for his or her economic policy or a journalist we perceive as anti-Christian, we unload our anger, deriving pleasure from the perception that we are fighting back. In this way, outrage functions as an odd catharsis for our insecurities, fears, and sense of powerlessness. Such anger becomes about *me*–my needs, wants, and desires–rather than about injustice.

3. **Outrage is *divisive.*** In this era of cultural polarization, outrage bends anger to serve a spirit of tribalism. Outrage rants and raves about *them*, their group, their ilk; about the injustice and evil of those politicians or communities, journalists, or even pastors. Conversely, when we are outraged, we can accept no criticism of our own team and are quick to explain or justify the same behavior in ourselves. Because of this, outrage will always ring hollow over time.

4. **Outrage is *visceral.*** In the digital age of rapid reaction, outrage is often produced by our uncritical gut reaction to things,

people, or ideas we perceive to be wrong or offensive. When we aren't thinking critically, we do not consider context or try to understand the why or what. Instead, we simply lash out. As the pace of our world increases, it can feel that we need to comment *as things happen* or risk being left behind. This lack of careful reflection inevitably transforms anger into outrage.

5. **Outrage is *domineering*.** Because its aim is to shut down, silence, or shame those who disagree, outrage is not interested in truth or nuance. The world is binary and defined solely by winning and losing. Often when we encounter pushback, warning, or calls for moderation—even from friendly voices—we respond by trying to berate others into submission. Hyperbole, insults, and even profanity become justifiable tools to ensure the battle lines are clearly drawn.

6. **Outrage is *dishonest*.** Outrage often cares only about scoring rhetorical points, not about giving fair and honest treatment. We use terms and descriptors to disparage others rather than their ideas. Complementarians are defenders of the patriarchy, while egalitarians are militant feminists. Those who vote differently from us are unpatriotic. And those who call for tightening US immigration policies hate all immigrants. While there may be legitimate reasons for disagreement and reasonable people continue to have substantive discussions about these issues, outrage cares more about getting good sound bites that disparage the opposition than affirming the dignity of others. Invariably outrage will digress to an attack on a flawed misrepresentation of an opponent's true position or argument in order to knock it down more easily.

We can determine that anger is devolving into outrage when it takes on these characteristics. Whenever our anger is disproportionate, selfish, divisive, visceral, domineering, or dishonest, we should exercise caution in ascribing any righteousness to it.

We Need to Call Outrage What It Is: Sin

I have always been a sucker for tourist-trap museums. I relish my role as *that* dad, and few experiences allow me to exercise my role as "embarrasser-in-chief" of the Stetzer tribe more than tourist attractions. Forget about forcing my kids to be in pictures with Mickey; *I'm* going to be in that picture too.

So for people like me, a trip to Branson, Missouri, is like hitting the jackpot. The town is filled with every tourist trap known to man, and my family's favorite is the Titanic Museum. It is hard to describe this museum, but picture a perfect replica of the *Titanic* with its front third cut off. Then imagine it stuck in a pond with a fake iceberg attached to the side of it.

It is cheesy. It is goofy. It is awesome.

I think one reason the museum is my favorite is that I'm fascinated by the story. The ship's owner, the White Star Line, was so confident in its durability that one of its employees boasted that "not even God himself could sink this ship."[3] I mean, at that point you're really just asking for it. But it wasn't a crash or a torpedo or a hurricane that brought the ship down—just a naturally occurring piece of ice floating in the water. For those of you who scoff at the educational value of such tourist traps, let me pass along one fact that stood out to me at the Titanic Museum. I'd never known how easy—or how catastrophic—it can be to underestimate the size of an iceberg. When it floats, only about 9 percent of an iceberg is above the water, and 91 percent is below. Ignoring this fact was the fatal flaw of the *Titanic* crew. They saw the iceberg but ignored the roughly 90 percent under the water.

This same lesson can be applied to Jesus' teaching in the Sermon on the Mount. One of the most challenging and complex pieces of Scripture, the sermon is Jesus' argument about how his followers can flourish. He explains that he did not come to abolish the law, but to fulfill it.[4] He reinforces this six times throughout the sermon when he says, "You have heard that it was said . . . , but I say to you . . ."[5]

His point is that the law is merely the tip of the iceberg for Christian living. As with an iceberg, there is so much more to the law hidden below our sight line.

While Jesus touches on many vices, I want to focus specifically on how he treats anger and hatred in Matthew 5:21-26. Jesus reminds his audience that, at the surface level, the law says, "Do not murder." But this is only 10 percent of the iceberg, and Jesus is, as Jonathan Pennington noted, "bringing out its fullest and truest sense." He continued,

> To "fulfill all righteousness" and to have a "righteousness that surpasses the scribes and the Pharisees," disciples must face the issue of the inner person. Not committing the physical act of murder is good and right, of course, but it is not the true litmus test of piety and alignment with God's nature, will, and coming kingdom; examining one's attitudes and speech are just as important as refraining from homicidal violence.[6]

Jesus invites his audience to understand that it is not enough to obey the letter of the law more often; instead, we need to experience a heart change reflected by inward concern and a changed attitude. We are to look beyond the rules without discarding them.

When Jesus discusses anger, we see that the 90 percent hidden behind the simple command "Do not murder" is far deeper than we could have imagined. He says, "I say to you that everyone who is angry with his brother will be liable to judgment, whoever insults his brother will be liable to the council; and whoever says, 'You fool!' will be liable to the hell of fire" (Matthew 5:22).

Jesus is interested in outward behavior only as it reflects the inward state of our hearts. While harboring anger against a brother was not technically against the law, Jesus teaches that insulting and raging against others is still intensely ungodly behavior.

Today we see a similar disconnect in our understanding of anger. Many people look for loopholes in the commands so they can feel a sense of self-righteousness in an attempt to justify themselves before God and man. The reality is, Jesus' teaching brings us to the heart of the law, not just the letter of the law. A heart that gives way to worldly anger is sinful and severely at odds with the Spirit of God. Such fury damages ourselves, our churches, our communities, and ultimately God's Kingdom. Excusing it as an "innocent social media comment" or simply "the way political rhetoric works" sorely misses the point.

This is why we must confront the lie that our outrage is righteous anger. When we treat such anger lightly and try to pass it off as holiness, we damage our souls.

Distinguishing between the Two

Given how far our culture has drifted from a Judeo-Christian perspective, we will rightly be concerned by much of what we see on the screen, hear on the news, or read on the Internet. In light of Jesus' words, however, how can we keep from unrighteous outrage? Let me offer three practical suggestions we can glean from Scripture.

1. **Be quick to listen and slow to anger.** Our world is constantly pushing us to respond quickly, to shoot from the hip. We are conditioned to believe that if we see something we like or dislike, we need to speak up immediately. Yet James 1:19-20 says, "Know this, my beloved brothers [and sisters]: let every person be quick to hear, slow to speak, slow to anger; for the anger of man does not produce the righteousness of God." The reason Scripture cautions against reacting too quickly is that for the most part, our initial response is stupid. Psychology and sociology are catching up to Scripture, recognizing that our intuitive responses are often not only wrong but destructive.[7] Step back, think, and pray about what was said; then reflect on what would be a God-glorifying response.

2. **Reject the impulse to right every wrong.** Righteous anger picks and chooses its battles with care and precision. Proverbs 26 tells us to both answer a fool according to his folly (verse 5) and to resist this response (verse 4); in other words, we need to use discretion and self-control. People who cannot resist responding to every poke or slight reveal through their lack of self-control that their anger is outrage rather than righteous anger.

   At this point in history, when everyone seems to be yelling all the time, the words of people who speak rarely and with intention carry the most weight. Watch for those who recognize the power in reserving their anger for truly important causes. Often these voices are the ones pointing us in the right direction. There is an ocean of wrongness and offense on the Internet; trying to correct it all is like trying to empty the ocean with a thimble. It is impossible and not what God has called us to.

3. **Think through what you are trying to accomplish.** What is your end game? Righteous anger is designed to rebuke and exhort the people of God to obedience or the world to repentance. Thus, its goal is reconciliation with God. Anger that merely inflames and divides without an eye toward this goal is deformed. While it might feel good to put people in their place with our perfectly placed sarcastic comment, this ultimately doesn't serve the Kingdom of God. While our culture celebrates "savaging" or "flaming" others as ends in and of themselves, righteous anger aims at Kingdom purposes. In other words, not only *what* we say but *how* we say it needs to glorify God.

Less than a year ago, California Assembly member Evan Low and Biola University president Barry H. Corey took opposite sides during a heated debate on legislation meant to address tensions between nondiscrimination laws and religious beliefs about sexual ethics. There was plenty of outrage and name-calling to go around.

Faith-based universities like Biola were fighting to uphold their beliefs about sexuality, while Low and other supporters argued that these religious institutions were searching for a loophole to give themselves a "license to discriminate." Words and tone quickly soured on both sides.

Due to some relationship building, the bill eventually was modified in a manner that religious colleges could support. This, however, did not resolve the persistent distrust between the two opposing political and religious sides.

What happened next surprised many. Low and Corey entered into a posture of listening and actually talked through their opposing viewpoints. They began to deconstruct the mistaken impressions each had, breaking many barriers between the two ideas. Their cooperation allowed for a different kind of discussion, one that promoted unity and peace.

While Corey could easily have taken an aggressive stance, rallied his base, and allowed his frustration to cause further division, he instead used this debate as a platform to show the heart of Christ in relationships. He decided to extend a hand relationally and work for the common good, even when it was uncomfortable and left him feeling vulnerable.

The two wrote an article together for the *Washington Post*:

> We both had notions that informed our initially defensive stances toward the other. It's amazing how quickly biases can be overcome when real relationships are prioritized, when you realize the person you once thought an adversary is in many ways like you, with a story and passions and fears, and a hope that we can make the world a better place.[8]

The idea that Christians are more interested in protecting their truth than listening and hearing out opposing viewpoints is quite prevalent. Corey, who wrote a helpful book, *Love Kindness: Discover the Power of a Forgotten Christian Virtue,* has modeled a better way–a more Christlike way–for many in the Christian community. He's not changed his views, but he has changed his relationships.

And in the age of outrage, that's the kind of model we all need.

CHAPTER 5

Lie #3: "_____ Will Save Me from the Outrage!"

- When asked to describe their feelings when each party held the presidency, evangelicals' top responses for how they felt during a Republican administration were protected (34 percent) and safe (33 percent). During a Democratic presidency, they said they felt fearful of the future (34 percent) and frustrated (29 percent). This difference suggests evangelicals, along with the rest of society, associate political control with the safety and stability of their community.

I HIT "PUBLISH" AND walked away from the computer.

Another major political controversy had erupted, and each side was quickly stirring up their bases to engage in another round of cyber yelling. Both were adamant that they had the solution to the problem.

"It's obvious," some screamed.

"You're an idiot," others yelled back.

Since taking my post at the Billy Graham Center, I have tried to be a unifying source and help Christians respond to such events in a way that glorifies God and enlarges our witness for the gospel. That morning I published an article that outlined the nature of the controversy and called Christians to respond with grace and love. I recommended that we resist the urge to fall back to political or cultural talking points completely irrelevant to the gospel.

After returning to my desk, I went back to a full day of work. I finally returned to my article later in the evening. As I scrolled through the replies, my heart sank. To some I was a dangerous heretic; to others I was a coldhearted Pharisee. I guess it takes talent to write a piece that enrages the left and right, Christian and secular, old and young.

My piece also attracted the attention of some major news organizations. That gave me the opportunity to explain the gospel to a wider audience, but even then I received hate mail and phone calls from people on both sides of the issue. Depending on who you talked to, I was either a liberal shill or a conservative bigot. In the end, I could only sit back in complete exhaustion, sighing, "What is wrong with the world?"

In his influential book *Not the Way It's Supposed to Be*, theologian Cornelius Plantinga Jr. examines the two forces at work in our world: shalom and sin. According to Plantinga, *shalom* means "universal flourishing, wholeness, and delight."[1] In other words, it is *the way things are supposed to be.* It is the world as God designed it, where man is reconciled to his Creator and dwells with him. In contrast, sin is the disruption of this perfection. Sin is "any agential evil for which some person (or group of persons) is to blame. In short, sin is culpable shalom-breaking."[2] This is Plantinga's source for the title of his book: A world in sin is *not the way it's supposed to be.* Something has gone horribly wrong, and God's perfect design has been corrupted.

Plantinga's book was influential when it was published during the Clinton presidency, and it remains a compelling exploration of the nuances of hamartiology (the study of sin). Reading it again recently, I was struck by how his words seem to resonate today even more than when I first read them in the nineties. Make no mistake, the sin of this world has always been apparent for those with eyes to see. Plantinga even highlights how systemic racism gave rise to slavery and Jim Crow, two particularly strident forms of "shalom-breaking" sin that reverberate today. Yet the current polarization combined with technology has produced a world in which the chaos and division of sin is not only loud but feels far more pervasive. Everyone has a megaphone and is emboldened to give voice to their sin in a way that feels wholly unique to our world.

In this sense, I am actually thankful for one thing in this age of outrage. No longer can this world deny what Christians have known for millennia: This is not the way things are supposed to be. Even as we contribute to the outrage, we recognize that something is wrong that needs to be fixed. We need help.

But at the same time, this has led to an equally troubling problem. I worry now that in our hunt for the solution, this world (and many Christians) will seek answers in the wrong places. Distracted and divided, we are too ready to jump at any and every possible solution. This is how the third lie of the age of outrage sneaks in: "_____ will save me from the outrage!"

The age of outrage has no shortage of ideas to put in that blank. Most Americans agree that anger, division, and divisiveness in our world are out of control, fanned by the flames of social media, religious hypocrisy, echo chambers, media bias, and the widening of political and social gaps. At the same time, there is no consensus on what to do about it. Everyone seems to point fingers at a "guilty party" while giving self-serving, simplistic, and biased solutions to "fix" the problem. These proposed solutions–whether technology, politics, therapy, economic redistribution, education, or political liberty–are often one-sided, causing even more outrage from those with opposing viewpoints. That prompts more "fixes," which cause more outrage. The age of outrage seems to pick up more heat and smoke from this vicious cycle: simplistic, ready-made solutions to the problems it has created and exacerbated.

Rather than seeking a silver bullet, a new invention, or a groundbreaking discovery, Christians at their best understand that the problems of polarization and division are due to the underlying condition of a world mired in the brokenness of separation from God. We recognize that the outrage we see around us is merely the visceral reaction of a world estranged from its heavenly Father. We recognize the truth that the only one who can save us from the outrage is Jesus Christ. Everything else will leave us more broken and outraged.

At our worst, however, we give in to the lie that something else can save us, and we throw our credibility behind unfulfilling solutions that this world offers. This chapter explores how the age of outrage has made an idol even out of solving the problem of outrage. Christians need to recognize that at the core of this lie is an idolatry problem. When we look for solutions apart from Christ, we obscure the truth that the only answer to our dilemma is the gospel–that the dysfunction, division, and disorder leading to outrage are fundamentally a sin problem.

Trading Living Water for Cisterns of Outrage

The prophet Jeremiah was called by God to speak to his people at the outset of their exile from Israel in the sixth century BC. The Old Testament book bearing his name is a humbling exploration of the tragic effects of idolatry. While Isaiah reasoned and Jonah raged, Jeremiah wept at the inability of Israel to turn from their idols. They had the living God who had led them out of bondage, but in their fear, arrogance, and confusion, they had turned to the idols of the surrounding nations to solve their problems. This was tragic in two respects: "My people have done two evil things: They have abandoned me–the fountain of living water. And they have dug for themselves cracked cisterns that can hold no water at all!" (Jeremiah 2:13, NLT).

In Jeremiah's day, hand-dug wells called cisterns were the most common source of water. Hewn from limestone and then lined with plaster, cisterns captured rainwater, which was often the only source of water during the dry summer months. The image of a broken cistern essentially meant death to people living in such an arid environment. No matter how many times these Israelites went looking for water, they would come back empty.

Jeremiah used this analogy to make two interconnected statements about idolatry. First, idolatry begins with rebellion against God (Jeremiah 3:13). The Lord had consistently proven to Judah that he was the "fountain of living water" who was able to satisfy and save. His joy-filled presence required no effort to maintain, and he offered unending rest and refreshment. Idolatry began when the people rejected this truth and no longer believed that

God was present, powerful, and good. Judah rejected their source of living water.

Second, Jeremiah defined idolatry not simply as rebellion against God but as submission to worthless substitutes. Despite the presence of living water, the people of Judah had dug out cisterns in their hearts. In other words, they had turned to the world around them to satisfy needs the Lord had already met.

We need to grasp the foolishness of this picture. It is like the farmer who, having a bountiful spring on his land, nevertheless digs out a shabby well that provides no water. Every day he gets up and walks past the flowing spring with his herd to get to his broken-down well, only to find that there is no water. Unsatisfied, he tries again the next day. And the next. And the next. Hoping to find a different result, he keeps going back to that empty well.

Notice the plurality in Jeremiah 2: The prophet notes that the people dug their own *cisterns*. That would be like the farmer, finally giving up on his first well, digging another one rather than going back to his spring. This second well, too, is broken, and the cycle repeats. From well to well the farmer goes, each time passing by the fresh water he needs, thinking that this next well will do the trick.

We laugh at the silly farmer for his idiocy, much as we shake our heads at the ancient Israelites who kept going back to idols. How could the same people who had escaped slavery in Egypt by walking on dry land across the Red Sea turn to some golden calf just a few chapters later? How dumb could they be?

Yet we do something similar every day in the age of outrage. Our idols are not golden calves or carved statues. Idolatry is not tied to any specific idol; it exists whenever we look to someone or something in the world around us to save and satisfy us. Just as every age has its own problems, each has a fresh cast of new idols it creates to solve them. We reject the refreshing and rest-filled salvation of the Lord and hew for ourselves cisterns that give the illusion of holding water but are really bottomless pits. Try as we might, every new cistern fails, and we are left looking for some new solution to our temptations, fears, anxieties, and self-righteousness. The insidious lie of idols is that they prey on our hope. Every day they demand our work and devotion, offering nothing in return but promising us that "just a little more" will do it.

The Idols of Outrage: Politics, Identity, and Personality

So what are the idols of our outrage? Where do we go looking for solutions?

The truth is that there is no shortage of idols. The apostle John identified several broad categories in his first letter: "Everything in the world—the lust of the flesh, the lust of the eyes, and the pride of life—comes not from the Father but from the world" (1 John 2:16, NIV).

Not only is there an endless number of false gods, but the sixteenth-century theologian John Calvin was exactly right when he described the human heart as an idol factory: "Stuffed as it is with presumptuous rashness, [it] dares to imagine a god suited to its own capacity; as it labours under dullness, nay, is sunk in the grossest ignorance, it substitutes vanity and an empty phantom in the place of God."[3]

In other words, our hearts are driven by sin to make idols. Whether out of ignorance, pride, or laziness, we can make idols out of anything and worship them. Common to each idol is our willingness to defend and justify its prominence. We are fond of pointing out others' idols, but the minute the lens turns inward we go on the defensive. Tim Keller speaks of this unique response to idols being threatened:

> When we center our lives on the idol, we become dependent on it. If our counterfeit god is threatened in any way, our response is complete panic. . . . This may be a reason why so many people now respond to U.S. political trends in such an extreme way. When either party wins an election, a certain percentage of the losing side talks openly about leaving the country. . . . They have put

the kind of hope in their political leaders and policies that once was reserved for God and the work of the gospel.[4]

While there are countless false gods in modern Western society, I see three key idols that Christians and non-Christians alike often embrace as solutions to the age of outrage. The idols of politics, identity, and personality most often tempt us to turn away from the life-giving wellspring of God's truth and seek to save ourselves. Then, when these idols are threatened, we easily slip into outrage.

Idol #1: Politics

Public politics wields one of the strongest draws on our lives, especially for conservative evangelicals in the West. The declaration that "this is the most important election of our lifetime" has appeared in countless fund-raising mailers, rally speeches, and commentaries in recent US elections. It seems ironic that the *next* election, regardless of other circumstances, always seems to be the most important. But it's not. That's foolish. Do we honestly believe elections today are more important than, for instance, those around the Civil War or in the early years of our newly birthed republic? American history is filled with elections that were "the most important election ever." Inevitably, the next one will likewise be sold using the same tired rhetoric.

At its core, this attitude reveals the idol that politics has become within American society. Christians and non-Christians alike place the hope of our future on donkeys and elephants. (Considering the importance we place on them, we might as well be lining up to offer our gold and silver to be melted down to make physical animals to worship.)

Few idols have wreaked as much havoc in the church and hurt our witness more than the way evangelicals have engaged in politics. To be sure, Christians have a long history of political involvement for good and ill that even predates modern democracy. However, the upswing in political polarization in culture in the past generation has slowly trickled down into the pews with disastrous effects. The near blind devotion of many evangelicals toward political parties has produced a litany of vicious anti-gospel rhetoric from the very people claiming to engage the world for the gospel.

Idolatry of politics and political solutions is evident in the way many people respond to legitimate criticism of their candidates or their party.[5] If you see your political party as never being wrong, there is a problem. Some Christians seem more interested in political loyalty than in love of neighbor. Rightly criticizing politicians does not call people's loyalty into question.

Let me be clear: I don't think everyone needs to speak up on every issue, but Christians have a moral obligation to have a prophetic witness and confront evil. We can lose that witness when we are unable to see (or speak to) the errors or failings of leaders. And if Christians feel the need to defend even an obvious and divisive mistake (and my Twitter feed is often filled with comments from people doing just that), they hurt the church's witness and tie it too closely to a person, not the truth. It shows the world that our loyalty is to the person on the ballot or in the office rather than the Person who said he is the Truth.

Billy Graham recognized this danger and once said, "I don't want to see religious bigotry in any form. . . . It would disturb me if there was a wedding between the religious fundamentalists and the political right. The hard right has no interest in religion except to manipulate it."[6]

When we recognize our reliance on politics to save us, we start to see the mechanism of idolatry inside us. It is really the lust of the eyes that looks out into the world and tries to find someone else to save us. To be honest, it's much easier to drift toward hoping a politician or political party will be our functional savior because that is something we have an illusion of control over. We feel our voice can sway a politician, as if he or she isn't really a human but rather an object we desire to control and use to meet our own needs. But this mentality causes us great spiritual harm because when we look to someone else to deliver us, we are rejecting Jesus as our true Savior. We also place roadblocks in front of friends and neighbors with opposing political viewpoints to whom we may give the impression that they must align themselves to our political views to be Christians. Finally, we set ourselves up for ultimate failure and disappointment because human politicians disappoint us in a way Jesus never will. When we give up the life-giving fountain of the gospel for the broken cistern of politics, we get the short end of the deal.

Idol #2: Identity

Modern Western society has made an idol of identity, which in many ways is connected to the idol of politics. This idol takes several forms. We seek salvation and liberation in the ways we identify ourselves, in the rights we claim, and from the communities we align with. Too many people aren't willing to give up—let alone acknowledge—their allegiance to various groups. In such a culture, the mantra "be yourself" has become one of our most treasured idols.

Unable to answer the question "Who am I?" in the wake of a collapsed Judeo-Christian worldview, society seems to have finally given up and said, "Whatever you want to be." Systematically we have witnessed sexuality, gender, and even race reduced to social constructs. I think this speaks to our deep desire to belong. Every person longs to fit in, to find a group of people with whom they have shared experiences and challenges. This is not to dismiss the very real identity challenges that these debates have provoked and the questions many people (including Christians) face over questions of sexual, gender, and racial identity. Rather, too many people expect settling questions about their identity will provide them with some refuge from the outrage of our world.

In addition, many people place their pride and identity in America and the freedoms we enjoy. When our perceived personal freedoms and rights are attacked, we often respond with vehement opposition, biblical justification, and conflation of being Christian with being American. This denies the truth of our ultimate allegiance and once again confuses non-Christians who wonder who or what we value most.

More recently, we have seen racism reemerge with the rise of the alt-right and conversation around racial identity. The news shows us horrific images of people marching and chanting Nazi slogans like "Jews will not replace us" or "Blood and soil." Many of these protesters call themselves Christians. The irony is clear. People who call themselves Christians while harboring prejudiced views are foolish; after all, Christians follow a dark-skinned, Middle Eastern Jew. (That's three strikes for racists.)

In his book *Under Our Skin*, NFL player Benjamin Watson, who is African American, talks about visiting the home of his high school friend Frank for the first time. After being greeted warmly by his friend's parents, the boys headed to Frank's room. Benjamin says he stopped cold when he saw a huge Confederate flag hanging over the bed.

While Benjamin saw the flag everywhere in South Carolina—it even flew over the statehouse—it was particularly hurtful to see it displayed proudly in the room of the person he considered a close friend. Benjamin took a risk by briefly explaining to Frank why the flag, with its association with slavery and oppression, was so offensive to him. Benjamin recalls how valued he felt the next time he walked into his friend's room and noticed Frank had removed the flag.[7] To many of us, the idol of identity is so deeply ingrained into our consciousness that we don't even realize the hold it has on us.

This idolatry of identity turns our inward feelings, passions, and rights into the gods we bow down before and worship. We are traveling a dangerous road when we look inwardly to ourselves to find meaning. This self-actualizing arrogance—especially when masked as patriotism within the evangelical community—indulges sinful, fleshly patterns and destroys our relationship with the God of truth and with our neighbor. When we trade our life-giving identity as a son or daughter of God for the leaking cistern of self-identity and national pride, we are left parched in a wilderness of our own making.

Idol #3: Personality

Truly one of the mystifying developments of the past generation has been our society's devotion to the cult of celebrity. While there have always been strong and attractive personalities, even within Christianity (think about Charles Spurgeon in the nineteenth century or George Whitefield in the eighteenth), our current political division and technologies have put this idol into hyperdrive. We live in a world that measures success and authority by the number of followers, likes, shares, and retweets.

We reason that certain people must be trustworthy or have something meaningful to say because they have the blue checkmark on Twitter or because their blog gets so many thousands of views. We place our trust in high-profile individuals–whether musicians or pastors, politicians or journalists–expecting them to show us the way.

Why is this so prevalent? Why do we line up to invest in and follow strong personalities?

In times of chaos and insecurity, people look to leaders who claim to have the answers. We are drawn to compelling communicators, those with vision for the way forward, and the polished images of people who are simultaneously idealized and approachable.

More concerning has been how I have seen this idolatry take root in the church. Just as dangerous as Christians actively idolizing celebrities outside the church is the way some Christian leaders use their celebrity to exert considerable power and control over ministries and their churches. In my thirty-plus years in ministry, the retort "This is my church" has sadly become common. I would be hard-pressed to think of a phrase that more accurately reveals pastors or elders who have allowed the power of their personality to become an idol.

Indeed, we are a church that long ago ignored Paul's exhortation to exalt Christ alone: "Who is Apollos? Who is Paul? We are only God's servants through whom you believed the Good News.

Each of us did the work the Lord gave us. I planted the seed in your hearts, and Apollos watered it, but it was God who made it grow" (1 Corinthians 3:5-6, NLT). The perception that a church is "ours" because we give money, service, loyalty, or legacy is absurd and anti-gospel.

The truth is that the personalities in whom we place our hope and trust are merely broken cisterns that will always disappoint. As with the church in Corinth, following personalities never solves outrage; it merely begets more division and hostility. That is why Paul needed to remind the Corinthians that Apollos and Paul were nothing and that Jesus was everything.

I am certainly not against impactful pastors. Many do have important and insightful contributions in theology and leadership that the church desperately needs to hear. However, only those leaders who consistently make much of Jesus are worthy of following. Only those who remember that they are "jars of clay," created to show the "surpassing worth of knowing Christ Jesus,"[8] are going to lead us through the age of outrage.

The power to solve our outrage comes from the gospel, not from human personalities.

The Gospel Solves the Problem of Idolatry

Let me be clear. Christians should be actively involved in the political process as well as their local churches. They should also be critical thinkers on issues of identity and community. However, we must avoid taking the good things God has given us and worshiping them as gods. When we forget that these are tools to accomplish the grander purposes of God's Kingdom, they start to become idols.

At its core, the age of outrage is the newest manifestation of people's sinfulness. It is the result of people's rebellion against and isolation from God. Forgetfulness and apathy always lead to idolatry.

But there is hope.

As Christians, we understand that the solution to this world's problems is found in the Good News of Jesus Christ. He came to be the true Savior. He is the Way out of idolatry. He is the Truth that speaks to our idolatry, and he is the wellspring of Life that nourishes and satisfies our lonely and forgetful hearts. Part of his Good News is that our work, energy, and striving are over. If our political, self-identification, or church systems require us to work and exert energy to maintain them, we are following the wrong god.

St. Augustine prayed, "You have made us for Yourself, and our heart is restless until it rests in You."[9] Jesus has come to give his people rest from work, toil, energy, and exertion from trying to do it right. Paul even says he works and struggles so hard "depending on Christ's mighty power that works within me" (Colossians 1:29, NLT). Being a Christian means it is Christ's energy in us and through us that solves the problem of our idolatry.

This rest is a cool drink of water on a hot day. It frees us from looking to politics to be our savior; we are no longer forced to defend and justify our political leanings. We can be free to fail and free to move between political camps or have dissenting views from the cultural or political norms. When we do, we are often more like Jesus.

Jesus' rest frees us from looking to identity as our savior. As Christians, we have a new identity, rooted in him and his work. The gospel guides what we shape our identity around, so we can freely lay down our rights, our thoughts, and our opinions of ourselves at Jesus' feet, knowing that he will mold and shape us as a potter does clay. He gives us a new identity that is secured and satisfied in his work on our behalf.

This rest also frees us from relying on power and control as our savior. We ultimately are under a new King and a new Kingdom. Jesus is in control of his church (global and local) and his world. His Kingdom is already present yet not fully expressed in the world, and he is much better at managing the world than we are.

In the gospel, God consistently draws us back to the fountain of life. He wants to break down our cisterns, take away our opportunity for idolatry, and satisfy us with his life-giving water that will never leave us thirsty.

The Gospel Changes How We View Others

Not only does the gospel reveal our own idolatry, it also changes how we see others and their idolatry, especially if we have previously perceived them as our enemies.

In June 2016, the Pulse nightclub in Orlando, Florida, which catered primarily to a gay clientele, was hit by one of the most heinous terrorist attacks in American history. A lone gunman entered the club, killing forty-nine people and injuring another sixty-eight during a prolonged standoff with police.[10]

Several of those inside barricaded themselves in various rooms in an attempt to keep the gunman out. Those who could sent voice messages and texts to loved ones—in some cases, the last communication family and friends ever received from them. Eddie Justice, for instance, texted back and forth with his mother as he and several others hid in a bathroom. Eventually Eddie's texts stopped, and he was later confirmed as one of the dead.[11]

At the time, my friend Mark Hausfeld was president of an Assemblies of God seminary. In the days after the attack, Mark found himself in a Colorado coffee shop that was a favorite of the local LGBTQ community. Shocked that one of the worst mass shootings in US history specifically had targeted their community, the people in the coffee shop were clearly hurting, defensive, and angry. My friend told me his thought process as he considered how to respond when the mood in the shop was so somber and fearful: "After about forty-five minutes, I realized I was the only male in the coffee shop. I noticed some ladies working on a chalk drawing with the names of the people killed in the Orlando massacre. I felt the prompting of the Holy Spirit to make the most of the opportunity to speak with the servers and the people sitting at the coffee bar."

Before assuming his role as a seminary president, Mark had served as a missionary to a majority Muslim nation for more than twenty years. He had experience in cross-cultural contexts among people with very different and even opposing beliefs and values. He understood that cultural division does not make witnessing impossible; it merely presents new challenges we have to meet with patience and understanding. To him, these women in the coffee shop were not his cultural enemies or political opponents. They were image bearers who were hurting.

Leaning in rather than putting on blinders, my friend requested permission to ask several of the servers at the coffee shop about the shooting, their feelings of pain and anger, and their perception of how Christians were reacting. As he listened, he found five common themes in the messages they asked him to take back to his students:

1. Do not single out homosexuality and ignore other sins.
2. Deal with your own sin before criticizing sin in others.
3. Ask questions and listen.
4. Protect us from hate and violence.
5. Love by words and actions.

I was struck by the fact that people in the LGBTQ community at a coffee shop in Colorado were telling Christians to act more like Jesus. There was not one thing on that list that every Christian should not affirm.

In the age of outrage, we are perpetually encouraged to view others purely in categories of friend or foe. Are they on my side or are they against me? Do they like my politics and politicians? Endorse my worldview? Embrace my ideology?

Outrage is a product of the flesh. It is selfish, divisive, wrathful, and chaotic. In some cases, outrage pretends to be righteous anger, but underneath the veneer, it is simply driven by our fleshly desires. In contrast, engaging the Spirit takes the focus off us (our tribe, our desires, our anger, our anxieties) and places it on God and his glory. When we experience forgiveness in Christ, God entirely transforms the way we see people and communities.

Before salvation, we saw others through the lens of our flesh; now we see them as new creations.

That's the answer to so much outrage today: Ask, as Charles Sheldon did in his 1896 book *In His Steps*, "What would Jesus do?" I can easily imagine Jesus walking into an LGBTQ-frequented coffee shop, listening, and sharing.

For too many Christians, though, LGBTQ people are their enemies. For some, maybe it is even easy to get to that view. Biblical theology is clear in its teaching on marriage, gender, and sexual identity. One major result of the cultural forking in Western culture has been that in less than a generation, this biblical teaching has moved from being nearly universally accepted to widely contested. As this trend continues, it is likely the traditional position on marriage and human sexuality will be the minority view in the not-too-distant future. From the perspective of religious liberty, we are, as Ross Douthat put it in the *New York Times*, negotiating "the terms of our surrender." He elaborates,

> I am being descriptive here, rather than self-pitying.
> Christians had plenty of opportunities—thousands of years'
> worth—to treat gay people with real charity, and far too
> often chose intolerance. (And still do, in many instances
> and places.) So being marginalized, being sued, losing tax-
> exempt status—this will be uncomfortable, but we should
> keep perspective and remember our sins, and nobody
> should call it persecution.
>
> But it's still important for the winning side to recognize
> its power. We are not really having an argument about
> same-sex marriage anymore, and on the evidence of
> Arizona, we're not having a negotiation. Instead, all that's
> left is the timing of the final victory—and for the defeated
> to find out what settlement the victors will impose.[12]

No one denies it is a tricky time. Douthat highlights the ways in which this is a complex situation for religious liberty and challenges us to think carefully about the future. No Christian I know believes a restaurant should refuse dinner to a gay couple. Yet many Christians don't think a baker should be required to use their artistry to write celebratory language on a same-sex wedding cake. And yes, this conflict has gone all the way to the US Supreme Court, with similar cases in other countries throughout the English-speaking Western world. However, labeling the LGBTQ community as our opponents is a symptom of polarization and tribalism. More important, it is the perspective of preserving cultural power rather than advancing Kingdom mission.

Twenty years from now, after lots of court cases across the Western world, I imagine those lines will be settled between religious liberty and LGBTQ rights. I hope the line will recognize that all people are created in the image of God and worthy of dignity and respect. And I hope (and will work toward) that line acknowledging and defending the religious liberty of those who now dissent from the majority view.

But for now, and in the future, I hope a lot of Christians will cross the line, as my friend Mark did, because while there are cultural and legal issues to discuss, we need to converse with those who think differently from us for the sake of Christ. You see, you can't hate people and engage them with the gospel at the same time. You can't war with people and show the love of Jesus. You can't be both outraged and on mission.

As Mark and I continued to dialogue about his conversation in the coffeehouse, he drove home the point that the gospel provides us with an alternative to the outrage of our world. He explained, "They didn't ask that I change being or believing as a theologically conservative Christian. They want the virtue of Christ to be exhibited to them. In my time with them, this is what I felt the Holy Spirit was impressing upon me: 'Love them.'"

Mark saw and engaged these women according to the Spirit. He rejected the hostility of outrage and brought the gospel of Jesus *into* their pain. He no longer saw the women as cultural and political enemies but as people who needed to see the love of Jesus in the midst of their grief. That's an outrageous gospel idea. That's living out the enduring truth at the core of the Christian faith.

The Gospel among Broken Idols

"How long will you waver between two opinions?"

This was the challenge of Elijah to the people of Israel at the top of Mount Carmel in 1 Kings 18. In the midst of a three-year drought, the people had again turned away from God to seek salvation in idols and false prophets. Fooled by the false promises of vain and sinful leaders, Israel had vacillated between serving God and serving idols, trying to have the best of both worlds.

The resulting conflict is described in one of Scripture's most memorable passages as Elijah faced off against the false prophets of Baal. When they failed to ignite their fire through their noisy prayers and rituals, the stage was set for Elijah. After drenching his sacrifice in water, Elijah called out to God, asking him to answer so that "these people will know that you, LORD, are God, and that you are turning their hearts back again" (1 Kings 18:37, NIV). Scripture records that the heavens opened and fire fell and burned the entire sacrifice, going so far as to "lick up the water."

Even today our world constantly seeks saviors and solutions. Nonbelievers search for these answers in the temporal, the finite, the unsatisfactory. They always turn to idols because that's all they know. One false god may seem to satisfy for a while, but eventually that idol will fail too. Yet Christians can also get caught in this temptation and, like Israel, waver between depending on God and depending on some worldly hope. We may go to church, pray some prayers, and read our Bibles, but in the end our actions and thoughts betray our belief that the solution to the problem of outrage in our world can be found in a worldly solution.

The problem, as we saw with Plantinga, is that this world is not the way it's supposed to be. That's why none of these solutions—no matter how powerful they seem, how much hope they promise, or what community they create—address the underlying issue, which is sin. Worse yet, Christians spark outrage when we get caught wavering between the gospel and some worldly power.

And the response is not to dig deeper into the well of human ingenuity, wisdom, or culture. If the disease is sin, the remedy is found at the Cross. Though the heart forges idols of politics, identity, power, and more, the gospel both overcomes those temptations and addresses the underlying outrage we wrongly thought they'd solve. The fountain of living water, flowing and bubbling up with rest, refreshment, and joy, satisfies the ultimate longing of our forgetful hearts. Not only does the gospel expose our idols, it changes how we view others, even in the midst of their idolatry. Going back to Plantinga, "For the Christian church . . . to ignore, euphemize, or otherwise mute the lethal reality of sin is to cut the nerve of the gospel. For the sober truth is that without full disclosure on sin, the gospel of grace becomes impertinent, unnecessary, and finally uninteresting."[13]

So let's get our first principles clearly on the table before we move to the more practical issues: The church stands no hope of engaging the age of outrage unless we root out the lie that the solution to sin lies anywhere outside of the gospel of Jesus Christ. He is "the true God and eternal life" (1 John 5:20). Salvation is not coming on Air Force One. And Jesus will not come riding on a donkey or an elephant. Those who fail to see such things have been lost to the idolatry of the moment.

It is only by clinging to Christ in the midst of the storm that we can resist the pull of idols (1 John 5:21).

CHAPTER 6

Lie #4: Mission Is Optional

- 42 percent of evangelicals agree that the divisive political climate in America makes it harder for them to share their faith. Only a small percentage said it was easier.

- 41 percent of evangelicals agree that the divisive political climate in America makes it harder for them to build relationships with neighbors, coworkers, or acquaintances.

ONE EVENING A FEW MONTHS AGO, I was studying Jesus' appearance to his disciples in John 20 with a small group. Most of the group focused on Jesus' followers hiding in fear behind a locked door following their Lord's crucifixion. Several shared times they'd experienced fear and isolation and explained how Jesus came and gave them peace. We all agreed that Jesus' presence brings peace and comfort.

I asked, "But what does Jesus say in this passage?"

Silence.

I pushed through. "Jesus doesn't just show up and be silent. In verse 21, he actually says, 'As the Father has sent me, even so I am sending you.'"

Silence.

"Jesus didn't go sit in the locked room with the disciples to make them feel better. He went in to get them out, to get them on mission, to send them into the chaos and anger from which they had locked themselves away."

Of course, the group rightly emphasized Jesus' presence as a comfort to the disciples. But we can't stop there. The passage doesn't end with Jesus showing up—it simply begins with his appearance. After speaking peace to his disciples, Jesus sends them (and us) on mission.

Individuals and groups tend to retreat when they sense hostility or opposition. Whether because of self-protection, confusion, or fear, our first instinct is to pull back. Like a toddler touching a hot stove, when Christians engage a post-Christian world and are met with hostility and bitterness, they think the lesson is to withdraw. Reflecting on the shift to a post-Christian culture, Christians breathlessly whisper to one another across their Chick-fil-A meals, "Weather the storm; protect your family."

When the alternative seems to be engaging in a yelling match with other religious or cultural communities or throwing our support behind unsavory if not explicitly immoral politicians who promise to be our strongmen, the idea of retreat doesn't look so bad.

The problem is that this path is founded on the fourth lie of the age of outrage: Mission is optional.

The insidiousness of this lie is that Christians agree that believers cannot opt out of mission. While they may admit that they struggle to identify with the three earlier lies, they agree 100 percent that mission is not optional. The problem is that they live as if it doesn't apply to them. In other words, a majority of Christians acknowledge we are called to mission, yet few actually live out their belief.

In a recent LifeWay Research study, 85 percent of all believers ages eighteen to twenty-nine agree they have a duty to share the gospel, and 69 percent feel comfortable sharing their faith. Yet only 25 percent of them look for ways to share the gospel, and only 27 percent actually build friendships with unbelievers to do so.[1] This means that even as most Christians recognize that mission is essential, they fail to act on this belief.

Of course, mission in the age of outrage is wholly different from that in past generations. There is no denying that when we see yelling, anger, and vitriol on our screens, the passion to share and show the love of Jesus can become muted. When it seems like everyone is so easily offended by everything, how do we evangelize? How do we care for others when people see us as uncaring? We may still believe mission is mandatory, but it's no wonder we function as if this is no longer true.

It's a tricky time, but the mission is still the mission.

Mission Is Fundamental to Our Christian Identity

Mission isn't for the days we feel like it. It isn't only for cultures that are accepting or make it convenient to share the gospel. It isn't reserved for people with seminary degrees, online followings, Super Bowl trophies, or home-repair shows on television. Politicians are not going to do the mission for you, nor is the legislation you hope they'll pass. Corporations do not absolve you of this obligation, no matter how much chicken they serve or how red their Christmas cups are.

While few would argue this point, throughout my ministry I have made this point repeatedly to virtually every church, Christian organization, and pastor I've met. At conferences and seminaries, discussion topics often focus on how to be effective in discipleship, how to manage diverse teams, or how to lead through crisis. These are all important, yet at the heart of what the church needs most is the drive to reclaim its call to mission. We cannot outsource it to parachurches, find some technology to do it for us, or entrust it to politicians.

The truth is, *God has given us a mission.* In John 20:21, Jesus says, "As the Father has sent me, even so I am sending you." This is not an optional assignment. It must be at the core of who we are as a community of believers. Without God's help we would not be able to accomplish anything. N. T. Wright reminds us,

> Left to ourselves we lapse into a kind of collusion with entropy, acquiescing in the general belief that things may be getting worse but that there's nothing much we can do about them. And we are wrong. Our task in the present . . . is to live as resurrection people in between Easter and the

final day, with our Christian life, corporate and individual, in both worship and mission, as a sign of the first and a foretaste of the second.[2]

Charles Spurgeon said that Christians who do not engage the world with the gospel are like those who have a treasure but hold on to it. "The world is starving, and they hoard the bread of life." Spurgeon argued that neglecting our mission is on par with the vilest heresies in the history of the church. Hearts that do not bring Christ to the world prove they do not actually love Christ: "If they loved Christ they must love sinners; if they loved Jesus they must seek to extend His kingdom and to let Him see of the travail of His soul!"[3]

Serving as the regional director for Lausanne North America, I am often reminded of one of the slogans central to the Lausanne Covenant. A testament to the unique yet complementary legacies of John Stott and Billy Graham, the organization states that *evangelization requires the whole church to take the whole gospel to the whole world.*[4] Notice the depth of the claim. There is no opt-out clause or half measure. There is no excuse or justification. In order to claim the whole gospel, we must be willing to bring the *whole* gospel to the *whole* world. Only then can we begin to transition from outrage to outreach, from disgrace to integrity, and from peripheral to essential.

Cultural Balkanization

It's hard to measure how and when people share their faith, but most observers think that the frequency has declined. When I was younger, there were evangelism conferences all over, churches regularly offered training, and many books were written on the topic. Today, just about the only time I hear someone talk about evangelism, it's to make fun of the way people used to do it.

An obvious question, then, is this: Why have Christian engagement and evangelism declined? There are many possibilities; however,

I believe one primary reason is that today's church doesn't know how to engage a post-Christian culture. For centuries, Christendom occupied a central position in much of Western culture. Now that our influence is waning, how can we possibly witness to our neighbors and proclaim truth? Yet facing a hostile culture isn't new for believers. In fact, the cultural milieu in most of the world today takes us back to the New Testament and early church era, when animosity and outrage toward Christians were commonplace.

Certainly, US culture is in a moment of transition that presents challenges for living out our mission. The cultural fork that is often a cause of the outrage around us has led to a point of *cultural balkanization.* Primarily a political term, *balkanization* refers to the splitting apart of small hostile states or people groups. It originates from the breakup of the Balkan states (Yugoslavia, Bulgaria, Greece, Albania, Turkey, and Romania) after World War I. Balkanization occurs when smaller warring factions within a country cannot agree and no central authority exists to bind them together. In our country, this process is primarily cultural rather than political and is the result of our dominant cultural identity becoming increasingly diverse and fragmented.

When faced with this new reality, some Christians, and even some non-Christians, begin to idolize the past homogeneous culture as a "golden age" of Christianity. From a position of cultural power, Christians were able to build ministries, evangelize the public, and speak into politics and society with considerable freedom and acceptance. We look back and see order and peace around *our* shared beliefs as something we need to reclaim.

This perception is deeply problematic, though, because it assumes the Christianity that dominated Western culture was *the* Christianity. Even a casual survey of our Christian brothers and sisters from communities traditionally marginalized from speaking into culture will tell you that this is a mistake. When one group sets the rules for culture, it invariably silences others.

More important, cultural power often produced rampant nominalism that lulled us into a false sense that we were actually accomplishing the mission. In the twentieth century, most people throughout the Western world self-identified as Christian because of their parents, their community, or their shared values. Yet most cared little for actual faith. This made preaching the gospel to a group of people who thought they were already "in" extraordinarily difficult. In today's world of cultural balkanization, the secularism once cloaked under layers of nominalism is finally out in the open.

This certainly presents a host of challenges, but it is not inherently worse than the situation in past generations. Yet the attitudes and methods that worked when culture was relatively homogeneous will prove ineffective when applied to a culture balkanized along political, economic, and ethnic lines. Instead, Christians need to think specifically about how we can live, engage, love, and serve in a home mission field that is so diverse. More important, we must consider how Christians can *defend* and *contend* for the faith, as Paul calls us to do (see 1 Timothy 6:12; Jude 1:3) without devolving into just another one of the voices yelling in outrage.

A Missional Community Transcends Cultural Outrage

Christians also buy into the lie that mission is optional because the church too often reflects rather than transcends the world's outrage. Instead of the church being a place that prepares us to face hostility, the church becomes simply another community group. Understanding the church as the point where cultural hostility and division are defeated is central to overcoming this situation.

The church is unique because it is both a place where we gather around a single identity as sinners saved by the gospel of Jesus *and* a place where we bring our unique culture and history into relationship with one another. This tension exists throughout Scripture. We are a "new creation" (2 Corinthians 5:17), yet at the same time the Kingdom of God includes members from every tribe, nation, and tongue (Revelation 7:9). Australian theologian Graham Hill reminds us that "God calls his church to be a distinct people, with a distinct ethic, a distinct story, a distinct peace, a distinct community, a distinct diversity, and a distinct witness. The church is a distinct gathered and sent people."[5] Wherever the diversity of this world has produced a cultural balkanization, diversity within the church is brought together under our overarching identity as worshipers of the same King. The church provides us a single theological/religious/spiritual identity within which we can engage, listen, and understand each other's perspective through love.

I recently had the opportunity to put this idea into action. In the fall of 2017, the National Football League became embroiled in controversy when several players began kneeling during the national anthem. This cultural protest had been initiated by then San Francisco 49ers quarterback Colin Kaepernick the previous season. I wrote a couple of articles in which I reflected on these protests and the ensuing controversy. In the first, I wrote that I believed this cultural protest was not the best approach to addressing racial injustice.[6] In the second, I echoed the words of President Obama in making this point.[7] My main point in the articles was that we should listen to the concerns expressed by the protest. I shared my appreciation for the athletes' using their platform to bring attention to the problems. However, I concluded that, unfortunately, their concerns had been overshadowed by their approach, which offended many people because it seemed to disrespect the flag and discount the sacrifice of service members. As a result, the protestors' message could be easily hijacked. And that's what happened.

My articles generated a lot of discussion, even within our office at the Billy Graham Center. John Richards, our managing director, and Michael Lee, one of our research fellows, pushed back against the way I framed the debate in the first article. They made compelling and insightful comments, so I published their perspectives. As an African American, John brought attention to the way protests in sports have functioned in American civil rights history. John was able to remind me that for generations African Americans have been told to find a "better way" to protest.[8] Michael wrote about his experiences as an Asian American of Korean descent, pointing out features of the controversy that may have been lost on both white and black Americans.[9] I thought that by publicizing our discussion, we could illustrate to Christians that disagreement can be an effective tool in our spiritual growth and that disagreement is not inherently wrong. This is what the church is *supposed* to model.

I was sharpened by their critiques to consider how I was living out the gospel. It was not necessary that we ended with complete agreement. Indeed, while they challenged me to think through the why and how of my position, I remained convinced that Kaepernick's approach was not creating a conversation that would help improve the issues about which Kaepernick was concerned; rather, it was redirecting it toward side issues and had been hijacked. However–and this is key–I was sharpened in my own thinking and love through the way John and Michael disagreed with some of my conclusions.

For instance, I was challenged to critique Kaepernick's approach in ways that did not echo language used to excuse the problems of systemic racism in our culture. By listening to John and Michael within the context of our shared belief, our disagreement refined my own position and prepared me to engage a hostile culture more effectively by helping me remove obstacles to such discussion.

The willingness of brothers and sisters in Christ to speak into our lives prepares us to go into the world and engage communities we sometimes see as our cultural enemies because we do not understand them and may even struggle to love them. The body of Christ is more than a refuge from the storm of outrage; it is the gateway by which we transcend the polarization and isolation of our world. As our society becomes increasingly multicultural, this is needed now more than ever if we expect to be successful in our mission.

If we can't disagree effectively with someone in our local church or faith group who is also committed to living out the gospel, how can we hope to productively engage someone whom the world assumes we hate? If we cannot demonstrate the humility and love necessary to listen to other perspectives *within the body of Christ*, we will never be able to engage those outside the church with the gospel.

Mission begins with demonstrating the gospel through our relationships *inside the church*, which equips and trains us to engage those *outside the church*. When we practice this in a context designed to abound in grace, it prepares us for the challenge of engaging the outrage. In many churches, personal viewpoints and preferences take center stage far too readily, which in time leads to diminished ministry and credibility of the Christian faith.

This has always been the case. Churches have split over preferences related to musical style or service times. Many of us have lamented these divisions for years. Now it is even spilling over into the political divide. Committed Christians who are anti-Trump cannot be with committed Christians who are pro-Trump, making me wonder if, for some, the most important loyalty is to a person and not to the Savior.

Outrage Is *Our* Mission Field

Christians see the surrounding culture as progressively hostile to traditional faith as well as distracted and isolated by technology. Furthermore, the church is frequently indiscernible from that culture. The result is a perceptible sense of impending crisis among Christians: *What are we going to do? The culture is worse than ever before! Will the church survive?*

This siege mentality overlooks the simple truth that every Christian lives in the midst of a mission field where God has called them to contend faithfully for the gospel. The age of outrage is no different. It is our mission field. It is both useless and destructive for us to pine for some lost golden age of cultural mission when God has set before us a culture that needs the gospel of Jesus. In this sense, the age of outrage is the context within which the gospel must take root.

Rod Dreher addresses this challenge in his provocative book,

The Benedict Option. Dreher named this proposed solution in honor of the sixth-century founder of the Benedictine monastic order, Benedict of Nursia (AD 480–547). In the book, Dreher calls on Christians to think through what Christian cultural engagement looks like in a post-Christian world. Dreher argues that American Christians "have to come to terms with the brute fact that we live in a culture, one in which our beliefs make increasingly little sense. We speak a language that the world more and more either cannot hear or finds offensive to its ears."[10] Dreher points out that Christianity has encountered this hostility before. He takes his cue from Benedict, who lived at a time when the Roman Empire was steadily declining, giving way to the Dark Ages. Disturbed by the licentiousness all around him in Rome, Benedict retreated to a cave and later founded a number of monasteries. Dreher suggests we follow the example of Benedict. In a sense, he recommends that the local church strategically withdraw from engaging the culture so it can focus on developing new forms of community, strengthening institutions, and more.

I appreciate Dreher's attempt to answer this question, and there may come a time when I agree that withdrawal is preferable to engagement. And to be fair, he did temper his "strategic withdrawal" language later. But when I reflect on the culture we face, my thoughts are drawn to a different monastic example: St. Columba.

For me, this situation presents us with an opportunity to think about what it means to be on mission from the margins.

Similar to Benedict, Columba lived in a hostile environment with limited resources. An Irish missionary after the time of Patrick, Columba traveled to Scotland and established a monastery in Iona with only twelve followers among the Scots and Picts. Yet in contrast to Benedict's monasteries, the community at Iona was consistently outward facing. After establishing a community of believers, Columba drew them out into the surrounding areas. He had established a community on mission, not a community of withdrawal.[11]

In his biography of Columba, Ian Bradley notes that two activities dominated Columba's public life: "forging relationships with kings and establishing a network of churches and monasteries."[12] Columba's time was marked by transition and cultural upheaval similar to our own. Though facing a foreign and hostile culture, Columba personally engaged community leaders while simultaneously training others to go and replicate the believing community throughout Scotland. Cultivating relationships with regional leaders wherever he could, Columba's most lasting impact was made in his missionary efforts. Bradley notes that most sources depict Columba as constantly on the move, replicating his community across Scotland as part of an overarching plan to convert the entire nation.[13]

While numbers are hazy, one nineteenth-century biographer argued that Columba was responsible for at least forty monastic communities. Connecting these churches to the Columba legacy, he concludes, "The names of these localities, or churches, give us . . . little evidence of the real work of Columba. It must have been far more extensive than these indications convey. There is scarcely a parish in the North and West of Scotland, or the West and South of Ireland, where his memory is not fresh and venerated even to this day."[14]

Not every community needs to be an exact replica of Columba's. Not everyone needs to be monastic, but we ought to take note of the way Columba was shaped by the gospel and then formed a community that was also shaped by the gospel, which went out and evangelized. There was no social media in Columba's day— he didn't have a Twitter account—but he did have an unwavering belief that the believing community was inherently missional and that the relationships we build within the body of Christ are designed to be replicated in other communities. Columba built relationships and established churches—not to protect himself and other Christians, but to train other believers to reach out as well.

Social media is an effective space in today's world for reaching people, understanding their positions, and building community. But even as it can help us form relationships, social media itself is not the goal. It is an imperfect and often biased tool that can be as destructive as it can be helpful. The goal needs to be Christian people in community with one another—and also with people who don't know Christ. E. M. Bounds says, "The church is looking for better methods; God is looking for better men."[15] This is a helpful reminder of the limitations of social media in our age and the necessity for personal engagement.

Missionaries of Outrage

In December 2017, the *Chicago Sun-Times* asked a panel of experts to name the most influential Illinoisans in the state's two-hundred-year history.[16] Not limiting their lists to native Illinoisans, the experts selected two hundred individuals who had shaped American thought and culture and who had a significant connection to Illinois. The list is a fascinating journey revealing various movements and ideas that inspired and even divided past generations. It includes athletes, politicians, social activists, business leaders, and musicians. As I reviewed their selections, two stood out to me: Dwight L. Moody and Hugh Hefner.

On one expert's list, they were right next to each other.

That Moody grabbed my attention is obvious. At the time of this writing, I preach most weeks at the Moody Church in downtown Chicago, where I am reminded on a weekly basis of his impact, not only on the city and country, but in the world. One of America's most impactful evangelists, Moody moved to Chicago in 1856 at nineteen, when he was a fresh convert to Christianity. Even as a young businessman trying to make a name for himself in Chicago, Moody understood that mission was not optional for Christians or a task to be left to pastors and missionaries. While attending Plymouth Congregational Church, Moody famously used his own money to rent four pews and fill them with whomever he could find on the streets and boarding houses.[17] Indeed, the impulse to ensure that everyone heard the gospel of Jesus became a driving principle of Moody's life, eventually leading him out of business and into full-time ministry.

Before you respond that we face a more hostile and divided age than Moody, consider the time in which he contended for the faith. He ministered throughout the Civil War, going so far as to join the Christian Commission that ministered to Union troops on the front lines of the war. Later he helped rebuild Chicago in the wake of the Great Fire of 1871, which decimated the city and forced the closure of many other ministries. He went into the slums and prisons produced by America's rapid urbanization during the Gilded Age. Moody did all of this while training an army of young men and women to follow his example of bringing the gospel of Jesus into the darkness of the world.

In his biography of Moody, Lyle Dorsett observes that the evangelist transcended the class and social divisions of an outraged world because he never lost sight of the fact that in each individual was a soul who needed Jesus:

> Rich, poor, educated, ignorant, male, female, they were as one to Moody. In England he hobnobbed with nobility and factory workers; in America he moved as comfortably in prisons as he did at Ivy League colleges. Stations in life or the places people lived gave Moody no pause except to be careful to communicate. He was able to reach men and women at all levels of society because he truly cared about their souls—and they sensed it.[18]

Moody did all of this while, as historian David Bebbington notes, showing "genuine humility."[19] Moody modeled to generations of believers that devoting ourselves to the mission of the Kingdom of God is the only means by which Christians can bring healing to the broken.

Hugh Hefner was a complete contrast to Moody in his message, but he was also an effective missionary for his worldview. For more than half a century, Hefner espoused a gospel of sexual freedom and liberation. Railing against the prudish norms he believed were damaging society and holding it back from experiencing true self-realization, Hefner built an empire giving people a look behind the curtain of sexual intimacy. Reflecting on his career, Hefner framed his life as merely one in a long line of innovators. In a 1974 *Playboy* interview, Hefner said,

> If we hadn't had the Wright brothers, there would still be airplanes. If there hadn't been an Edison, there would still be electric lights. And if there hadn't been a Hefner, we'd still have sex. But maybe we wouldn't be enjoying it as much. So the world would be a little poorer.[20]

In the wake of Hefner's death, the Internet was flooded with testimonies to his influence and stories of admiration about the "sexual icon." For many, the man in the smoking jacket symbolized some ideal of modern sexuality, a goal to shoot for or a trailblazer to follow.

There is no denying Hefner's influence. He was, perhaps, the greatest missionary for his worldview during the second half of the twentieth century. Yet as the world celebrated him, Christians rightly grasped the utter destruction he left in his wake. In his article for the *National Review* on Hefner's legacy, David French wrote,

> The cultural harm done is even now ripping kids from parents and husbands from wives. When I think of Hugh Hefner, yes I mourn, but I mourn because the bitter fruit of his life's work has helped poison the families of people I know and love. He is gone, but his legacy lives on. And his is a legacy of despair.[21]

Over the course of his life, Hefner won millions to his "gospel" and in the process redefined morality and sexuality for many. He was a missionary for pornography, selfishness, and hedonism. His legacy is the ruin of sexual identity and morality he has left behind.

Yet Hefner is not alone. Missionaries fill our world, each selling a different gospel. We must recognize that evangelism is going on every day in countless ways. Our call to engage our mission field of outrage is in part because we, like Moody, are to be lights in this darkness. If we reject this call, not only are we withholding bread from the starving, as Spurgeon warned, but we are leaving the broken and hurting to the missionaries of false gospels that will bind them in heavier chains.

Keep Calm and Carry On

In Jesus' commission of his followers in John 20, we understand there was ample reason for the disciples to be afraid of mission. Their leader had been killed, crucified by a stunning coalition of Roman and religious leaders. Forget trying to engage the world; earlier that day the disciples had been concerned with their own survival.

The age of outrage can produce a similar sense of isolation and hostility. With any significant cultural shift, there is a temptation to retreat in our witness. We see this today in those who prioritize the reclaiming of cultural Christianity, trying to bring back the familiar and comfortable blanket of nominal Christianity.

Kevin Ezell notes that many churches in North America have "responded to the cultural crisis by going into survival mode. [They] have taken a defensive position—hunkering down in their churches hoping the immorality of the culture does not creep in." But this posture is nothing more than a "circling of the wagons," which inevitably leads to an "us versus them" mentality.[22]

Into a room filled with a similar atmosphere of isolation and fear, Jesus began his commission in John 20 with one crucial word of comfort: peace. While it is understandable for us to withdraw in fear or confusion, Scripture consistently teaches and models a better way. Even when the world looks its most hostile, difficult, and intimidating, God is greater still, and his gospel will not be contained. Paul gives theological flesh to this pattern:

> God chose things the world considers foolish in order to shame those who think they are wise. And he chose things

that are powerless to shame those who are powerful. God chose things despised by the world, things counted as nothing at all, and used them to bring to nothing what the world considers important. As a result, no one can ever boast in the presence of God.

1 CORINTHIANS 1:27-29, NLT

Or as Andrew Murray summarized, "We have a God who delights in impossibilities."[23]

In that locked room days after his death, Jesus gave us the way forward. We are to go out *as he first went out.* Just as the Father sent him, he now sends us. Again and again, he leads his people into a place of faith where they recognize this world is nothing compared to him. It is into this fear, this crisis, this outrage, that Jesus both comforts us and calls us to action. In the midst of the storm, Christ reminds us not only that he is sending us, but that he first blazed the pathway forward.

So why is mission not optional?

Because God has called us. Because we live in a broken and fragmented world in need of the Good News of Jesus. Because if we ignore our calling, there are a legion of false missionaries to take our place. Because the God who did not spare his own Son for us has given us a mission and promised victory.

We are not commissioned to retreat into our buildings to form holy huddles and talk about the good old days. In his omniscience, Jesus knew he was sending his followers into hostile territory. Nevertheless, he commanded them to go into the world (Matthew 28:18-19), be fishers of men (Mark 1:17), and tell people everywhere about him (Acts 1:8). Just before his ascension, in fact, Jesus commissioned the church to fulfill God's mission. Reflecting on Acts 1:8, Ezell argues, "The church does not simply have mission as one of its objectives; the church is *always* to be on mission."[24]

Our calling ends only when Jesus returns. Until then, remember what God told Joshua as he prepared to enter the hostile territory of the Promised Land: "Be strong and courageous . . . for the

LORD your God is with you wherever you go" (Joshua 1:9). God did not promise ease; he promised his presence.

So dig deep, get ready, and let's now consider how we can engage our age of outrage for the Kingdom of God.

PART 3

The Outrageous Alternatives to Outrage

Death by meeting.

It's both the title of a well-known book by Patrick Lencioni and what will likely be the cause of my own demise. Meetings are crucial to a team's success because they ensure that everyone is on the same page, provide vital feedback and collaboration among team members, and are efficient ways of disseminating information. At least, that's what meetings are in theory. In reality, they are more like what I imagine Catholics believe purgatory to be: the glare of fluorescent lights, the smell of stale coffee, and the discomfort of sitting too long in an overused chair that is not nearly as cushy as it looks.

I was in a meeting recently where everyone was discussing the troubles of higher education (actually, I've undoubtedly been in hundreds of these meetings). Everyone voiced their anxiety about rising costs, declining enrollment, and on and on and on. For hours we discussed all the problems, the reasons for the problems, our feelings about the problems, and those responsible for the problems. By the end of the meeting, we had a pretty good idea of what the problem was, but we were no closer to understanding what we should do about it. We ended with no direction as to where to go from here. We had hopes, possibilities, and ideas for sure. But no practical advice, no strategic plan or next steps.

Too often we are content with merely the diagnosis. Leaders believe they have contributed by simply pointing out that we are in the middle of a desert without offering any vision for moving out of it. The world is filled with people who will stand on the sidelines and point out the problems. Indeed, the church is filled with theologians, pastors, and ministry leaders who have carved out careers by critiquing and complaining about the flaws of Christians. There is a place and a time to be critical, to challenge people and communities to think through their actions and attitudes. But simply pointing out problems without offering some kind of road map back to effective gospel ministry is neither helpful nor pastoral.

Let me be clear: It is not enough to point out failure. Anyone can do that. Anyone can see where the train went off the tracks.

The purpose of this book is not only to understand why and how we got here but also to use that understanding to better engage others in our age of outrage as servants of Jesus Christ. In other words, I want to offer some constructive direction for Christians rather than simply pointing out where culture and the church have gone off the rails. So in this final section, I offer a number of factors that I believe will make us effective witnesses today. These components are interconnected, and the neglect of even one, I believe, contributes to the apathetic witness of many American Christians today.

As the volume turns up and the insults begin to fly, there is the inevitable temptation to either shrink into the background or match the level of intensity around us. While this "fight or flight" mentality is second nature, we have to grasp that it is killing our witness. Those who fight drag the church down into the gutter, and those who flee abandon the world to its hopelessness. At the root of either choice is the desire for ease. It is easy to insult and yell. It is easy not to rock the boat. Engaging the world is hard. It requires intentionality, faithfulness, love, courage. But I believe it is what God calls every believer to do. So let's dig in.

CHAPTER 7

A Worldview Shaped by the Gospel

- 62 percent of evangelicals attend a religious service at least once a week compared to only 15 percent of non-evangelicals.

- 39 percent of evangelicals say their pastor uses Scripture to address political topics at least once a month, perhaps showing that such topics are not often addressed.

- Only 43 percent of evangelicals agree that their pastor should address issues currently being debated by politicians, while the largest share of respondents (31 percent) *strongly* disagree, perhaps showing that many people adamantly oppose their pastors weighing in on political issues.

OVER TWO HUNDRED MILLION. That's the number of people Rev. Billy Graham is thought to have preached the gospel to in person. This doesn't include the tens of millions who read his books, magazines, and newspaper articles; watched him on television and film; and heard his messages via radio. An untold number of people came to faith in Christ as a result of Graham's commitment to his Savior and his pursuit of the call of God on his life.

His impact on modern global Christianity in the twentieth century—and continuing to this day—is unparalleled. And yet his life calling was one of simple obedience. "My one purpose in life," Rev. Graham once said, "is to help people find a personal relationship with God, which, I believe, comes through knowing Christ."[1]

Graham was so successful that we are tempted to think it was inevitable. We forget that in 1946, three years before his Los Angeles tent revival, the National Association of Evangelicals published an article listing evangelical leaders who had been "best used by God" in the five years since the NAE's founding. Graham's friend and fellow evangelist Charles Templeton was prominently featured in the article while Graham did not make the cut.[2]

So what changed? While we can only speculate, Graham was convinced he knew the answer.

In the months before the pivotal LA revival, Graham famously came to a point of crisis in his own spiritual journey. Templeton had walked away from his faith due to his belief that the Bible could no longer be trusted. The event shook Graham to his core and pushed him to a singular moment of decision.

Years later in his autobiography, Graham recounted the night he was walking through the woods at a retreat center in the San Bernardino Mountains. Finally stopping and getting on his knees, Graham laid his Bible on a tree stump in front of him and launched into a prayer that would define his life and ministry:

> O God! There are many things in this book I do not understand. There are many problems with it for which I have no solution. There are many seeming contradictions. There are some areas in it that do not seem to correlate with modern science. I can't answer some of the philosophical and psychological questions Chuck and others are raising.[3]

Unloading his anxieties and fears to God, Graham eventually came to a conclusion:

> Father, I am going to accept this as Thy Word—by *faith*! I'm going to allow faith to go beyond my intellectual questions and doubts, and I will believe this to be Your inspired Word.[4]

In his own words, Graham crossed a major bridge from doubt to faith, submitting his worldview to divine revelation over his own understanding.

The truth is, if you try to engage the age of outrage with a wrong or malformed worldview, it will *eat you alive.*

The purpose of this book is to challenge Christians to be servants of Jesus Christ who shine the light of the gospel into the age of outrage, as Billy Graham did so successfully.

I hear Christians of every denomination, tradition, and community trying to figure out how to engage the age of outrage. Yet in Graham's story, we see a simple truth that is the beginning for Christians who want to bring their best to a world entangled in outrage. Graham understood that in order to engage the world for the gospel, you need to have a worldview wholly submitted to the gospel, a view of authority and action that is surrendered to the Word of God.

He would engage the world from a tent in Los Angeles, but he had to address his doubts first. He had to go through the challenge to get to the mission. And we do too.

So let's do the hard work of making sure we have the right worldview in order to bring the gospel into the age of outrage.

Forging a Worldview

On February 26, 2015, a picture of a black-and-blue dress was posted to the social networking site Tumblr. However, thousands of viewers didn't see the dress as black and blue but as gold and white. In the first week, more than 10 million tweets addressed the starkly different perceptions of the same image.[5] Theories to explain this mystery abounded: Perhaps it had something to do with the different ways humans perceive color, or the simple fact that the dress might look different depending on the device it was viewed on.

To me, the incident is a clear illustration of how people can look at the same thing and see it quite differently. When my wife, Donna, sees a sunrise, she sees it as a beautiful start to a great day. When I see one, I see that I am up too early. Ugh.

Fortunately, while the dress incident prompted more befuddlement than outrage, this was largely because of the silliness of the problem. After all, it's hard to get too worked up about the color of a dress (not that a few brave Internet trolls didn't try to stir up some angst). True problems develop, however, when we begin to see more important and personal issues—such as morality, justice, and fairness—in fundamentally different ways. Many times two people have intensely opposite responses to moral issues. The same event has the power to provoke wildly different reactions from different people, and this is due to more than a difference in taste. Want proof? Go stand outside the Supreme Court when a controversial ruling comes down, and you will see two competing crowds, each with a polar opposite response to the same event.

At a more basic and less controversial level, think about a sunrise again. Upon seeing a Grand Canyon sunrise, religious people and people of no faith may have different reactions determined by their worldviews. Some might ascribe praise to the general idea of God, where others might marvel at the results of scientific explanations like the big bang theory. In contrast, Christians will praise a specific God: the one who created and sustains the world. He is both the awesome and all-powerful Creator who carved out the Grand Canyon and the intimate Savior who died and rose for their sins. The majesty of the natural display is paired with the intimacy of the God they know in their prayers and trials. Our worldview, then, informs how we see and respond to everything, from Supreme Court rulings over life and equality to the beauty of the Grand Canyon.

What Is a Worldview?

Simply stated, a worldview is a set of fundamental beliefs that inform the way we see and engage the world. It is the framework through which we interpret everyday life and make decisions. N. T. Wright describes worldview as the "lenses through which a society looks at the world, the grid upon which are plotted the multiple experiences of life."[6] It is, as Charles Colson liked to describe it, "the sum total of our beliefs about the world, the 'big picture' that directs our daily decisions and actions."[7] The questions at the center of our worldview revolve around how we understand God, ethics, truth, and reality. Does God exist? What is truth? How do we distinguish between good and evil? What is the meaning and purpose of my life? The answers to these and similar questions comprise our worldview.

Our physical sight helps us see, interpret, and interact with the physical world, while our worldview helps us understand and interact with the moral, social, and spiritual elements of life. When we respond negatively to a new Supreme Court decision, it is our worldview telling us that this ruling is a bad idea. When we derive joy from seeing an athlete praising God after winning a championship, our worldview tells us this is a morally praiseworthy act. From how we vote to the friendships we develop to the news channels we watch, our worldview is responsible for the hundreds of reactions and decisions we make every day. In essence, our worldview is the machine running in the background of our thinking that influences us at all times.

Our worldview is also a *product* of our decisions, habits, and influences. The cultures and communities we live in can have a profound effect on our answers to the fundamental questions above; therefore, many of us have worldviews similar to those around us.

However, our worldviews can evolve and change over the course of our lives. Change can come quickly or over a long period as we forge new habits and acquire new sources of influence. Think of the Christian who, after years of putting it off, finally begins to read God's Word every day. Over time, her values and beliefs shift as she learns and applies biblical lessons to her life. Conversely, a worldview change might be sparked by a singular event that radically reshapes the way someone sees the world. Think of the man who tragically loses a child at a young age. We rightly call such events "earth shattering" and "life altering" because they have the potential to radically reshape the way we see the world. Thus, our worldview shapes us, and we shape our worldview.

Perhaps most important, our actions often uncover the *truth* of our worldview. While many people claim to have a certain worldview, their habits and reactions paint a different story. As Philip Ryken points out,

> The way other people respond reveals *their* worldview—their faithfulness in keeping a commitment, for example, or their unbelief in the existence and providence of God. Ideas have consequences. Even ordinary interactions reflect our commitments and convictions about the basic issues of art and science, work and play, family and society, life and death. Whenever we bump into the world, our worldview has a way of spilling out. It comes out in what we think and love, say and do, praise and choose.[8]

How we respond to the challenges and questions of life *exposes* our worldview. This is crucial. Our worldview might not be what we think it is. An atheist might scream and rage against those who believe in God, but when turbulence shakes his plane in a thunderstorm, a prayer may slip from his lips.

Defining a "Gospel-Shaped" Worldview

Scripture calls us to set our minds on things above (Colossians 3:2) and to be shaped into the image of Christ by the Spirit (2 Corinthians 3:18). A true Christian worldview that leads to such transformation has certain emphases. I often talk about it being gospel-shaped and mission-driven. Being mission-driven is a theme throughout this book, so I won't rehash that here. When we live out a gospel-driven Christian worldview, the gospel is not just something we grasp at conversion; it is something that influences how we see and respond to the world in all areas of our lives.

When Christians participate in an unhelpful way in this age of outrage, this transformation has not happened; instead, they have allowed their worldview to become infected. Some of these Christians are nominal believers, perhaps more Christian-ish than Christian. Other Christians have not been discipled to follow Christ. They may neglect the disciplines God uses to sanctify and mature our minds and hearts in favor of harmful habits that negatively shape the way they see and engage with others.

Even those who strive to follow Christ closely may unknowingly be influenced by a secular outlook. When confronted with the major questions of life and identity, they might give the correct answers characterized by a Christian worldview. Yet if they did an honest inventory of their time and thinking, they, too, might recognize that their worldview has become disordered. The shouting headlines of cable news, the latest post by some Instagram celebrity, and the scare tactics of a negative political campaign ad can easily influence their gospel-shaped worldview. In essence, they have ignored Paul's exhortation, "Don't copy the behavior and customs of this world, but let God transform you into a new person by changing the way you think. Then you will learn to know God's will for you, which is good and pleasing and perfect" (Romans 12:2, NLT).

In a culture awash in a sea of outrage, Christians frequently do not look very different from those with secular worldviews. We have the same addictions, indulge in the same selfish political games, and ultimately reveal the same fears and anxieties as our neighbors, coworkers, and leaders. When our worldview is markedly similar to that of a person who does not know Jesus, what does that say about us? Should not the reality of Christ's redemptive work, the indwelling of the Spirit, and our adoption as coheirs to the Kingdom of God be manifest in a profoundly different worldview? Instead of appearing changed and renewed, Christians too often appear conformed. It is little wonder that Christians feel challenged by the age of outrage. We need to hear Paul's exhortation to the Ephesians:

> But that isn't what you learned about Christ. Since you have heard about Jesus and have learned the truth that comes

from him, throw off your old sinful nature and your former
way of life, which is corrupted by lust and deception.
Instead, let the Spirit renew your thoughts and attitudes.
Put on your new nature, created to be like God—truly
righteous and holy.

EPHESIANS 4:20-24, NLT

The Dutch theologian Herman Bavinck argued that "all good,
enduring reformation begins with ourselves and takes its starting
point in one's own heart and life."[9] While we might be distraught
or even angry at the level of outrage in the world, our first task is
putting off the old and putting on the new in ourselves. We must
first consider which of our own habits and influences may be responsible for pulling our worldview away from Christ, then reflect
on how we can course correct.

We must develop the inputs and outputs for our lives that will
shape our worldviews according to God's truth. What habits have
we developed? The answer to this question reveals the truth about
our loves and, in turn, what is shaping our worldviews.

A problem of quality: outraged voices

I have a game I play when I watch a young preacher.

Because I speak at dozens of conferences and events each
year, I've been able to listen to some of the best and most popular
preachers of our time. I've developed a sense for many of their
mannerisms, customs, and peculiarities, including the way they
tell stories, drive home applications, and even move their bodies.
Every preacher has a distinct speaking pattern.

So when I watch young preachers, I try to determine from their
mannerisms what other preachers they are listening to, whose
podcasts and YouTube clips they are downloading, and who they
might have trained under at seminary. If I get the chance to bring
it up in casual conversation, I usually ask them these questions
and see if I was right.

Why do I do this? Because young preachers are incredibly

impressionable, and they will naturally incorporate the tics and tendencies of those they respect and value. More often than not, they don't even know they're doing it. In one case, I remember noticing how a very influential pastor would start every sermon rolling his head to stretch out the ear microphone cord so it didn't pinch his neck. Sure enough, when I saw some of his protégés preach, several of them rolled their heads the same way. Only problem: They weren't using those types of ear mics! There was nothing to fix. They had subconsciously picked up a behavior from the established preacher without knowing it and for no logical reason.

Although mimicking others can be humorous, it can be a good thing in many instances. In a way, this mirrors Paul's encouragement to Timothy to follow him (2 Timothy 3:10). Of course, it can be taken too far, but for young preachers trying to find their voice and style, looking for quality models to follow is wise.

When we begin to look at why people, including many Christians, are giving in to outrage, an important place to start is the voices speaking into their lives. Simply put, when we choose to follow leaders who contribute to rather than stand against the outrage, we will become like them.

Scripture consistently warns us about the quality of voices we allow into our lives. What we see and hear is depicted as the gateway to what we love and worship. The psalmist outlines the ways Scripture guides and protects us against sin. Yet just as important as meditating on God's Word is his exhortation to "turn [our] eyes away from worthless things" (Psalm 119:37, NIV). Jesus expounds on this idea in the Sermon on the Mount: "The eye is the lamp of the body. So, if your eye is healthy, your whole body will be full of light, but if your eye is bad, your whole body will be full of darkness. If then the light in you is darkness, how great is the darkness!" (Matthew 6:22-23).

When we read Paul's list in Philippians 4:8 ("whatever is true, whatever is noble, whatever is right, whatever is pure, whatever is lovely, whatever is admirable–if anything is excellent or praiseworthy," NIV), we can characterize it as simply a poetic list of nice things. However, Paul ends it with the commandment to "think about such things." Paul is calling us to reflect on our influences, challenging us to consider whether they align with the characteristics of God's holiness. Paul connects the quality of our influences to the quality of our spiritual lives, which is why we must think through how we are shaped by the people, media, and activities we experience.

I remember religiously listening to the conservative radio host Rush Limbaugh more than twenty years ago. I even called in to the show once and sat up a bit taller when he asked for "Ed from Erie, Pennsylvania." All of my friends called me, and I felt like a mini-celebrity for a day.

Limbaugh was (and is) bombastic and brash (but also entertaining), and I resonated with his conservative politics. Even if you reject his politics, if you listen to him for only five minutes, you understand that he is a remarkably gifted communicator.

But Limbaugh makes his living on political division and anger. Limbaugh has a long history of going after anyone he sees as politically to his left in a tone that is at best unfriendly and often condemning. I enjoyed his arrogance, energy, and irreverence, unable to recognize how his tone and mentality were affecting my ability to transcend political division as a young pastor.

The proverbial scales fell off my eyes when I realized that I was more interested in listening to Rush Limbaugh than in praying for President Bill Clinton. That insight was so momentous to me because it was obviously against what Scripture calls us to do in praying for our leaders. At this point, I was struck by the realization that voices such as Limbaugh's were promoting a vision of the world in which political identity is everything. Faced with the choice between obeying Scripture or listening to Limbaugh, I realized I needed to stop tuning in to him.

Now before you search for my Twitter account and post a message about how outraged you are that I'm calling for a boycott of Rush Limbaugh—please know that I'm not doing any such thing.

My point is not that you should stop listening to Rush, but that you should recognize the voices that may be influencing you to join the outrage. It became clear to me that listening to his voice was not helpful in my discipleship. What political, cultural, and spiritual voices help, and which ones hinder your own walk with the Lord?

A problem of quantity in a binge culture

The trap was set for a Saturday night.

Our kids were out of the house, and my sermon was prepped and ready for the next day. With a little bit of time to spare before bed, my wife and I settled in to watch some television. Now I'm not a big TV guy, but in my role as dutiful husband, I agreed to watch a new show we'd heard about called *This Is Us*. Little did I know what I had signed on for.

I swear this show was genetically engineered in a lab to pull on our heartstrings. No . . . not pull, more like rip. I picture a room full of scientists huddled together brainstorming about what needs to go into a program to elicit the correct balance of viewers' tears and laughs. Not too much sadness, not too much laughter. Don't let it get boring, but avoid pure chaos.

Before I realized it, we had watched late into the night. More to the point, over the next few weeks, we kept returning to pick up where we'd left off until we'd caught up with the most current episode. Even now, my wife is waiting to watch an upcoming episode with a big reveal about a character's death. If this can be a safe space for a moment, I'm super pumped.

But what happened to us? How did we go from not caring to being so invested that we binged through episode after episode?

Speaking of the word *binged*, have you noticed how the accepted definitions of that word have changed recently? Emil Steiner highlighted this transition:

> Until 2012, the noun binge connoted unhealthy behavior—
> a period of uncontrollable excess. As a verb it is still

commonly associated with binge drinking and binge eating–psychological symptoms associated with a pathological loss of control. Despite appending the same modifier, binge-watching has mostly been depicted as a liberating experience, the worst side-effect of which is poor personal hygiene, in the more than ten thousand newspaper and magazine articles mentioning the behavior since 2012. The rapid transformation of binge-watching from obscurity to ubiquity has stretched popular understanding of binge.[10]

Over thirty years ago, Neil Postman sounded the warning bells about a culture he feared was enslaving itself to entertainment and leisure. Published in 1985, Postman's *Amusing Ourselves to Death* was prophetic in arguing that the way Americans created and consumed media was ultimately destructive. Focusing specifically on television (it was the eighties, after all), Postman argued that the medium actually discouraged reflection and made its viewers into passive consumers rather than critical engagers. In the intervening years, the factors that Postman first drew attention to have increased. Even as new media emphasize audience involvement, every facet of our media engagement is aimed at pushing us toward the next show, the next podcast, the next article. To update Postman's assessment, I believe we're bingeing ourselves to death.

In a University of Michigan study of binge watching, researchers noted a large majority of viewers don't actually want to binge. The study notes, "Binge viewing appears to be unintentional: reports indicate that 71% of binge viewing happens by accident, when people wound up watching more than they wanted to."[11] At one time, the credits rolling signaled the end of a show. Now when the credits roll on many streaming services, we have seconds to decide to stop watching or continue with the following episode. Some services automatically start the next episode so the viewer must actively decide to stop watching before that program launches.

The entertainment industry is always studying ways to hold our attention for the longest stretch of time. Whether companies are trying to entice us to go from one show to the next, one article to the next, or one blog post to the next, they will not let our attention go without a fight. The root of the issue is this: *They are fighting for our discipleship, for our love.*

While the cognitive and social effects of media and binge consumption are concerning, in my opinion, those pale in comparison to how they shape our spiritual walk. Media is constantly trying to condition us, train us, and shape our worldview.

Before we start blaming "those media-obsessed millennials" for this trend, we must recognize that every age demographic has seen dramatic increases in the amount of time they spend on social media and binge watching.[12] In fact, the heaviest users of social media aren't millennials, but Generation Xers like me (born between 1965 and 1980), who clock almost seven hours per week on social media compared to millennials at six hours.[13] In 2016, Americans consumed almost eleven hours of all media *each day*. This is a staggering new reality.

Let me be clear: I'm not saying that watching any particular show is sin, but rather that the uncritical embrace of an emerging culture that not only accepts but approves of entertainment bingeing will deform your spiritual walk. The issue is not "How does it?" but rather "How could it not?" In a new reality where there is more content than we can possibly consume, we need to develop the necessary discipline to recognize the danger in drinking from a bottomless mug. There is *always* another podcast, *always* another Instagram post, *always* another television series.

It's easy to assume that we have avoided the more caustic elements of our outrage culture because we do not consume the most popular programs. We point at others who listen to *InfoWars* or *Pod Save America* and shake our heads, wondering how they could let such politically divisive voices speak into their worldviews. This fails to acknowledge that the six hours in a single day we spent watching the latest trending show or scrolling through social media pictures can be just as destructive in the long term.

Ancient Paths: Spiritual Disciplines
Shape a Gospel Worldview

Rooting out bad habits is not enough. If we merely attack what is wrong, we create a vacuum that will inevitably be filled by some new behavior or addiction that does not shape our worldview according to the gospel. The solution, I believe, is discipleship, the process of becoming more like Christ.

Eugene Peterson describes the Christian life as "a long obedience in the same direction."[14] Few lines so neatly summarize the relevant factors that go into discipleship: the importance of obedience rather than emotion; the sense that this is a process rather than an instant transformation; the reminder that discipleship is not perfection but a progression in one direction. More than anything else, Peterson repeatedly points out that obedience is not intrinsically powerful in itself; the one whom we obey is the source of life-transforming power. Discipleship is empowered by and aimed at God.

In this time of instant gratification, faster-than-light processing speed, and transactional politics, Christian discipleship stands out as something distinctly radical. It cannot be downloaded, bought, or won. We do not stumble upon it, nor can others give it to us.

Philip Nation is right when he says the foundational truth of discipleship is this: "*Love is the central discipline of the Christian life.* Everything else will flow from that as the centerpiece of spiritual formation."[15] James K. A. Smith adopts a similar perspective, imploring Christians to recognize the intimate connection between discipleship and habit: "If you are what you love, and love is a habit, then discipleship is a rehabituation of your loves. This means that discipleship is more a matter of re*form*ation than of acquiring *in*formation."[16] The answer for Christians in the age of outrage is not some silver-bullet study that will give a new piece of knowledge. Rather, it begins with looking at our habits, the things that we love every day through our choices and actions.

In thinking through the challenge of spiritual disciplines in the age of outrage, I find the prophet Jeremiah instructive. Perhaps no other biblical author had greater reason to throw up his hands and give up. At the best of times he was simply ignored, while the worst times brought universal derision and persecution. God gave him a message of rebuke and warning for his people, but they ignored him to carry on with their ways of injustice and hedonism. After calling the Jewish people back to God, Jeremiah famously wept when they rejected what he knew was their final warning. In one of the saddest passages of Scripture, Jeremiah wrote, "My soul will weep in secret for your pride; my eyes will weep bitterly and run down with tears, because the LORD's flock has been taken captive" (Jeremiah 13:17). The old prophet's admonition comes earlier in the book and hearkens back to the old ways:

Thus says the LORD:
"Stand by the roads, and look,
    and ask for the ancient paths,
where the good way is; and walk in it,
    and find rest for your souls."
JEREMIAH 6:16

Walter Brueggemann rightly noted that Jeremiah is not calling us back to "a nostalgic return to 'old-time religion' or 'the good old days,' but a return to a more radical and dangerous memory that serves to end all present complacency and to subvert all present certitudes."[17] It is a return to the theological traditions that are central to the formation of a correct worldview. For those in Jeremiah's time, this was a return to the Torah and their covenantal relationship with God. For us, I believe this is a call to return to the spiritual disciplines.

To be sure, all spiritual disciplines as historically practiced are necessary in the life of every believer. When we practice them, we are heeding Paul's encouragement to Timothy to "discipline yourself for the purpose of godliness" (1 Timothy 4:7, NASB). While believers are new creations upon their coming to faith and repentance, the work of godliness is a lifelong pursuit. Given the focus of this book, I want to consider three spiritual disciplines as particularly relevant to counteracting the creep of outrage thinking into our worldview. We may think of them in terms of inputs, outputs, and necessities.

1. Scripture: inputting spiritual/gospel truth

How do we fight back in a world filled with meaningless data? In an age when every politician and blogger promises to enlighten us?

In times when "truth" seems like a commodity peddled on every street corner, we need to grasp the power of the foundation we have in Scripture. While many readers will say "yes" and "amen" to this, the sad truth is that Bible reading is low even among those who frequently attend church. A 2015 study by LifeWay Research found that only 45 percent of people who attend church regularly read the Bible more than once a week. More than 40 percent of church attenders read their Bibles occasionally, about once or twice a month. Almost one in five churchgoers say they *never* read the Bible, which is about the same number as those who read it every day.[18]

As noted earlier, a worldview is not defined by what we say but what we do. Our confession that the Bible is the divine Word of God capable of training us in godliness and preparing us for engaging an outraged culture is an empty statement unless our habits align with the claim.

If we are to begin to push back against this, we have to understand how meditating on God's Word is central to worldview formation. As Christians, we believe Scripture is the central and authoritative input by which we engage with and learn from God, and the lens through which we interpret all events and trials. In this respect, a Scripture habit develops and reinforces our Christian worldview in two practical ways.

First, reading the Bible provides a *daily reorientation of our worldview.* In Joshua 1:8, God told Joshua: "Study this Book of Instruction continually. Meditate on it day and night so you will be sure to obey everything written in it" (NLT). Remember the context of God's command: Moses was dead, and Israel was preparing to head into a foreign and hostile territory. In fact, God encouraged Joshua to "be strong and courageous" three times in the first nine verses of chapter 1. Joshua faced an unknown obstacle and was in charge of a people who had already revealed their proclivity to wander. Now they would come into contact with other gods, other customs, and other systems of government, all of which would try to tempt Israel away from God. The exhortation to daily reflect upon the law in this situation was a reminder to Joshua that the only way he could successfully navigate these challenges was under God's direct guidance.

Second, reading the Bible is *identity forming*. Sadly, many Christians fail to grasp this crucial truth about discipleship. We think of Bible reading the way we might think about charging a battery; we expect time in Scripture to recharge our engines so we can face the world. We assume we need a little jolt once in a while and then we'll be good. As a result, when our pastors or small group leaders encourage us to get into God's Word for ourselves, we think of it as a way to gain knowledge rather than a means to form our identity:

"I know the Gospel of Luke. Pharisees are bad. The humble tax collector is good."
"Ten plagues in Egypt. Got it. Hasn't changed since the flannelgraph lesson when I was a kid in Sunday school."
"How many times does this cycle of judgment in Judges repeat? I get it already!"

Yet when we read Scripture, we are entering into a community of the Word. It binds us to other Christians and other Christian disciplines.

A few years ago, I was asked to speak at the Q Conference, a gathering of educators, politicians, and Christian leaders designed to stimulate curiosity and ideas on how to advance the common good. The other speakers presented their thoughtful ideas on ways to change the world. President Obama even sent a video. But my talk was a bit different. They had asked me to speak on discipleship that leads people to serve others, so I reported on our research at LifeWay. Our study had uncovered the one factor that correlated to a greater practice of serving others: reading the Bible.

Actually, reading the Bible was the factor that had the highest correlation with *every other factor of discipleship.* Now when people ask me, "How do we get people to witness?" "How do we get people to serve others?" or "How do we get people to pray?" I give them the same answer: Get people to read the Bible.

It is even more important in the formation of identity in young Christians. In a study released in 2017, LifeWay discovered that 29 percent of the young adults surveyed read the Bible regularly while growing up. "On average, that group has 12.5 percent higher spiritual health than otherwise comparable individuals."[19] Young adults are at a crucial point in life because they are developing lifetime habits and choosing what influences they will allow to speak into their lives, so regular engagement with God's Word is formative.

2. Prayer: outputting spiritual/gospel concern

Outrage is most often the result of anxieties and insecurities bubbling to the surface, but the Christian faith has a ready-made alternative: prayer.

When we pair our prayers with Scripture, we effectively merge our inputs and outputs. We remind ourselves of God's truth in the midst of our trials while simultaneously laying God's own truth before him, asking him to be faithful to his Word. In prayer, we bring to Jesus those anxieties and insecurities that would otherwise fuel our outrage. The discipline of prayer prevents us from venting, flaming, or savaging others, either in person or online. I've never seen people go after someone they're praying for.

When Scripture calls us to "pray without ceasing" (1 Thessalonians 5:17), it envisions lives saturated in prayer and invites us to bring God all of our challenges, opportunities, and complexities of life.

All politicians tell us to "trust them," pledging things will get better if we just win the next election or raise the most money.

All commercials and pop-up ads tell us to "trust them." If we buy these companies' products or install that new technology, we can overcome the anxiety and outrage of the world around us.

All newspapers tell us to "trust them." If we read their articles or follow their reports on social media, we can gain control by staying up to date on all the latest news headlines.

Every industry, discipline, and leader is vying for our attention. They want us to cast our needs and wants upon them, promising they have the solution that will bring peace. The problem is that when they fail—which they all inevitably will—the fallout is a ratcheting up of the outrage.

In these situations, we should pause to remember that God also tells us to trust him with our anxieties, insecurities, and fears. Paul says this best in Philippians 4:6-7.[20] In the first part of the passage, God provides an alternative to anxiety and outrage: "Don't worry about anything; instead, pray about everything. Tell God what you need, and thank him for all he has done." In the second half, God gives a promise that is more powerful and secure than anything this world can offer. He says, "You will experience God's peace, which exceeds anything we can understand. His peace will guard your hearts and minds as you live in Christ Jesus." The discipline of prayer actually guards our hearts and minds in Christ.

The Bible also depicts prayer as the necessary practice *prior* to engaging the world.

1. Nehemiah prayed before asking the king for permission to return and build Jerusalem (Nehemiah 1:4-11).
2. Jesus prayed for God's will prior to the Cross (Luke 22:41-44).
3. Prior to his mission, Paul asked for prayer that God would open a door for evangelism (Colossians 4:3).

Prayer plays a critical role in preparing our hearts for engagement. In essence, we cannot hope to engage the age of outrage unless we are properly devoted to the habit of prayer. Without it, we will inevitably succumb to the temptations and pressures that give rise to outrage rather than proclaim the victory and peace of Christ.

3. Fasting: disciplining spiritual/gospel reliance

Fasting is by far the most neglected spiritual discipline, with roughly 80 percent of churchgoing Protestants saying they have not fasted in the past six months.[21] I believe, however, that where outrage is often a product of mindless, instant response to things we do not like, fasting, at its root, is a reminder that God is the answer to every need we have.

Too often, people in our culture (and I include Christians) do not know how to separate need from want. We *need* to order that item that popped up in our timeline. We *need* to watch the new trending show. We *need* to engage in an online fight. Our world is exceptional at making us believe all these things are necessary. The lesson of fasting is nowhere more relevant than in a society where we have lost the concept of delayed gratification. God gives us many blessings and gifts that satisfy our bodies and minds, but our souls–the part of us that is actually us–long for God as we thirst for water (Psalm 42:1).

Let me be clear on one point: Biblical fasting does not necessarily require a total "technology unplug." While psychologists and sociologists are quickly catching on to the health benefits of taking breaks from our plugged-in world, these are the benefits of a fast, similar to the weight lost when someone fasts from food. Fasting is designed to reorient our hearts to God and to reveal our dependency upon him and the complete insufficiency of this world to meet our needs. To fast without intentionally focusing on God is to take something off without putting on what matters in its place. We may root out destructive habits, but we will not have done the spiritual work of replacing the vacuum with worship.

Spiritual disciplines lead us away from outrage

Dedicating ourselves to Scripture reading, prayer, and fasting enables us to reset our minds, steering us away from the road toward outrage and onto the path of peace. Jeremiah's listeners ultimately rejected his exhortation to walk in these ancient paths and seek "the good way." A prideful and stubborn spirit led them to respond, "We will not walk in it" (Jeremiah 6:16). The truth is they, like us, did not want to do the hard work of returning to these pathways of faithfulness and obedience.

Jeremiah's words are similar to Jesus' call to come to him for this same rest:

Come to me, all of you who are weary and carry
heavy burdens, and I will give you rest. Take my yoke
upon you. Let me teach you, because I am humble
and gentle at heart, and you will find rest for your souls.
For my yoke is easy to bear, and the burden I give you
is light.
MATTHEW 11:28-30, NLT

As believers, we need to recognize that the power in these disciplines is in how they draw us closer to Christ. These paths do not have mystic power to combat outrage, but it is down these pathways we walk with Jesus.

Through Scripture, we hear Christ's voice speaking into the outrage, giving us wisdom rather than forcing us to seek it from the chaotic masses.

Through prayer, we cast our anxieties and fears upon Christ rather than pouring them out into a vat of outrage.

Through fasting, we remind ourselves of the soul's dependence upon Christ and the insufficiency of everything else.

Are you weary of the pace of this world? Does the never-ending deluge of information from the media wear you out? God promises that when we meet him, we find our true rest along these ancient paths—not in a new technology, a new medication, or the passage of new legislation, but through *intentionally* and *habitually* coming to Jesus and casting our burdens upon him. Only there do we find *true* and *enduring* rest. When we submit our inputs and outputs to the gospel, we will find that the voices of outrage dim and the peace of God grows.

Tempered Voices: Spiritual Teaching Shapes a Gospel Worldview

When we start listening to the wrong voices, our worldview can easily become distorted. While I'm not much of a sports fan (shocking, I know), I was invited to the 2017 Orange Bowl to watch the matchup between Wisconsin and Miami in one of the year's most important college football playoff games. The stadium was so loud that I couldn't hear my friend standing next to me trying to describe the game. I can explain the story of Boniface and the Sacred Oak of Thor, as well as its relevance to modern missions, but somehow I missed the train on the whole sports thing. When something major happened that night, I needed my friend to yell the explanation into my ear. Just to participate in the event, I needed an interpreter who could cut through the volume.

"What happened?"

"Miami got a touchdown."

"Is that good?"

[*Vigorous nodding*]

In the age of outrage, the sheer volume of yelling and anger can be deafening, just like the Orange Bowl crowd. The most challenging issue is cutting through the noise to listen to the right voices. Everyone is claiming to be an authority, everyone claims to have the answers, and everyone has a platform to try to grab our attention. The result can be chaos as Christians try to live out the gospel. More than ever, we need to think intentionally about the voices we listen to and the authorities we let speak into our lives.

Pastoral leadership

In 1998, I was walking to my car when my cell phone rang. Imagine my shock when the familiar voice of Rick Warren greeted me. I knew the voice well from his preaching tapes (those rectangle things with two holes in the middle that fill the basements and attics of churches across the United States today), but I was still caught off guard. Not one to be slowed down, Rick jumped right into his reason for calling: He had a job he wanted me to take.

Now I'll cut you some slack if you don't know that cellular technology has come a long way in twenty years. Back then I did not have an iPhone with unlimited data. I don't remember the brand, but I am sure it had a built-in antenna and flip cover and was just awesome.

But it was also expensive to use.

You can imagine my situation as Rick continued to talk. Warren, now a friend, was more of a distant, digital mentor then. Warren's *The Purpose Driven Church* was a big influence on me and how I did ministry, helping me apply a systematic approach to discipleship and engaging culture. So I did not want to rush him off the phone. On the other hand, a massive cell phone bill for a pastor on a tight budget in the nineties was no joke.

As Rick laid out his vision for a job he wanted me to take as a professor of church planting, I watched the minutes tick by on my watch. Finally, I asked if I could call him back on my phone (that's what the kids call a "landline" today, but we just called it a "phone," in contrast to the mobile phone in my hand). He soon wrapped up the call (and my life was now on a new trajectory).

Warren's book was so impactful because his pastoral voice cut through the chaos and noise of the world with godly truth. Warren simply made the case for building a culture of discipleship, for engaging your community, and more.

Just as Rick Warren influenced my ministry, Christians need to learn from discerning voices. We need mature believers who will speak truth, guide us through trials, and teach us about God, ministry, and culture. A major part of the problem in the age of outrage is that we are looking for answers in the wrong places. When we turn to the voices of our culture for wisdom—Fox News or MSNBC; celebrities or athletes; musicians or pop psychologists; or the self-help section at the bookstore or on our podcast app—we give platforms to people with no allegiance to or love for the gospel. One of the major ways to combat this and ensure our worldview is shaped by the gospel is by listening to voices that lead us toward holiness. In other words, we can decrease the platform we give to the Rachel Maddows and Sean Hannitys and fill the vacuum with the voices of pastoral leaders.

The good news is that there has been an explosion in Christian publishing. We have an abundance of quality resources that touch on every doctrine, trial, experience, and culture. In past generations, Christians struggling to answer complex issues like systemic racism, mental health, or addiction could find few or no quality pastoral resources. Local churches were responsible not only for preaching, pastoring, and leading their communities, but also for guiding Christians through these questions.

I suggest that Christians think about exploring five categories:

1. Resources to help Christians understand God and his Word. You could spend a thousand lifetimes studying theology or the nuances and beauty of Scripture, but it is often shocking to me how little Christians know about the faith they profess to hold. The trick in reading books on theology is choosing books that match your level. While it's good for mature Christians to think deeply about weightier truths, pastors can turn off new believers by giving them a giant tome of systematic theology to read. There are important books that are more accessible:

> Examples: Christopher Wright, *Knowing Jesus through the Old Testament*, and Jen Wilkin, *None Like Him*
>
> Wright is a first-rate Old Testament scholar who excels at bridging the gap between the church and academy. For Christians struggling to understand the Old Testament or

its connection to Jesus, Wright is an able and compelling
guide through Old Testament theology and its importance
for faith today. Likewise, Wilkin is a winsome writer
who discusses major, complex ideas about God typically
reserved for a seminary classroom, making them practical
for everyday believers. Wilkin's work shines because she
demonstrates that buried in the complexity of Christian
doctrine is a robust and beautiful faith ready to meet every
challenge and trial in our lives.

2. Resources to help Christians in their fight against sin. The
mark of any good spiritual resource on Christian living is its ability to *both* convict us of sin and strengthen our faith in the power
of God to continue his sanctifying work in us until it is completed.
Such materials reveal our flaws and point us to Jesus.

Example: Timothy Keller, *Counterfeit Gods*
A Keller book could fit every category, but his work
on idolatry is a great starting point for Christians trying
to understand and fight against sin. Keller explains how
idolatry worms its way into our loves with false promises
of fulfillment when only the gospel can satisfy. Not content
to uncover the personal idols Christians love to hide,
Keller probes the depths of the cultural and societal idols
we often excuse or pretend don't exist.

**3. Resources to help readers engage in ministry, in both their
churches and their communities.** Ministry is not only for pastors.
All Christians are called to evangelize, care for their neighbors,
and serve in a community of local believers. However, learning
how to be effective in ministry is a lifelong pursuit, and Christians
should be willing to learn how to be more loving and fruitful.

Example: Trillia Newbell, *United: Captured by God's Vision
for Diversity*

There has been an outpouring of powerful works on how Christians and churches should engage with the issue of racial reconciliation and intentionally cultivate multiethnic communities. While I could pick a dozen that have shaped my thinking, at the top is Newbell's advocacy for diversity within the united body of Christ. Through her own story, Newbell invites Christians to see how God can use ethnic diversity to advance his Kingdom and unify his church.

4. Resources to answer complex questions about life and morality. Many of us view issues like in vitro fertilization or suicide only in the abstract. We may discuss them with friends over coffee, but rarely do we engage with them at a deeper level. For some people, however, these questions are intensely personal and can become unfathomable weights as they try to reconcile life with their faith. In these times, Christians need to lean on faithful voices who have prayerfully and biblically addressed these complex questions.

Example: Matthew Stanford, *Grace for the Afflicted: A Clinical and Biblical Perspective on Mental Illness*
A neuroscientist and psychiatrist, Stanford tackles a subject that many in the church are either ill-equipped or tentative to engage: mental illness. Stanford's medical expertise and astute theological reflection guide patients through the complexities of mental health, while always pointing readers back to their identity as God's creations. For pastors and lay leaders struggling to understand how to love and serve those with mental illness, Stanford provides both solid application and a vision for the role of the church in meeting this need.

5. Resources to help believers understand our world and evolving culture. I have spent most of my life trying to help Christians understand and engage culture in ways that advance the Kingdom of God rather than surrender to the methods and objectives of this world. In the age of outrage, Christians need to be wary of voices that buy into the polarization and seek those that challenge us to consider how we can live in the world without becoming part of it.

Example: Alan Jacobs, *How to Think: A Survival Guide for a World at Odds*
In this exploration of today's political and cultural division, Baylor professor Alan Jacobs breaks down how much of the hostility today stems from our inability to think well. By connecting poor thinking to biased judgments of events and other people, Jacobs challenges readers to consider their own blind spots and thinking processes. Gracious yet convicting, Jacobs winsomely engages topics of politics and culture where other Christian leaders fear to tread.

I draw attention to these five categories simply to reinforce the point that Christians have a staggering depth and breadth of resources on which to draw. Whatever the topic, countless mature believing voices have thought deeply and prayerfully on how to pastor God's people toward righteousness. The challenge is sorting the wheat from the chaff; seeking those godly, pastoral voices who will build up rather than those who sow seeds of division and polarization.

In times like these, local churches are a vital resource for believers. Pastors, elders, and ministry staff don't have to know everything or solve every problem. Rather, one of the most fundamental ways they can lead is by pointing believers to those who can give gospel-shaped answers. This is, in part, what I try to do by publishing book reviews and promoting the work of Christian leaders. Whether it's a book, a podcast, a video, or an Etch A Sketch drawing, Christians need quality resources to help walk the life of faith.

Embodied discipleship

The rise of podcasts, social media, and online streaming can leave the impression that we are actually *being discipled* by the leaders we follow. For sure, leaders who excel in these formats can help foster our discipleship growth, particularly in locations or circumstances where there are few alternatives. However, we need to understand that these resources are at best supplemental to our spiritual discipleship. Discipleship is necessarily embodied; that is, discipleship is an exchange or dialogue between Christians. It is a personal investment on the part of mature believers in others with the overarching purpose of equipping them for righteous living and Kingdom ministry (Ephesians 4:12).

We see this consistently demonstrated in Scripture, most clearly in the example of Apollos in Acts 18:24-26. Apollos was a preacher in Ephesus who experienced considerable fruit due to his skillful teaching. But when Priscilla and Aquila heard him in the synagogue, we're told that "they took him aside and explained to him the way of God more accurately" (verse 26). Apollos had learned enough about Jesus on his own to preach, but he needed others to come alongside and teach him more about the faith.

Paul understood the place of relationship. Many times in his epistles, he confessed his desire to *be with the church.* His letters, even though supernaturally inspired, were not all that was needed. Churches could choose to ignore parts of them (as Corinth did). They could misunderstand them (as in Thessalonica). Or they could be less effective than Paul hoped in relieving problems (as with Ephesus and Timothy). When writing to the church in Rome, where he hadn't been, Paul reflected on his longing to visit so he could properly help the believers there grow strong in the Lord.

While we are the beneficiaries of Paul's letters, it is clear that he considered his writings to be authoritative, but also to be engaged in the context of personal discipleship. The book of Acts highlights just how often Paul traveled. After his initial trip when he founded a series of churches, Paul spent most of his travels visiting established churches so he could effectively encourage and build them up in person. Whenever I want to complain about my travel schedule, I think of Paul hoofing it around the Mediterranean so he could properly disciple churches.

The reason Paul desired to be with his churches in person–and the reason we need to seek out embodied discipleship–is because of its intimacy. In effective discipleship, we can be held accountable when we allow wrong thinking and habits to sneak into our lives, and we can then be encouraged to press on toward godliness. Our absence from small group or church will also be noticed and challenged.

The truth is, no matter how good the online sermon or the discipleship podcast, in the absence of an embodied discipling relationship, we are always one mistake away from changing the channel. If a leader says or does something we don't like, we can easily move on to another source with no consequences. Digital and mass discipleship are inherently one-way models. A preacher or leader may be speaking truth into your life but only insofar as they are speaking truth to everyone.

Church history

One of the most neglected voices within modern American Christianity is church history, which can play a vital role in shaping a Christian worldview and is an invaluable repository of spiritual wisdom. When we make a mental list of our godly influences, we tend to include the thinkers or preachers who draw crowds and followings today. After all, if we want to learn how to engage in this age of outrage, we need to listen to people who are living through it and are familiar with its challenges and opportunities. Yet in listening to the voices of our collective past, believers retrieve the truths of our faith that have endured for centuries. This is perfectly captured by the nineteenth-century church historian Philip Schaff:

> Church history shows that God is ever stronger than
> Satan, and that his kingdom of light puts the kingdom

of darkness to shame. The Lion of the tribe of Judah has bruised the head of the serpent. With the crucifixion of Christ his resurrection also is repeated ever anew in the history of his church on earth; and there has never yet been a day without a witness of his presence and power ordering all things according to his holy will. For he has received all power in heaven and in earth for the good of his people, and from his heavenly throne he rules even his foes.[22]

Schaff reminds us here that God has supernaturally guided his church for two thousand years. He has overcome every obstacle as if it were nothing, raised up courageous believers to accomplish tasks others thought impossible, and protected his church and Word from every means of attack. Nothing in history has surprised him or come close to overwhelming his power to uphold us. Even as the alarm bells of today are ringing loud that the end is near, that Christianity is near collapse and the church is dying, church history reminds us that these same false alarms have rung many times. Church history reminds us that God is sovereign and in control during this age of outrage, just as he was in the Middle Ages, the Reformation, and the Enlightenment. It confirms that there is actually no reason to be outraged. Merely faithful.

Reading church history and allowing it to influence our worldview reassures us not only that God has promised to be with us, but that he has delivered on this promise *to every generation of believers regardless of the trials and tribulations of their time.* Armed with this truth, we can better live out our worldview in the confidence that Christ is with us as he was with Martin Luther, Charles Spurgeon, C. S. Lewis, and Corrie ten Boom. In a later passage, Schaff reminds us that not only is church history a "storehouse of wisdom and piety" but more important, it is "the surest test of [Christ's] own promise to his people: 'Lo, I am with you alway [sic], even unto the end of the world.'"[23]

But before you run out and buy your copy of Calvin's *Institutes* in the original Latin, I want to suggest some good entry points into church history so that you won't become overwhelmed. Here are three means by which you can incorporate the wisdom of the historical church into your worldview:

1. **Biographies.** When reading a biography, we enter a different era of church ministry with its own difficulties and opportunities. Good church history biographies present real historical figures with all their victories and failures; using the former to inspire and the latter to remind us that God uses imperfect vessels to accomplish his will. More important, reading about their sinful blind spots (as with Jonathan Edwards and slavery) can be a powerful reminder of our own community's potential to have cultural blinders to sin. One of the most impactful twentieth-century biographies is Roland Bainton's study of Martin Luther's life, *Here I Stand*.

2. **Devotionals.** One of the greatest resources of the church is its devotionals. The greatest thinkers, pastors, and leaders throughout history recognized the importance of spending time praying and meditating on God's Word. Church history is filled with devotional material that pulls us out of the ruts of our own time and context and into the timeless truths that connect us to earlier Christians. One devotional that has become popular again over the past few decades is Arthur Bennett's *The Valley of Vision*, a catalog of prayers by Puritans. Saturated in Scripture and deeply poetic, this book and others like it are a major encouragement to Christians who struggle in knowing how to pray by leading us through some of the church's greatest prayers.

3. **Theological histories.** Popular books by Christian historians and theologians often enable us to examine a small

slice of church history and then connect it to our spiritual walk. They can also provide helpful guidance before we dive into historical works. An excellent example is Kyle Strobel's *Formed for the Glory of God*, which introduces us to Jonathan Edwards by considering his spiritual disciplines and habits. Strobel then shows how Edwards's thinking has significant meaning for the church today. In Strobel's hands, Edwards's work is not an old, dusty Puritan tome but an accessible and warm encouragement to believers.

Where Do We Go from Here?

Effectively engaging the age of outrage requires that we recognize that each of us has a worldview that is shaped and influenced by what we consume. For that reason, we must consider how what we consume disciples us for godliness or for sin.

As the illustration of the blue-and-black dress proved, we all see things differently. As tempting as it is to insist that our way is the only way, we must intentionally begin to see the world as Jesus would have us do.

The apostle Peter wrote to "God's chosen people who are living as foreigners" (1 Peter 1:1, NLT) in their time, much as we are in ours. His words still ring true:

Prepare your minds for action and exercise self-control. Put all your hope in the gracious salvation that will come to you when Jesus Christ is revealed to the world. So you must live as God's obedient children. Don't slip back into your old ways of living to satisfy your own desires. You didn't know any better then. But now you must be holy in everything you do, just as God who chose you is holy. For the Scriptures say, "You must be holy because I am holy."
1 PETER 1:13-16, NLT

Those words are quite simple, but profound for us today. They are a reminder to

1. prepare our minds,
2. exercise self-control,
3. avoid slipping into self-satisfaction, and
4. be holy.

We can, and must, *prepare our minds* for the moment we are in. That means being intentional about what we consume, as well as being more discerning about what we believe. We have to be prepared for a world—and often even for people with whom we agree—driving us toward a God-dishonoring outrage.

We've got to *exercise self-control* in how we respond. Yes, it does feel as if our beliefs are under attack at times. Yet adopting a siege mentality is not the answer; exercising self-control and doing what Jesus said are.

Let's be honest. It feels good to vent. And most of us live in places where we are encouraged to speak our mind. It's our right as citizens. But we must *avoid slipping into self-satisfaction*—speaking our minds only to feel better, to "get it off our chest" rather than to glorify God in our lives.

The message is clear: We are to *be holy*. Being holy literally means to be set apart. Although many people are going along with the crowd now, stocking up on offense and outrage, there is a better way. It's the way of Jesus. It's the holy way.

Let's consider that black-and-blue dress one more time. Scientists finally confirmed that it truly was black and blue, not gold and white as many thought. In the midst of all the debating and millions of posts, there really was one right way to see it. It was black and blue, even though scores of people insisted it was white and gold.

Now as followers of Jesus, we have to decide how to live in light of the truth. We believe he is the true King of the whole world.

He offers the right way to live in our world. Whether or not most Christians follow that path, we must.

It's time to live as people shaped by a gospel-centered worldview.

CHAPTER 8

Kingdom Ambassadors
in a Foreign Land

- Politics were identified as *extremely important* to a greater percentage of evangelicals than to non-evangelicals (30 percent to 18 percent).

- A significant majority of evangelicals (67 percent) agreed that a Christian can benefit from a political leader even if that leader's personal life does not line up with Christian teaching.

IN THE EARLY 2000S, I had the opportunity to serve for a few years as the interim pastor of a large, traditional, Southern church. I had planted several churches in the late eighties and nineties, but nothing had prepared me to lead a church of nine thousand members. Exchanging the relaxed and intimate environment of a church plant for choir robes and members calling me "Brother Ed" was a bit of a transition, to say the least. Despite the culture shock, the church was persistent in its love of my family. My kids still remember that Tennessee church as a crucial part of their spiritual journey.

After I left that role, another church in the area asked me to help them during a period of transition. A group of members had begun questioning many aspects of the church's leadership. The conflict became public and ugly, and everything came to a head during a contentious meeting on Mother's Day 2009.

Eventually the pastor left, and the successful megachurch dwindled to six hundred people, split evenly between a traditional service and a contemporary service. This may not sound so bad, but the sanctuary held three thousand. Simple math says that only 10 percent of the seats were filled in any given service. The first Sunday morning I preached, the people were spread out like

BB pellets rolling around in a minivan. The church's finances were in shambles as well.

As the remaining church members were trying to salvage their situation, they invited me to be their interim pastor. Fun times. My instinct was to say no. Nothing burns as hot as church conflict, and I was reluctant to jump into that inferno. The infighting of this church had made the front page of the local paper five times and the national news once. Instead of using their significant platform to preach the healing power of the gospel, they were airing Christian outrage.

My wife, Donna, is *way* more godly and discerning than I am, and she thought I should reconsider the invitation. After much prayer, we decided to pitch in. The first goal was to stop the bleeding that threatened to take this church to the grave. Because of the financial crisis, I didn't take a salary, honorarium, or reimbursements. I didn't want it to be a distraction, and I wanted the freedom to make decisions as someone not receiving any financial benefit from the church. One of the first things I did was let a couple of dozen people go. We started along a hard road, and other than the sudden staff shifts we had to make, Sundays were the most difficult. Remember, there were just three hundred people per service in a three-thousand-seat sanctuary.

Over the next year, the church began healing and saw growth to almost one thousand people coming on any given Sunday. We prayed together about renewing our presence in the community but had an extremely difficult road ahead of us, given the public nature of the implosion.

Our regional paper, the *Tennessean*, ran a front-page story about our efforts:

> The key to the turnaround is getting back to the basics of Christianity, says interim pastor Ed Stetzer. That means focusing on sharing their faith and treating one another with respect and love.

It also means sending church members out to do community service projects.

Since last fall, he's been preaching the same message.

"We want to be known for what Jesus was known for," said Stetzer. "We are building a new reputation for sharing and showing the good news of Jesus Christ."

A reporter for a local TV news station came, and one of our staff members repeated that objective: "We are building a new reputation for sharing and showing the good news of Jesus Christ."

But God did something in the midst of this—he accelerated our endeavors.

On May 1, 2010, we were having a "servolution" day at the church, taking on about a dozen different service projects in the community. My family and I, for instance, were cleaning the baseboards at a local high school. All day long, it rained. But we worked on because we were there to show and share the love of Jesus in our community.

Well, it kept raining. And raining. It rained like it never had in recorded history there.

A flood, the likes of which had not been nor will be seen in a thousand years, hit the city of Nashville. More than 13.5 inches of rain fell within forty-eight hours. The Cumberland River crested over fifty feet, flooding highways and interstates and killing twenty-one people in Tennessee. Our church was located on a hill right across the highway from the Gaylord Opryland Resort and Opry Mills shopping mall, both of which were completely inundated. The following day when I drove there, I couldn't take my usual route because the streets had flooded. But the church was safe.

And the question we asked was this: What are we going to do? Immediately, the church agreed to become the evacuation site for the hotel. It also became a command center for the city of Nashville. The church even hosted two performances of the Grand Ole Opry because the theater was several feet deep in flood waters. (Charlie Daniels performed, and so did Ricky Skaggs, but my friends were amused by a quote in one article: "Stetzer said Opry officials assured him the content of programs will be appropriate for a church setting."[1])

This church, which had earned a bad reputation, opened its doors to the community. We began to say that we were stepping into this time to show and share the love of Jesus. And that phrase, "show and share the love of Jesus," gained a foothold in our congregation. I took time off work, mucked out houses that had been swamped with mud and mire, and became a de facto chaplain to the community around us. Our church gathered water bottles and school supplies in backpacks and went door-to-door with these gifts. It was hard work, but good work.

The first Sunday after the flood had ended, the church was a literal mess. It was in complete disarray as organizations including the city government were still operating out of our buildings. Before church in the early morning, we were in the community serving, so our people showed up wearing overalls, shorts, and muddy shoes. And as I started to walk on stage, I remembered what day it was: Mother's Day—the one-year anniversary of the worst moment in the church's history.

But now, despite our muddy boots and fatigue, we were becoming something different: a church showing and sharing the love of Jesus. This was a Mother's Day to remember. This one would be burned into our collective memory.

When I had first arrived, the church was known for fighting, contention, and difficult relationships. It had been on a mission of self-preservation, longing for its bygone glory days. It was a place where outrage was cultivated, embraced, and wielded like a weapon in ways that made nonbelievers blush. What we represented was not aligned to our mission and values.

After the flood, we became known for showing and sharing the love of Jesus in the midst of a broken and hurting world. We were known as a community on a mission for the gospel and as ambassadors for Jesus. By leaning into hospitality and graciousness, we were renewing our church's presence in our community.

Every church and believer must ask: What are we known for in the community? What do we represent?

Becoming Ambassadors to the Age of Outrage

In the previous chapter we established the importance of knowing what we believe and cultivating a worldview from which to properly understand the age of outrage from a gospel perspective. This chapter shifts the focus from what we believe to who we are: What does it mean to be ambassadors to the age of outrage?

No longer representative of the dominant culture, Christians need to rethink the way we understand cultural engagement, mission, and evangelism in a newly post-Christian society. While Scripture gives us many ways of understanding mission, I think the most helpful for our purposes is in Paul's second letter to the Corinthians. In describing himself and those with him, Paul uses a term that describes us as well:

> All this is from God, who through Christ reconciled us to himself and gave us the ministry of reconciliation; that is, in Christ God was reconciling the world to himself, not counting their trespasses against them, and entrusting to us the message of reconciliation. *Therefore, we are ambassadors for Christ, God making his appeal through us.* We implore you on behalf of Christ, be reconciled to God. For our sake he made him to be sin who knew no sin, so that in him we might become the righteousness of God.
>
> 2 CORINTHIANS 5:18-21 (emphasis mine)

Paul begins by proclaiming the gospel—the good news that Christ came to reconcile us to God. He was describing the Christian worldview. In fact, it is crucial to recognize that everything we do—every act of cultural engagement, every opportunity for evangelism—starts from the reality that Christ has reconciled us. He started the work, he does the work, and he finished the work of reconciliation when we were "dead in [our] trespasses and sins" (Ephesians 2:1). His grace to us shapes how we extend grace to others.

But we don't stop with the reality of our present state before God. Paul notes that Christ has *given* this ministry of reconciliation to us. He allows us to not simply receive this grace, but also to participate with him in extending it to those who are still unreconciled: those who are lost, without purpose, and lonely. This is, according to Paul, why we are *ambassadors* for Christ.

Today we think of ambassadors as the people who represent their countries abroad and whose job is to help avert crises or generate goodwill. In Paul's time, Rome did not send out ambassadors; they sent out armies. As British theologian Martyn Percy explains, other countries sent ambassadors to avoid the armies and to entreat Rome toward peace and reconciliation:

> In the first century, an ambassador was an ad hoc representative, usually of a community, though occasionally of an association or individual, commissioned to carry out a particular task and who returned to the community, association or individual on completion of the task. Almost invariably, at the heart of an ambassador's task was an appeal to the person or community who received him.[2]

In his study of ambassadorship language in the New Testament, Anthony Bash highlighted four crucial functions of an ambassador in the Roman Empire in which early Christians lived.[3] Ambassadors, he noted, had a specific task to accomplish; traveled to a specific place to accomplish this task; were dedicated to the interests of the one who sent them; and did not return until the task was completed.

Ambassadors were more than just messengers or heralds. They were representatives with a mission, endowed with the responsibility to engage a different government or culture on behalf of their sovereign. This means they didn't stay home. To accomplish their king's task, they left and lived in foreign countries–studying the culture, learning the language, eating the food, and seeking to build bridges to communicate their king's message with clarity and zeal. With these functions in mind, it is little wonder Paul used this language to refer to our Kingdom mission. God has given us a task and called us to a mission field. We are to persist until he returns or we are called home.

Similarly, Christians study the culture while seeking to understand how the mechanisms of the foreign land are opposed to the Kingdom of Jesus. While doing this, we are given a heart of compassion by God's Spirit for a people who are also far away from home and living unreconciled to him. This is what motivates us to work for the good of others in both spiritual and practical ways.

Much of this chapter will focus on the metaphor of what it means to be Christ's ambassadors to a foreign land, living as heaven's representatives in a world working against the very assignment we have been given. Let's further explore what these terms mean and why we use them.

So what does it mean to be ambassadors for Christ to the age of outrage? In this chapter, I want to explore three distinct ways of understanding our "sentness" as ambassadors for Christ:

1. We are sent with an allegiance to the King.
2. We are sent with a message of reconciliation.
3. We are sent to a foreign land with a mission to complete.

What Does It Mean to Be Ambassadors?

Ambassadors sent by a King

At a fundamental level, our identity as ambassadors begins with the one who commissions us and sends us out. In this way, being ambassadors of Christ speaks to the nature of God. He is not distant, removed, or isolated from his creation. While sin has put an obstacle between us, Scripture reveals God to be on a mission of reconciliation. This is a profound truth that missiologists describe in the unfolding story of the *missio Dei* (the mission of God).

And just as this says something about God, it speaks to our relationship with him. Simply put, we are a sent people. The message of the *missio Dei* is that God is on mission to glorify himself by means of advancing his Kingdom on earth through his people, empowered by the Holy Spirit, who proclaim and demonstrate the gospel of God's Kingdom in Jesus Christ. David Bosch, a South African missiologist who died tragically in 1992, reminded us that "to participate in mission is to participate in the movement of God's love toward people, since God is a fountain of sending love."[4]

Again, we are a *sent* people. And that identity carries with it the idea that someone is sending us; a King to whom we owe allegiance.

This identity was central to the New Testament authors even in the way they spoke about themselves to others. One of the most common titles Paul adopts to refer to his ministry is that of servant. We can and should learn much from this. Despite being one of the crucial leaders of the church, an apostle who saw Jesus on the road to Damascus, and the founder of many churches throughout the Roman Empire, Paul framed his identity as a servant of Jesus Christ (Romans 1:1; 1 Corinthians 3:5; 2 Corinthians 4:5; Galatians 1:10; Philippians 1:1). Far from using it as a self-deprecating term, Paul attaches significant honor to this title, calling other believers to follow him (2 Timothy 2:24) and celebrating those who demonstrated themselves to be good servants of Christ (Romans 16:1; Colossians 1:7; 4:7; 1 Timothy 4:6). James began his epistle in the same way, identifying himself simply as "a servant of God and of the Lord Jesus Christ" (James 1:1).

What Paul and James understood so clearly was that they were not their own and that all they did was a result of God's reconciliation and his calling on their lives. As ambassadors of Jesus Christ, they were consumed with the task given to them by God. Any authority and influence they had were not their own, or even connected to their brilliance or dynamic leadership strategies.

Rather, they were servants of the King. Their allegiance was to his priorities, and they discerned the many ways they could walk in obedience to show and share the gospel in a world of great need.

Our Kingdom mission as ambassadors is bound up in our devotion to the program of the King who began and oversees our work. Mission is the privileged participation of the servants in the Master's grand plan.

We rightly "call out" soldiers, traitors, or mercenaries when they switch sides or abandon a post when it looks like defeat is inevitable. The name Benedict Arnold is infamous in American history precisely because he swore allegiance to the Continental Army yet ultimately lacked an embodied fealty. At a time when other American colonials professed, "Give me liberty, or give me death" (and some were hanged), Arnold talked the talk but could not walk the walk. The age of outrage has countless temptations calling for our allegiance and testing our willingness to place loyalty to them above the gospel. Even as we support and work for many different people and varied causes, our ultimate allegiance is solely to Jesus and his Kingdom. Thus, when and where people and causes step out of line with our King's will, we are called to speak out as his representatives.

Our interests, goals, and ambitions must be centered on the all-embracing task the gospel sets before us. Paul describes this in Romans 15:20: "My ambition has always been to preach the Good News where the name of Christ has never been heard, rather than where a church has already been started by someone else" (NLT).

Ambassadors sent with a message of reconciliation

The mission of the church is defined for us. Scripture leaves no room for interpretation, no basis for debate, no ambiguity as to its purpose. Just look back to the 2 Corinthians 5:18-21 passage I cited earlier. Paul directly tells us: "God . . . through Christ reconciled us to himself and gave us the ministry of reconciliation . . . entrusting to us the message of reconciliation." Paul leaves no room for doubt regarding the content of our message. Even as theologians disagree on the nature and method of Kingdom mission, there is no refuting this one truth: We have been given a mission of reconciliation.

What do we mean when we say *reconciliation?* In Ephesians 2, Paul outlines four central truths about reconciliation:

1. There is hostility and division between God and man.

   As for you, you were dead in your transgressions and sins, in which you used to live when you followed the ways of this world and of the ruler of the kingdom of the air, the spirit who is now at work in those who are disobedient. All of us also lived among them at one time, gratifying the cravings of our flesh and following its desires and thoughts. Like the rest, we were by nature deserving of wrath.
   EPHESIANS 2:1-3, NIV

2. God is the initiator of reconciliation.

   Because of his great love for us, God, who is rich in mercy, made us alive with Christ even when we were dead in transgressions.
   EPHESIANS 2:4-5, NIV

3. The work of Jesus Christ is the sole solution to this hostility and division.

   It is by grace you have been saved. And God raised us up with Christ and seated us with him in the heavenly realms in Christ Jesus, in order that in the coming ages he might show the incomparable riches of his grace, expressed in his kindness to us in Christ Jesus. For it is by grace you have been saved, through faith—and this is

not from yourselves, it is the gift of God—not by works,
so that no one can boast.
EPHESIANS 2:5-9, NIV

4. Our reconciliation is not the end but the beginning of our
   transformation, setting us on mission as active participants
   in the reconciliation of others.

We are God's handiwork, created in Christ Jesus to do
good works, which God prepared in advance for us to do.
EPHESIANS 2:10, NIV

These truths reveal a full, grand picture of the message of reconciliation we are sent to bring into the world. It begins with God
reconciling us through Christ's death into saving life, bringing us
back into a right relationship with himself by his own work, power,
and energy, even while we were enemies of God. This inspires us
to rejoice, having a joy that is not in the comforts of our foreign
land, but rooted in the salvation of our King. Notice that this message is both transformative and personal. It is not simply that God
reconciles but that he has reconciled *us*. It is not that we are simply
redeemed but that we have been sent so that he might redeem
others through us (Romans 5:10-11; Colossians 1:19-22).

Jesus' death on the cross for our sin and in our place accom-
plishes the peace that now marks our relationship with our heavenly
Father. Through God's divine purpose and intent, Jesus has broken
down the wall of hostility that existed between man and God. He
becomes our peace, both for our own relationship with God and also
for our interaction with the world around us.

God is building his church in communities and through leaders
who grasp the singular power of this message of reconciliation. One
powerful example is Brian Warth, pastor of Chapel of Change in
Southern California. In his autobiography, *Young Man Arise!*, Brian
recounts his life growing up in the gang culture of Los Angeles in
the late eighties and early nineties. His older brother was killed at

fifteen, and two other brothers survived multiple shootings. Brian joined a gang at twelve and was arrested and convicted of murder at sixteen. Tried as an adult, Brian began serving a life sentence. While in prison, Brian heard the gospel and surrendered his life to Christ. In the years that followed, Brian was discipled by prison chaplains. Eventually, God's message of reconciliation and redemption transformed Brian from an enemy of the cross into an ambassador of Christ, giving him a vision to enter the ministry and begin serving and teaching Bible studies to other inmates. Sixteen years after he'd begun serving his sentence, Brian was released.

Brian explains how his own narrative of redemption and reconciliation to God has shaped his ministry and preaching:

> God is using my story of extreme redemption and
> restoration as a modern-day example of what his power
> can do. My teaching and preaching deal a lot with the
> themes of fresh hope and freedom from guilt and shame.
> And this aspect of the gospel is resonating in the hearts
> of many broken people in our broken generation.[5]

Once out of prison, Brian continued his vision of bringing Christ's message of reconciliation to the lost, planting the Chapel of Change in south Los Angeles, one of the most diverse areas in the country. Into this community, which Brian describes as one of "extreme and deep brokenness,"[6] the message of redemption, freedom, and hope is resonating with people from all generations.

Although Brian's story is dramatic, we were all broken and separated from God because of our sin. Only those who have experienced the breakdown of hostility and relational disconnect with God and have then been restored through the work of Christ will be effective agents of reconciliation. We are now a part of God's family and a part of his delegation sent back into the world. Because of Christ, we are presented holy and blameless before an infinitely holy God.

Our renewed relationship with our Creator becomes the

catalyst for how we live as ambassadors in a world that displays varying degrees of hostility and outrage to the gospel. We can have peace, knowing God is sovereign over his salvation of the world, while also earnestly working with all the energy he has placed within us to deliver his message of reconciliation.

Ambassadors sent to a foreign land

Finally, being ambassadors for the Kingdom of God means that we are sent *into* a foreign land. This is not unique to our age of outrage. This imperative has been placed upon every generation that has sought to pick up its cross and follow Jesus. Just as Paul and the Corinthians were Kingdom ambassadors, so were Augustine and Billy Graham—and so are you.

Though the mission does not change, the culture into which each generation is sent as ambassadors does. Every society and culture has tried and failed to solve this problem of the unsatisfied and restless heart outside of Jesus. We need to study our culture like ambassadors so we can effectively show and share the gospel.

Behind every expression of outrage in our age is real need, brokenness, and destruction that our message of reconciliation through Jesus is meant to address. The age of outrage may be defined by its anger and polarization, but beneath these self-defense mechanisms are real and valid underlying questions as people try to understand their origin, identity, purpose, and path in life.

People have never been more engaged, busy, and connected than in this cultural moment. Yet this flurry of activity is a thinly veiled attempt to cover a crisis of identity, purpose, and belonging. The foreign land to which we have been called is in a crisis of lost identity, misplaced purpose, and chronic loneliness.

CRISIS #1: LOST IDENTITY

In chapter 5, we considered how identity has become one of the primary idols today. In a post-Christian world, the search for meaning and belonging takes on a new sense of importance and urgency.

While the problem seems particularly acute now, in the seventeenth century Blaise Pascal already recognized the despair and crisis of meaning that occur when people base their identity on anything except Christ himself:

> What else does this craving, and this helplessness,
> proclaim but that there was once in man a true happiness,
> of which all that now remains is the empty print and
> trace? This he tries in vain to fill with everything around
> him, seeking in things that are not there the help he
> cannot find in those that are, though none can help, since
> this infinite abyss can be filled only with an infinite and
> immutable object; in other words, by God himself.[7]

Our culture has been fixated on the dual identity questions of "Who am I?" and "Where do I belong?" Identity politics and polarization are inevitable outcomes when people arrive at different answers. The community and mission of Christ are the alternatives this world needs. We find healing and restoration in our search for identity when we look to the person and work of Jesus. He gives us an identity that transcends the temporal and ultimately pointless political and cultural identities.

As we seek to share our message of reconciliation, we cannot limit our evangelism to online tools and apps. We need more than mere association. As people who have found their identity in Jesus, we need to fully engage with and participate in the lives of those still seeking their identity. This is how we bring God's Kingdom to a broken world.

CRISIS #2: MISPLACED PURPOSE

In 2015, *Time* magazine ran the provocative headline "You Now Have a Shorter Attention Span than a Goldfish." The accompanying article summarized a study from Microsoft that revealed "the effects of an increasingly digitalized lifestyle on the brain" had resulted in a decline in one's attention span to merely eight seconds of concentrated focus. This came in just a shade lower than the goldfish's nine seconds.[8] Goldfish everywhere were unavailable for comment, but I'm sure they were excited.

At first glance this is a humorous statistic, drawing a line between the wide-eyed fish that dart in every direction and people's tendency today to constantly jump from article to blog to video. But reflecting on the *Time* article for a minute (thus proving I'm not a goldfish), the truth is that this is deeply troubling when we consider that the people around us are increasingly feeling lonely, disconnected, and distracted despite being more digitally connected than ever before. We have knowledge and data, but no communal context to process and engage with this knowledge in a way that delivers meaning and satisfaction. There is a major crisis of purpose in the world. And it doesn't stop there.

In the study from *Time*, 77 percent of those aged 18 to 24 said that when there is nothing to occupy their attention, the first thing they do is reach for their phone.[9] Many people of all ages are unable to resist looking at the latest notification, unable to resist the pull of checking social media posts, unable to look away (even for a moment) from the latest political feeds. Our world has an insatiable desire for information, recognition, and personal attention. We celebrate superficiality over reality and keeping up appearances over being real and transparent.

Boredom and a search for fulfillment are the results. Human beings are hardwired by God to work (see Adam and Eve in the Garden). When we have no clear purpose, we often drift toward whatever will make us happy in the moment, and we adopt words like *boredom* to explain our ennui.[10] After all, when we lack any meaningful engagement toward goals of high value, we risk distraction and disconnection as we fill our time with insignificant, unsatisfying actions. In the end, this can lead to a sense of meaninglessness and a compulsive anxiety in the search to find some purpose.

The nineteenth-century German philosopher Arthur Schopenhauer once observed, "For the nonappearance of satisfaction is suffering; the empty longing for a new desire is languor, boredom."[11] The boredom experienced by so many in our culture leads to outrage and harm toward others. Outrage, then, becomes a misplaced substitute purpose.

Christians who are living as ambassadors must see how the internal pain of boredom is connected to outrage and anger that is redirected externally. When the world around us doesn't know how to move forward from or process those emotions of purposelessness, boredom and outrage become normal reactions.

But the gospel enables our identity and purpose to transcend our own whims and desires. Jesus rescues us, giving us a new reason for living: reconciliation. We have a new calling: to go back into a world that is now foreign to us. We have a new assignment and a new job: to be ambassadors for the new King over our lives. This results in lives filled with purpose and meaning, transcending the crisis of boredom, superficiality, and misplaced purpose.

CRISIS #3: CHRONIC LONELINESS

In January 2018, the British government announced they were creating a new cabinet position with the sole aim of combating one of the gravest social threats facing the country. Not terrorism or drug addiction, the new position was dedicated to aiding the more than nine million British adults who suffered from "chronic loneliness."[12]

To be sure, there are important elements to this campaign that get lost in the novelty of it—for example, the government is particularly concerned with the elderly who have voiced a sense of loneliness and isolation that society has ignored for generations. However, we must step back and reflect on the fact that in an age when online communication and rapid transportation are praised for shrinking our world and strengthening relational networks, we are facing an epidemic of loneliness. Everyone is available all the time and in multiple formats, yet feelings of isolation have steadily increased to the point that people of all ages are beset by chronic loneliness.

As God's ambassadors, we must engage with a reality that scholars and theologians have been warning of for years: Although interpersonal connectedness has skyrocketed thanks to social media, there has been a corresponding increase in chronic loneliness.

John Cacioppo defined chronic loneliness more specifically in his research on human nature and the need for social connection:

> We can all slip in and out of loneliness. Feeling lonely at any particular moment simply means that you are human. . . . The need for meaningful social connection, and the pain we feel without it, are defining characteristics of our species. Loneliness becomes an issue of serious concern only when it settles in long enough to create a persistent, self-reinforcing loop of negative thoughts, sensations, and behaviors.[13]

Sound familiar? The symptoms of the age of outrage and chronic loneliness go hand in hand, and much of the anger we see is actually a response to a profound loneliness and the pain that goes with it. As ambassadors, this should drive us to feel compassion for our neighbors and friends who live apart from the freedom of the gospel and so fall into broken patterns of living.

In an attempt to build communities that can overcome chronic loneliness on their own, society has come up with mechanisms apart from the gospel. David Brooks focuses on these attempts at solutions, noting that "secular individuals have to build their own communities. Religions come equipped with covenantal rituals that bind people together, sacred practices that are beyond individual choice. Secular people have to choose their own communities and come up with their own practices to make them meaningful."[14]

In an odd turn few would have anticipated, the society that gave rise to McDonald's and Krispy Kreme has begun to find community in fitness and health groups (among many other avenues as well). Organizations formed around shared interests such as CrossFit, essential oils, and health affinities pride themselves on their ability to create a broad community through a specific shared activity. None of these groups focus solely on their original agenda, but rather seek to build a lifestyle, brand, or following that closely mimics a church. It happens in many environments, but to illustrate, let's show how CrossFit can mimic Christian community to battle chronic loneliness.

CrossFit has its own places of worship–gyms with specialized equipment. People come to these "temples" to the human body and experience shared pain, shared success, and shared experiences that draw them closer together. They also have an authority structure, but in place of pastors and seminaries, they have "coaches" and trainers with specific certifications. They have guiding documents, but in place of the inspired Word of God, they have programs, memorized workouts, literature, and books describing why this "way" is the best. People "evangelize," sharing stories of how their lives once lacked meaning but are now fulfilled because of these specific programs and communities.

Let me be clear, there is nothing inherently wrong with these communities–and I need some time at the gym! The problem arises when they become a distraction from the main thing. All of these communities are merely a substitute and a shadow of the true church. On their own, they are a cheap reduction that leaves people empty, dry, and lonely. What happens when a person simply can't make the cut? What happens when someone fails? Literally breaks a leg? If hope lies in a community based on anything other than Jesus, it will eventually fail and result in crisis.

The mission of a Christian is one of incarnation, and the church, unlike any other entity, has the power to relate to a world in need of authentic relationship, restoration, and renewal. We have the power as ambassadors to communicate the joy, peace, and reconciliation the world is looking for. It's been freely given to us, and we can freely offer it to others.

This is the Good News we carry as ambassadors to a foreign world: Jesus has reconciled us with a Father who loves us, adopts us into a new family, and forever gives us a home and a community. This is healing balm to the chronic loneliness of those so desperately longing to belong. We now are responsible as ambassadors to show and share this gospel with a lonely world that simply wants to come home.

The Outrage of Distracted Ambassadors

So much of the outrage against Christians can be traced to us taking our eyes off our identity as ambassadors of the King. When we use our authority or influence to advance some other mission, we are in danger of not completing our assignment well. Whether with good intentions or thinly veiled pride, if we advance any mission other than the one Christ gives, we forfeit the healing power of the gospel and risk fostering further disunity, division, disagreement, and ultimately outrage.

When we do this, we fall victim to what we call mission creep, a military term. In their report *Operations Other than War*, Jennifer Taw and John Peters wrote, "In mission creep, new or shifting political guidance requires military operations different from what the intervening force initially planned."[15] In other words, mission creep occurs over time when people add objectives or purposes to the original mission. It's unfortunate when leaders and churches deviate from God's mission and are carried away with their own ambitions. Mission creep is a sad reality for many churches.

In *Well Sent: Reimagining the Church's Missionary-Sending Process*, Steve Beirn and George W. Murray provide an excellent window into how mission creep can infect our Christian witness: "Mission creep occurs when objectives are expanded well beyond original goals. It dilutes the original purpose and broadens efforts, which results in a loss of priorities."[16]

When I was appointed executive director of the Billy Graham Center, I was thrilled at the opportunity to work for a historic institution with a long history of Kingdom work that existed to be "a world hub of inspiration and training for mission and evangelism."[17] One of my responsibilities as director was to ensure that every part of our ministry was focused on equipping Christians for evangelism and mission.

I spent my first year looking at every program. Each time I asked a simple question: How does this advance the mission of the BGC? At the same time, I made sure that every staff member and volunteer knew exactly what our mission was and how their work contributed to our success. Just as in any good organization, Christians can fall victim to mission creep and lose sight of their original mission.

Unfortunately, one of the most pressing issues for Christians today is confronting mission creep in the church. If we look at how the image of Christians has taken a beating, it is largely because of the way Christians have added some political, cultural, or social goal to the gospel.

In the second letter to the Corinthians, the apostle Paul wrote to a people whose reputation and commitment to living as ambassadors was being challenged:

> We don't go around preaching about ourselves. We preach that Jesus Christ is Lord, and we ourselves are your servants for Jesus' sake. For God, who said, "Let there be light in the darkness," has made this light shine in our hearts so we could know the glory of God that is seen in the face of Jesus Christ.
>
> We now have this light shining in our hearts, but we ourselves are like fragile clay jars containing this great treasure. This makes it clear that our great power is from God, not from ourselves.
>
> 2 CORINTHIANS 4:5-7, NLT

This is a powerful testimony to the frailty and insufficiency of individuals, and equally to the transformative power of the gospel.

Like the Corinthians, many Christians today have engaged in, rather than offered the antidote to, our age of outrage. The world is filled with people pursuing their own missions, forging communities around a shared mission for an alternative kingdom, and ultimately coming into conflict with one another over their competing missions and agendas.

This always ends with a damaged witness because it unnecessarily places obstacles between Christians and their neighbors. As our country continues its march toward social, economic, and political polarization, mission creep opens the doorway for these divisions to slip into the church and into our gospel proclamation.

In light of these issues, Christian faithfulness begins with an honest self-assessment of how well we are living out our mission among our neighbors. When those in our community or workplace know us as anything other than followers of Christ, in some way we have allowed a peripheral mission to creep into our identity. When we are living as ambassadors for Christ, those around us should not be surprised by our values and beliefs. Who we are and what we do should reflect our highest priority for God's mission in a foreign world. An ambassador knows how to stay focused on the goal of reconciliation and faithfulness in a world that values everything but that mission.

Compassionately Love the People

Being an ambassador is more than simply knowing our mission and our mission field. It goes beyond a commitment to proclaiming the message of Christ's Kingdom. Fundamental to our role as God's ambassadors is an abiding love for those to whom we have been sent and a commitment to see them as Jesus does. Just as we must remember our sentness, central to our success as ambassadors is responding with compassion to the lostness of others. We see this modeled most powerfully in Matthew 9:35-38, where the disciple tells us that Jesus, having gone through "all the cities and villages" (verse 35) teaching and healing, paused and reflected upon the pressing crowds. Seeing their need, Scripture records that Jesus "had compassion for them, because they were harassed and helpless, like sheep without a shepherd" (verse 36).

The Greek word we translate here as *compassion* carries a far deeper meaning than in English. Technically meaning to be moved in one's bowels, the idea is a gut feeling that stirs our hearts. When Matthew wrote his Gospel, it was commonly believed that the gut was the seat of emotions, the place where deep and powerful feelings took root. While science has long held that emotions are connected to brain activity, the ancient world was actually on to something: Researchers now know that the brain and digestive system are quite closely connected, and emotions affect both. We all know, for instance, that we seem to feel strong emotions in the pit of our stomach. Thus, when Matthew says Jesus had compassion when he saw the people harassed and helpless, he describes Jesus having this deep "gut reaction."

When I read this, I think about my experiences as a father, watching over my three daughters. Nothing hits me more than times when they are hurt or struggling. Every fiber of my being wants to do whatever I can to fix the situation, to take the burden on myself, and to put them back on solid ground. In moments like these, we see the intimate connection between love and compassion. Christ's love for the people translated into a deep compassion and therefore an engagement that sought to heal their pain, fix their brokenness, and redeem their hearts by reconciling them to the Father. And following Jesus' example, we are not dispassionate ambassadors but are called to love the foreign land to which we have been called.

The purpose of the story in Matthew is not simply to reveal Christ's compassion for the lost and oppressed, but also to call us to a similar love. Having been reconciled ourselves, we are given the same Spirit Jesus had, allowing us to have a deep love for those who remain slaves to their sin. Just as we have found peace and satisfaction in loving God, we must have compassion for those whose hearts are still restless and unfulfilled.

We are not disinterested ambassadors. We are ambassadors

who actively engage in the land in which we find ourselves, particularly through prayer and action.

Compassion through prayer

As ambassadors in a foreign land, one of the ways we grow in our compassion for others is through prayer.

This compassion is rooted in seeing people as Jesus did, as sheep without a shepherd. Notice the progression of what Christ told the disciples: "The harvest is plentiful, but the laborers are few; therefore pray earnestly to the Lord of the harvest to send out laborers into his harvest" (Matthew 9:37-38). From this we observe that

1. The foreign land is broken, desolate, and in great danger.
2. There are not enough ambassadors to meet the need.
3. We need to pray for God to send more ambassadors of Jesus Christ.

When we pray, we see how others are truly in desperate need of the Good Shepherd for their souls. Prayer pushes us toward compassion, and compassion so identifies with the needs of others that we must act.

While many Christians acknowledge this truth, statistically they do not live it out. When I worked for LifeWay Research, we asked Christians if they agreed or disagreed with the following statement: "I have a personal responsibility to share my religious beliefs about Jesus Christ with non-Christians."

Our study found that 80 percent agreed either strongly or somewhat with this position. Seventy-five percent of responders said they agreed to some degree with the following statement: "I feel comfortable that I can share my belief in Christ with someone else effectively." In other words, nearly eight out of ten American Christians recognize they have a personal responsibility to evangelism, and three-quarters profess a willingness to live out that responsibility. A large majority of Christians, therefore, not only recognize their calling to be ambassadors, but also believe they are capable of living out this task.[18]

Good, right? We have been praying for laborers in the age of outrage, but the problem emerges in the respondents' answer to the follow-up question: "In the past six months, how many times have you personally shared with someone how to become a Christian?"

The most common answer was zero, with 61 percent confessing they had not told anyone how to become a Christian in the previous six months.[19] When the question was adjusted to focus solely on times when Christians invited unchurched people to church rather than personally witnessing to them, the numbers weren't much better (48 percent had invited zero people in the past six months).[20] That's six months . . .

26 weeks
182 days
4,368 hours
262,080 minutes

. . . without mentioning just one time how to become a Christian.

It is hard to reconcile a belief in the importance of mission with this ambivalence to its execution. Why the disparity between our heads and hearts? I think that when we ignore Jesus' exhortation to pray, we become apathetic in our Christian duty to live as ambassadors. We need to regain a greater sense of compassion for the lost by remembering we were once lost. We need to remember that we have been truly and faithfully loved. We need to hurt for those who don't know Christ by remembering that he went on a rescue mission for us. Remembering our own salvation will spark the compassion that shapes us, changes us, and sends us on mission.

To Jonathan Edwards, prayer was the great divider between believers and posers. (Edwards actually called them hypocrites, but I like to think of the prim and proper American Puritan calling people posers.) Those who persisted in prayer revealed that God had truly changed their hearts and his Spirit indwelled them. Of those who did not pray, Edwards said, "The neglect of the duty of prayer seems to be inconsistent with supreme love to God. . . . True love to God seeks to please him in every thing."[21] Prayer is the fundamental building block of faith, and when Jesus calls us to pray for the harvest, he is asking us to take the first step as ambassadors of his gospel.

When Jesus prayed for workers for the harvest, the reality is that the worker is you. It's the missionaries who go into "foreign" lands on assignments from their King and seek to develop and foster the kind of compassion they were shown. That's what happened to the disciples; that's what's true today. When we pray for the harvest, we not only reveal a heart for the lost, we are praying for ourselves, the sent ones. We pray that our own hearts will remember that we are ambassadors as much in need of the gospel as the "heathen" down the street.

The content of our prayers, then, reveals the prominence of the mission in our hearts. In partnership with Max Lucado for his book *Before Amen: The Power of a Simple Prayer*, LifeWay Research published a study that asked the basic question: "What have you ever prayed for?"

41 percent prayed for people who mistreat them.

37 percent prayed for their enemies.

21 percent prayed to win the lottery.

13 percent prayed for their favorite team to win a game.

5 percent prayed for someone to get fired.[22]

Americans who pray typically pray for family or friends, their own problems, and their own sin. Thank God for that 42 percent saying they pray for their own sin, or the 38 percent who pray for people in natural disasters, or the 37 percent who pray in thanksgiving for God's greatness. Maybe they're worshiping and praising, and that's great![23]

We found that 20 percent said they regularly pray for people

Among Americans who pray:

Have you ever prayed for . . .

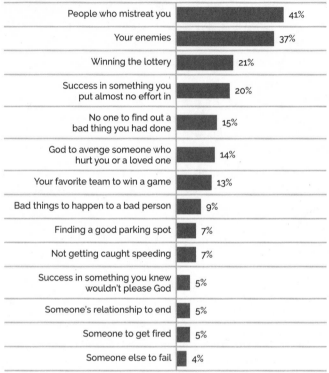

People who mistreat you	41%
Your enemies	37%
Winning the lottery	21%
Success in something you put almost no effort in	20%
No one to find out a bad thing you had done	15%
God to avenge someone who hurt you or a loved one	14%
Your favorite team to win a game	13%
Bad things to happen to a bad person	9%
Finding a good parking spot	7%
Not getting caught speeding	7%
Success in something you knew wouldn't please God	5%
Someone's relationship to end	5%
Someone to get fired	5%
Someone else to fail	4%

LifeWay Research. Note: Participants could select all that apply.

of other faiths or no faith. This is significant because 21 percent say they've prayed to win the lottery. Don't miss this: Jesus tells us to pray for workers and for the harvest, but more people say they've prayed to win the lottery than are regularly praying to win the lost.[24]

Even as high percentages of Americans prayed for family, friends, or themselves, the lost were not a major focus during prayer. Yet effective ambassadors are focused on the mission from our King, pray in light of his Kingdom, and are compelled by his love for the lost, which transforms our prayers outward toward others.

Compassion through action

One danger of theologically minded approaches is that we sometimes miss the practical application. When it comes to the body of Christ, it makes for a pretty disproportional body. It's like forgetting to exercise the legs when doing a full-body workout. We need more gospel sharing to balance the other practices within our Christian life.

If we're praying for a harvest and for workers, we cannot sit back and expect pastors and Christian leaders to do all the work. In the community from which my family recently moved, we intentionally sought to engage our neighbors because I truly believe that is essential to the Christian life. We actually made a map of the eight nearest neighbors who didn't know the Lord and began to share the gospel with them on a regular basis by building relationships with them. I later had the privilege of leading one family to Christ and baptizing the mom and dad. I had the privilege of seeing them place their trust in the Lord and eventually become leaders in the church I planted. (To learn more about the map and the list, turn to page 274.)

As the world becomes more secular and resistant to the good news of the gospel, taking those steps of faith will make all the difference. When you start praying, "Here I am, Lord, send me" (Isaiah 6:8), he will send you, and he will send others, too. It begins with one step of obedience, one yes to God. We can't tell people to reach their neighbors if we aren't first doing it ourselves, going across the street or next door. God uses prayer focused on the great commission in powerful ways.

Too often, our solutions are indiscernible from those of the world. We are willing to demonstrate grace and healing to those who look, act, and struggle the same way we do, but condemn and alienate those who look, act, or struggle differently. As a result, when people in our churches, whether out of curiosity or need, seek to discuss uncomfortable topics like racial injustice, they are often met with scorn or simplistic responses meant to quickly dismiss the conversation and silence "the other" because of the discomfort the topic creates. Such responses are profoundly unloving.

In these moments, the church no longer serves as a community of gospel healing but merely becomes another platform of the world's outrage. It has embraced a worldly identity defined by politics rather than fulfilling its supernatural and God-given design as a transcendent outpost for the coming Kingdom.

Those who have been silenced will naturally seek out some other community where they can find a salve for their identity pain. In these instances, we have ceded our opportunity for gospel mission to the world, driving those who need King Jesus into other kingdoms that don't give life and do not satisfy. The sad truth is that while these other communities will offer love, they cannot provide the healing the gospel does.

One story that Brian Warth, pastor of Chapel of Change, told has stuck with me. Not long after planting his church, Brian faced the challenge every pastor dreads: He was asked to officiate at the funeral of a young person who had been killed in a street shooting. Her mom had been involved in gangs and introduced her daughter to the lifestyle. It was a tragedy compounded by guilt and shame that only a parent can fully appreciate.

In the midst of that pain, Brian lived out his calling as an ambassador of the gospel by enduring in his compassion and love for those broken by sin. The woman who lost her daughter eventually surrendered her heart to Jesus and is now the Celebrate Recovery ministry leader at Chapel of Change. Brian brought Christ's message of reconciliation into the community's pain, and in the process he watched as God raised up new ambassadors out of what this world tells us is only despair.

Reflecting on his ministry, Brian noted that his own story of redemption changed the way he sees people: "I can empathize with people on a deeper level, which helps me view them with the eyes of a doctor rather than a judge."[25] His comment reminded me of Jesus' rebuke to the Pharisees in Mark 2:17. Asked why he ate with tax collectors and sinners, Jesus replied, "Those who are well have no need of a physician, but those who are sick. I came not to call the righteous, but sinners."

As ambassadors sent to a foreign land, we cannot be content with sitting in our comfortable churches and hoping to ride out the cultural storms and upheavals. We need to study the crises in our culture, uncovering the causes of pain and brokenness and then gently and lovingly combating them with the truth of the gospel in hope-filled anticipation that others will respond in faith. To do this, we must have the compassion of Christ, which flows out of prayer, action, and acts of reconciliation and understanding.

Asking ourselves, "What are we known for in our community?" leads us to a mirror and a door. First, we are faced with who we are: Christ-followers who are far away from home and called to be intimate students and compassionate intercessors for our community while representing a King who brings a much-needed message of reconciliation for the world. This is the mirror. We must understand ourselves and our communities.

We are also presented with a door that leads into a country that is not our own, a foreign land hostile to our message, our mission, and our King. Yet it also longs for the very thing Jesus provides. So we walk out the door and into the world, armed with the gospel of grace and strengthened through fervent prayer to God's Spirit, who gives us compassion, and through God's church, which gives us community.

What are we known for in our communities? How will we reach this age of outrage with the gospel? Every church and each believer must focus on the answers to these questions if we are to stay on course. Many churches and believers need to transition from destructive infighting and mission creep to being on God's mission within their neighborhoods and around the world.

Change is possible. The church I described at the start of this chapter was once known for fighting, contention, and being full of difficult people. After that beautiful, muddy Mother's Day anniversary, we were known for showing and sharing the love of Jesus to a broken and hurting world. We were known as a community on a mission for the gospel–ambassadors to the outraged for Jesus and his Good News.

CHAPTER 9

Winsome Love

- Over a third of evangelicals (35 percent) say they disagree with their friends and family up to half of the time. Evangelicals disagree with their *friends and family* often. We have to learn how to disagree winsomely or our witness and relationships will suffer.

In 1967, THE BEATLES MADE a proposition that encapsulated the hopes of their age: "All you need is love / Love is all you need."[1] The inviting message was set to a carnival-like rhythm, similar to many other hits that the Beatles churned out in their prime.

In their song, we find a grain of truth that speaks to the human condition. Not only do we all love, but we are innately drawn to the idea of *being loved*. We understand the power of our own desires and therefore long to be the objects of the desires of another. All the components of love—dignity, respect, affirmation, encouragement, service—are magnetic, even if the sin and brokenness of this world distort how we interpret them.

No wonder this Beatles hit captures the modern imagination almost as powerfully as it did in the sixties. Some churches even seem to have picked up on the sentiment in this anthem, repurposing it with phrases such as "Love Everyone, Always."

Perhaps no writer grasped the profound importance of love to the human soul as deeply as Augustine. To Augustine, our love and desire to be loved constitute our animating principle, the underlying drive of our human nature. In one of the earlier sections of his autobiographical work *Confessions*, Augustine said this directly: "What was it that delighted me? Only loving and being loved." For the unconverted young Augustine, this had been a major problem. Without the indwelling of the Spirit to orient these desires toward God, Augustine's loves were disordered. The result, Augustine wrote, was that these twin needs "swirled about together and dragged me, young and weak as I was; over the cliffs of my desires, and engulfed me in a whirlpool of sins."[2] The problem, as Augustine saw it, was not that he loved and wanted to be loved but that these desires were directed at ends that led him to pain and misery. The problem was in *what* he loved and the way in which he looked to sexual love to fulfill his deepest needs.

Even today our world *craves* love. And this should encourage us as Christians because, like Augustine, we recognize that only the gospel can satisfy this desire of our hearts. Yet there remains considerable resistance and even hostility to the gospel. Why is it that a people who long for love reject a message of fulfilling love?

The first reason is that the message of the gospel is offensive to a world broken and ruled by sin. Jesus tells us that the world will hate us just as it first hated him (John 15:18-25). Consequently, the world also despises the gospel message. Disciples are to expect suffering and persecution from this world when they proclaim the Good News of Jesus Christ. This stems directly from Christ's message: repent and believe. The world around us cannot stomach that (a) there is something inherently wrong (sin) and (b) there is an exclusive solution (belief in Jesus as Savior).

The idea that the gospel is offensive is everywhere in Paul's letters, and he gives four reasons why this is the case:

1. It preaches God's judgment of human wickedness and false righteousness (Romans 1:16-32; Philippians 3:7-9; 1 Thessalonians 1:9; and 2 Thessalonians 2:11-12).
2. It rejects the wisdom of this world as foolishness (1 Corinthians 1:18-25).
3. It is the catalyst of the spiritual battle between the forces of darkness and the forces of light that rages all around us (Ephesians 6:12).

4. It is focused foundationally and immovably upon the
   death and resurrection of Christ–insisting that mankind
   is fallen, that our current behavior is a reflection of
   our fallenness, that we need to be reconciled to God,
   and that Christ is the only means by which this can be
   accomplished (Philippians 3:3-10; Galatians 3:1-6).

When we try to discount the offensiveness of the gospel, we
may lower the exclusive and necessary claims of Christ along
with God's call to holiness. History is replete with examples of
professing believers, often with good intentions of witnessing to
those in sore need of the gospel, trying to make it more palatable.
For instance, some have shied away from condemning the sins of
greed and materialism to make Jesus seem friendlier to those in
the middle and upper classes.

Yet there is a second reason that unbelievers often will not hear
the good news of God's redeeming love, and this one makes us
uncomfortable. Even as Christians proclaim a message of love,
the unloving actions and words of Christians toward others contradict our witness. There is a fact about the way we sometimes
communicate the gospel that is difficult to swallow but important
to ingest and digest: Negative impressions of Christians stem from
Christians simply being unloving.

When we encounter rejection or anger, we tend to use the
"offensiveness of the gospel" as a shield for our unloving and cal-
lous response. But the offensiveness of the gospel does not give
license for Christians to be offensive. When we respond to pushback from others with hostility, it is *not* the offensiveness of the
gospel that damages our witness and reinforces negative stereo-
types of Christians–it's us! We laden the gospel message with our
own baggage–cultural biases, racial animosities, personal insecurities, and spiritual immaturity. In essence, we wrap the gospel in
our offensive packaging and then decry our neighbors when they
are less than enthusiastic about Jesus and his church.

During an appearance on *CNN Headline News*, I was asked to

comment on a recent LifeWay Research poll that had been causing a stir. At the center of the discussion were two questions on
cultural attitudes of unchurched Americans toward Christians and
Christianity. The poll revealed that

> 79 percent agree (somewhat or strongly) that "Christianity
> today is more about organized religion than loving God
> and loving people."

> 44 percent agree (somewhat or strongly) with "Christians
> get on my nerves."[3]

Why, if the gospel of Jesus is so amazing and if Christians are
called to love and serve, did a majority of Americans complain
that the organized church was less interested in love than in ritual
and that Christians are annoying if not unloving? The poll results
hardly seemed like a great starting point into a conversation about
the love of Jesus for a hurting world. But facts are our friends, and
then (as now) we need to face the reality that one of the biggest
obstacles to seriously engaging the message of Jesus is the character and conduct of its messengers. We must acknowledge that the
watching world does not sense that we are engaging them with a
winsome love.

Christians contribute to the outrage around us when we behave
badly rather than lovingly communicate the Good News of the
gospel message.

For instance, some Christians post Bible verses professing the
love of Christ, only to follow that with hostile if not derogatory
insults against some political, cultural, or religious figure. When
claims to being joy filled are mixed in with disparaging comments
about a politician, it strikes onlookers as oddly disjointed. People
believe our love is worthless when we cheapen it in this way. More
important, they assume Christian love must be contingent upon
political, economic, or cultural positions. This reduces our claims
to merely another form of tribalism.

This is not to say that Christians who mix messages *want* to come across as unloving or even recognize how their actions could come across that way. Rather, it shows a disconnect in our thinking when we are unable to recognize how such hypocrisy can destroy our witness. When we claim to *have* the love of Christ but don't *show it* to others through our actions and words, we demonstrate that we have not been truly gripped by grace and our own desperate need of it. Our lack of love is theological at its core, and this denial of the gospel by our actions damages our witness and the witness of Jesus in the world.

In his book *The Sermon on the Mount and Human Flourishing*, New Testament scholar Jonathan Pennington argues that Jesus' anger toward the Pharisees' hypocrisy was because "they are not unified in heart and action." Pharisees may have done good things, "but they are not the right kind of people because their hearts are wrong."[4] They appear to be good by doing good, but inwardly they are spiritually dead, nothing but "whitewashed tombs" (Matthew 23:27). Scripture reveals that God does not want our religious action for its own sake if it does not arise from truly changed hearts (Hosea 6:6). Loving action toward others must flow out of hearts enthralled by God's love for us.

Thus, if we do not actually love the lost around us, we demonstrate that we have missed the point of the gospel itself. No wonder our witness is so anemic! We don't appear to understand that what we preach applies to ourselves first and foremost! We disqualify our right to bring a message of love by being unloving in the very way we live and proclaim the gospel, and so deny the compelling power of the Good News. We cannot reach people and hate people at the same time.

So Christianity in a broken and rebellious world is going to be offensive. But we aren't supposed to be. Even as there is genuine offensiveness to the gospel, we can never lose sight that Jesus and his message are *equally* (if not more) attractive to this world. The gospel is the salve for this world's pain, brokenness, and anger.

The Good News is meant to be exactly that: hope of a cure to a spiritually dead world.

In John 10:9, Jesus proclaims, "I am the door. If anyone enters by me, he will be saved and will go in and out to find pasture." This is quickly followed with the promise that Jesus has come that we might "have life and have it abundantly" (verse 10). In our culture, where materialism (with the mantra of "I don't have enough") and nihilism ("Everything is worthless") are paramount, Jesus' words offer a powerful image of fullness and satisfaction. What does Jesus mean? What is attractive about the gospel? It is the source of

life for the dead (Ephesians 2);

liberation for the addicted and imprisoned (Romans 6:15-23);

reconciliation for even the most dysfunctional relationships (Philemon);

elevation for the humble and marginalized (Matthew 20:16);

the promise of an impending Kingdom free from prejudice and fear (Luke 4:16-27);

identity as a chosen child of God (John 1:12);

community as one body, beyond mere tribalism or shared interest (1 Corinthians 12:27); and

purpose in building a Kingdom that cannot be shaken (Hebrews 12:28).

Nowhere is there a love that overcomes the barriers of death, sin, captivity, separation, fear, alienation, and purposelessness except at the Cross. There is hope for racial reconciliation, for peace between the sexes, for ethnic harmony, and for healing when we rally around a common identity in Christ, love him as our Redeemer, and serve his Kingdom. As Christians, we have become well-versed in the offensiveness of the gospel. We know *why* it is rejected and *why* we encounter persecution and opposition. Yet we need to recapture just how attractive the gospel is and how central its truth is to our witness.

Writing in the 1950s, the British evangelist Roy Hession summed it up this way: "The glorious, central fact of Christianity is that God has made a full and final revelation of Himself which has made Him understandable, accessible, and desirable to the simplest and most fearful of us."[5]

Christians are called to demonstrate this profoundly attractive love in a way that testifies to the gospel and counters the lies, brokenness, and violence of sin. The way we interact with others will dramatically affect whether the world is drawn to Christ's love.

For Christians to be at our best, we must put ourselves in the position of accepting that demands will be made on our love. Yet that love must be real and evident to the world. It must be genuine and sincere. At its heart it must be winsome—a quality that draws people in rather than repulses them. People who love in this way view others through a specific lens:

Empathetic. They understand that this world is broken and in bondage, so people *need* Jesus, not rejection.

Humble. They preface cultural engagement with humility rather than hostility and tribalism.

Image Bearing. They perceive and value all human beings, even those who hate them, as image bearers who are entitled to *intrinsic* worth and dignity.

Sacrificial. They speak boldly into systems and acts of injustice rather than shrinking back in fear or confusion.

This is the kind of love Jesus shows: love that is compassionate, meek, respectful, and courageous. In this chapter, we will examine these four elements of winsome love and consider how each looks in real life. When we engage with others empathically, humbly, respectfully, and sacrificially, we will better communicate a love that is worth telling, worth witnessing, and worth receiving.

Empathy: The Polar Opposite of Love Is Disgust

For reasons that are too gross to share, I once ended up in a tank of manure and waste. I was fully and thoroughly disgusted.

Even decades later, whenever I hear or see someone say they are disgusted, my mind goes back to that moment. Like stepping in raw sewage, disgust points to a visceral reaction to something, an inability to be close to the object of our repugnance. Unsurprisingly, when someone conveys disgust toward me, it's not a great feeling. But more important, I know our conversation is over. That person can't hear anything else I would say because that feeling of disgust and revulsion destroys empathy, which is essential to any communication.

Unfortunately, many Christians I know truly are disgusted by people who don't know Christ. The real danger is that they don't think they are disgusted, but their words and their actions betray them. It takes little effort to uncover what people truly believe about one another because it comes to the surface like oil on water. And ultimately none of us can hide our feelings of revulsion. Disgust smells. And people catch the scent.

When we are asked what the opposite of love is, we often run to emotions like hate or anger. But I would argue that the opposite of love is disgust. When something disgusts us, it is virtually impossible to love it at the same time. For Christians to truly be at our best in this age of outrage, we must practice empathetic love and fight disgust.

The real problem of disgust

In her influential book *From Disgust to Humanity*, philosopher Martha Nussbaum argues that disgust often seeps into our perception of others, particularly in regard to their moral worth. In her opening illustration, Nussbaum points to a young gay student at an evangelical school who had "learned to feel horror and disgust at the behavior he desired and to think of it as base or animalistic, not suited to the full dignity of a human being."[6] Now I disagree with much of where Dr. Nussbaum takes her argument, but I also think that she has tapped into an underlying problem that pervades our world and fuels our age of outrage. This problem is what the young man took away from the evangelical environment: that he was less than human. Disgust whittles an entire person down to one struggle, one sin, one issue. Disgust is dehumanizing and not of Jesus.

The real problem with disgust is twofold: It destroys engagement and distorts our view of our sin. It's both practically destructive and theologically revealing. Let me explain.

Disgust halts any and all engagement. Like a bad odor or a revolting sight, disgust stops us in our tracks and prevents us from getting any closer to someone. One author categorized disgust as an emotion similar to fear and hatred. While we fear things out of self-preservation and hate things that have wronged us, disgust is an emotion of avoidance and repulsion. He wrote, "To be disgusted by something is, crucially, to want to avoid contact with it–either by sight or touch or smell or taste. . . . However invulnerable you may feel with respect to a certain stench, and however blameless you take it (or its producer) to be, you still wish to escape its influence–to put distance between yourself and it."[7]

Disgust will pervade our interactions, inform our quick dismissal of others, and even justify the harsh language we use to describe others. This is practically destructive to mission and highlights Christians at their worst.

Not only does disgust halt engagement, but it also distorts our view of our own sin. The reason raw sewage is disgusting is that it is foreign to us. We are not meant to smell those smells or be immersed in that putrid muck. And when we feel disgust toward other people, we reveal that this is how we feel about their sin and brokenness: We think we are worthy and good while they are unworthy and bad. We cannot feel disgust without stating an opinion about ourselves in the process. This is why the young gay man felt as if he were less than human when he struggled with sin openly. Those evangelicals who showed disgust toward him clearly didn't recognize that their sin was just as offensive to God.

And this is truly the theologically revealing heart problem behind disgust: We don't see our own sin and need for a Savior, and thus we place ourselves in the seat of judge and jury. That steals God's glory, robs us of joy, and shipwrecks our mission to the world. Now *that* is disgusting.

Most distressing is how this problem of disgust so easily infiltrates Christian thinking and engagement. It is crucial that we grasp how this attitude invalidates our claims to love. It transforms what should be a gospel-centered love for sinners as potential vessels of God's mercy into a conditional love predicated upon our cultural and political fears. We stand at the water's edge of society, yelling at the objects of our Kingdom mission to clean themselves before we can come any closer. This is not Christian love, and as such it is neither winsome nor effective. Sadly, Christians who engage in this deficient love are often puzzled as to why their witness, which is defined by avoidance and contempt, is proving insufficient to counteract the world's outrage.

The real antidote to disgust: Jesus

So how are we to respond to this sinful disgust in our hearts? Jesus offers a framework for interpreting sin, not with disgust but with an empathetic love that winsomely welcomes the broken to come to him. In Hebrews, we see how Jesus demonstrates this kind of love.

> For we do not have a high priest who is unable to empathize with our weaknesses, but we have one who has been tempted in every way, just as we are—yet he did not sin. Let us then approach God's throne of grace with confidence, so that we may receive mercy and find grace to help us in our time of need.
> HEBREWS 4:15-16, NIV

Notice that the author of Hebrews does not paint God as remote or uninterested in our struggles. Rather, through his incarnation as fully man, Christ is able to "empathize with our weaknesses."

The picture is of a Savior who is simultaneously enthroned in heaven yet intimately familiar with our trials and temptations. In other words, Jesus is both all-powerful and eminently approachable. And it is *precisely because of this empathy* that the author of Hebrews implores us to "approach God's throne of grace with confidence." Christ disarms our suspicions and emboldens us to approach him to find the love and reconciliation we crave.

This is the solution to our disgust: cultivating the same love toward the world that Christ shows us. This empathetic love–the ability to understand and relate to the experiences of others–is powerfully winsome in its ability to draw people in.

We do not need to sacrifice our revulsion of sin, but rather reframe how we see those caught in its power. We know the corrosive yet alluring power of sin that entangles this world (Hebrews 12:1), and we know the freedom and relief that come from being reconciled to the Father. We need to use that understanding to demonstrate an empathetic love to the lost, ensuring that they know they can approach us with confidence that they will receive the mercy and grace that was first shown to us.

In his letter to the Ephesians, we see how Paul was motivated to evangelism because he recognized that he–like all people–had once been dead in his trespasses and sins. In Ephesians 2:1-3, he unpacks this truth:

We once followed the course of this world.
We once followed the prince of the power of the air.
We once were sons of disobedience.
We once lived according to the passions of our flesh.
We once were children of wrath.

Now *that* is repulsive. *That* is worthy of disgust. And if we stop reading here, it is hopeless. But winsome love always includes a "but," and so Paul continues by moving the narrative from our sin to God's mercy: "But God, being rich in mercy, because of the great love with which he loved us, even when we were dead in our trespasses, made us alive together with Christ–by grace you have been saved" (Ephesians 2:4-5).

Our empathy and compassion, therefore, are informed by the recognition that, if not for God, we are worse than the objects of our disgust. Christians in the age of outrage don't say, "Love the sinner but hate the sin"; instead they say, "Love the sinner, as I have been loved."

Empathy in action

I can think of no better example of the shift from disgust to empathy than the eighteenth-century African American minister Richard Allen. He is perhaps most famous for leading the lengthy walk-out of black parishioners from St. George's Methodist Episcopal Church in Philadelphia. Though both blacks and whites worshiped at St. George's, the black parishioners protested the limitations placed on them, which included segregated seating. Eventually, Allen led the group in founding Bethel African Methodist Episcopal Church and subsequently became the founding bishop of the African Methodist Episcopal denomination. Despite his determination to end discrimination within the church, he was known for his winsome love.

In 1793, the year after Richard Allen walked out of St. George's, Philadelphia was hit with a yellow fever epidemic. Dr. Benjamin Rush (a signatory of the Declaration of Independence) wrote to Allen and other black ministers begging them to step in and help the sick (due to the mistaken belief that yellow fever didn't affect African Americans). Despite Allen's and other ministers' heroic and sacrificial service during the epidemic, some people charged that the African Americans had used the sickness as an opportunity to profit from the disaster. Allen responded with *A Narrative of the Proceedings of the Black People during the Late Awful Calamity in Philadelphia in the Year 1793*. In his refutation, Allen detailed story after story of African Americans who, because of their deep faith in Jesus, sacrificed for the dying and sick. (Some of them even died from the fever.)

Despite the overt racism he faced, Allen modeled an empathetic approach to loving his neighbors. Allen and his fellow volunteers were heartbroken over the suffering of the sick. They resonated with those patients who had been cast out by their white families: "Many of the white people, who ought to be patterns for us to follow after, have acted in a manner that would make humanity shudder."[8] Because of their own unique suffering as a people, Allen and his fellow caregivers were able to identify and love those who had been shunned and expelled, segregated and alone.

Later in life, Allen explained the motivation behind his service: He looked on those who condemned him with pity. In a series of letters Allen wrote to slaveholders and those who defended slavery, he wrote of the coming judgment of God and begged them to renounce their heresy of racism and embrace the gospel of Christ:

> The meek and humble Jesus, the great pattern of humanity and every other virtue that can adorn and dignify men, hath commanded to love our enemies; to do good to them that hate and despitefully use us. I feel the obligations; I wish to impress them on the minds of our colored brethren, and that we may all forgive you, as we wish to be forgiven; we think it a great mercy to have all anger and bitterness removed from our minds. I appeal to your own feelings, if it is not very disquieting to feel yourselves under the dominion of wrathful disposition.
>
> If you love your children, if you love your country, if you love the God of love, clear your hands from slaves; [burden] not your children or your country with them.[9]

Allen had every reason to be disgusted by those around him. He had been kicked out of his church, had risked his life and asked others to do so as well, and then he'd been accused of stealing during his relief efforts when he served those who thought he was less than human. Despite this, Allen never lost sight of the truth: Those around him were lost and needed Jesus. His empathy informed his witness, and it is one reason why the AME grew and his name is remembered today.

What is often ignored in our age of outrage is just how many Christians follow Allen's legacy. Christians across the United States and the world are living out this empathetic love, building bridges with people who are different from them at great personal expense with an eye to gospel proclamation. From church-planting alliances to hurricane-relief efforts to simple dinner invitations extended to their neighbors, Christians are working to counteract the misrepresentation of Christ by drawing closer to the broken rather than withdrawing and giving in to disgust.

Our compassion and empathy toward others also moves us to the next element of winsome love.

Humility: Counteracting the Hindrance of Pride with Love

Carl Henry, the founding editor of *Christianity Today* and a well-respected evangelical theologian, famously opened his book *The Uneasy Conscience of Modern Fundamentalism* with the line, "The present tendency of conservative Christianity is to make much of the embarrassment of religious modernism."[10] Writing just after the end of World War II, Henry recognized that American Christianity had come to a crossroads. On the one hand, mainline Protestants, in their pursuit of modernism, had incrementally walked away from doctrines Henry believed were central to the Christian faith. Henry correctly recognized that this pathway was destined for failure and rejected their theological liberalism.

On the other side were the fundamentalists, members of the group he called "conservative Christianity" in the quote above. Henry affirmed their orthodox theology but was deeply disturbed by their posture of hostility and divisiveness. It seemed to Henry that they defined themselves more by their theological enemies than by the truth and love of the gospel. This had led fundamentalists to ignore pressing social evils in their commitment to defending their theological purity against any signs of modernism. They robbed the "social Peter" to pay the "theological Paul," and it damaged the church and people in the process.

But the core of the fundamentalist church's struggle after the Second World War was a lack of humility. It became a contest to see who could be the most committed to the Bible, who was the most theologically accurate, and who was the most biblically astute. As Henry observed, this was a critical mistake. By ignoring "the injustices of the totalitarianisms, the secularisms of modern education, the evils of racial hatred, the wrongs of current labor-management relations," fundamentalism had failed to draw out the social implications of the gospel for the world to see.[11] They had allowed the world to see the Christian faith as aloof or unconcerned with the problems of *this* world. As a result, fundamentalists were now seen as *fundamentally* unloving. Their entire worldview seemed to be grounded in trying to win a theological debate rather than winning converts to the love of Jesus. This pride led to the beginning of the downfall of what we know as "cultural Christianity," long before anyone saw the external evidence of the cultural shift.

This lack of humility hinders the church's winsome love. If our faith doesn't translate to real life change that makes practical sense in the real world, it becomes irrelevant, vain, and prideful. When the cult of celebrity supersedes a culture of service, we lose our relevance to a world that watches us to see Jesus. And all of this diminishes our ability to love others well. Whenever Jesus interacted with people, he always put them at a crossroads: They could continue as they were or experience a true life change. And he did so with a smile and an open invitation, in true humility. This is what humble engagement and humble love do.

The expression of pride: hunting for the "nightmare"

I loved watching President Ronald Reagan. I started to think about politics as I watched his election. And while most historians today focus on his economic plans or foreign policy, we forget how effective he was as a communicator. Two examples from his presidential debates stick in my mind. In the first, Reagan famously fended off

Jimmy Carter's charge that he opposed Medicare by simply shaking his head and saying, "There you go again." Similarly, in his 1984 debate against Walter Mondale, Reagan responded to a quip about his age with the joke, "I will not make age an issue of this campaign. I am not going to exploit, for political purposes, my opponent's youth and inexperience."[12] In both cases, policy or logic didn't win the argument; Reagan's ability to turn a quick phrase did.

And I loved it. We naturally enjoy those moments when we catch someone off guard. Those quips of Reagan helped him win those elections and the affection of much of America (he won the electoral college in 1984 by a staggering 525 to 13). The tendency to deflect criticisms and trip up opponents has exploded with the introduction of social media and cable news. Every politician and journalist, every tweeter and blogger, is on the hunt for the witty "gotchas" to discredit and defeat others.

It is the hunt for the moment when we render someone speechless, unable to offer a rebuttal, and we are, by default, in the right. Some of the most celebrated public voices today are followed solely for their ability to "destroy" their political opponents. This is textbook pride. Driven by our own insecurities, we often seek someone else's "nightmare" without stopping to consider whether this is an effective way of engaging the culture.

When this thinking invades the church, it results in apologetics whose aim is not to present rational defenses of Christianity, but to defeat and humiliate other faiths and moralities. We justify this pride and egoism, baptizing it in Christian language such as "defending Christianity." In reality, however, we are more interested in stomping on others with witty sound bites.

We often take an all-or-nothing approach to engagement that demands, "You have to agree with me or you are [blank]." And each community fills in that blank with whatever pejorative term applies: racist, un-American, ignorant, bigoted, elitist, heretical, unchristian, liberal, conservative.

This is where the lack of love comes into play. When we are prideful, arrogant, and especially skilled at debate, we no longer express the winsomeness of the gospel but become blinded by our own personal victories and others' personal nightmares.

How the humility of Jesus kills our pride and revives true dialogue

Jesus is the ultimate model of humility, so we must learn practical and theological ways to translate his example into our own experiences.

First, it is important to accept a radical premise: It is okay to disagree. God gave Adam and Eve choices in the Garden of Eden. He gives us choices now, and he respects and honors those choices because of the dignity bestowed on every human made in his image.

The simple reality is that people will disagree, and yet we still have to breathe the same air. Mind-blowing, right? Winsome love doesn't mean that we must accept and embrace other people's positions; it simply means we avoid the hostile debate that defines online engagement. Winsome love doesn't speak to *whether* we disagree; rather, it shapes the *way* in which we disagree. Too often our engagement is characterized by an all-or-nothing debate that we are determined to "win." And this is where it gets practical: It's not about winning or losing; it's about sharing Jesus and inviting others to follow him. The following story is a perfect example.

There have long been tensions between the fast-food company Chick-fil-A and the LGBTQ community. These stresses have deep, sensitive roots stemming from disagreement about beliefs about marriage, specifically same-sex marriage, as well as the company's donations to certain organizations. The restaurant's president and COO, Dan Cathy, is open about his Christian beliefs, including his opposition to same-sex marriage. Shane Windmeyer is an activist for the LGBTQ community and the founder and the executive director of Campus Pride, which he calls "the leading national organization for lesbian, gay, bisexual, transgender (LGBT) and ally college students."[15] He is also an openly gay man.

Because of their different worldviews, we would expect Cathy and Windmeyer to consider each other enemies and to be open about their outrage. This type of behavior is, after all, common when two sides disagree, even on issues less central to people's lifestyles. Windmeyer and Cathy, however, consider themselves friends, and their friendship was born out of dialogue that happened in the midst of disagreement.

In 2012, at the height of the controversy between LGBTQ activist groups like Campus Pride and Chick-fil-A, Windmeyer received an unexpected phone call from Cathy. This private phone call led to a series of calls, texts, and in-person conversations. Both men listened and treated each other with respect. Although neither changed his core beliefs, they had a productive dialogue that led to a friendship. "We learned about each other as people with opposing views," recalled Windmeyer, "not as opposing people."[14]

Eventually, Cathy invited Windmeyer to be his personal guest at the Chick-fil-A Bowl on New Year's Eve 2012. Both risked fallout from their respective supporting groups by being seen together, but they chose to do so anyway. Their dialogue has had an impact in other ways: Chick-fil-A pledged to avoid contributing to some organizations, and Campus Pride suspended its campaign against Chick-fil-A. The example set by these two men proves that it is possible for change to occur when groups are willing to listen to one another with mutual respect. This is the path Jesus calls us to, and it is a much better alternative to outrage.

Perhaps no one grasped this truth better than the apostle Paul. In his letters to the Corinthian church, Paul set out plainly where he disagreed with their theology and practice. Yet Paul recognized that his goal wasn't simply to correct their aberrant theology but to win them to the true gospel. Thus, while Paul could confess, "Woe to me if I do not preach the gospel!" (1 Corinthians 9:16), this obligation in no way countermanded his mission to win the lost. In fact, Paul was able to connect so well with multiple cultures because of his underlying mission philosophy: "I have become all things to all people, that by all means I might save some. I do it for the sake of the gospel, that I may share with them in its blessings" (1 Corinthians 9:22-23).

Thousands of pages of dense theology have been written on Paul's meaning in this passage, but none have come as close as the church father John Chrysostom. In his sermon on the passage, Chrysostom explained that Paul is modeling for us the intersection of humble love and mission:

> [Do not think] that you lower yourself, when for your brother's sake you submit to some abasement. For this is not to fall, but to descend. For he who falls, lies prostrate, hardly to be raised up again; but he who descends shall also rise again with much advantage.[15]

This is key. Humility is not losing. It is not weakness or cowardliness. It is a lie of our outrage-fueled culture that meekness and humility are inferior to the screech and bellowing of the arrogant.

In contrast, Paul paints an example of humble love that is submitted to Kingdom mission and is incredibly powerful. The willingness to lower yourself by listening and understanding the culture, worldview, and background of those you engage opens doors for communicating the gospel of love. It reveals that you are interested in winning the person instead of the debate.

Such humility requires one other characteristic: forbearance.

The humility of forbearance

Forbearance is an old word with deep roots in theology. Essentially it means to endure with others, to *bear* their weight as our own out of love. In his book on the topic, James Calvin Davis proposed that Christian forbearance "is the active commitment to maintain Christian community through disagreement, as an extension of virtue and as a reflection of the unity in Christ that binds the church together."[16] It is a concept, Davis argues, that pervades Scripture and sets the tone for Christian relationships. We are to bear with one another (Colossians 3:13; Ephesians 4:2) in recognition that God through Christ first forbore with us (Romans 3:22-25). Indeed, Paul goes so far as to say that we "have an obligation to bear with the failings of the weak" (Romans 15:1). This is not merely a recommendation as to how we might settle conflict but rather a demand of our faith.

Yet we are not to have this disposition only toward those within the church. In Philippians 4:5, Paul tells us that we are to "let [our] reasonableness be known to everyone." While the term for *reasonableness* is fraught with translation difficulties, Paul is exhorting the community at Philippi to a gentle forbearance in the midst of significant adversity. Paul exhorted the Philippians to not only forbear in their love *within* the community of God but to *everyone.* Paul rightly understood that this kind of love defied human expectations and, in time, would draw others to the underlying power of Christ.

In this respect, it is easy to see how love and forbearance intersect so crucially in the lives of believers. It is only when we truly love others, whether they are our brothers and sisters in Christ or our unsaved neighbors, that we can endure through conflict without walking away or giving in to the outrage. If the Christlike response to the age of outrage lies in our ability to disagree in love, a crucial first step is our commitment to forbear with others, whether with Christians who may not be as mature as we are, or with the lost who are captive to an incomplete and distorted worldview. This kind of love can forbear with others only because it remains transfixed upon the mission of building the Kingdom of God.

My friend Heather Davis is a Lutheran writer and theologian who lives in Los Angeles, a city not known for evangelicalism or forbearance. She shared the following story with me:

> Last year, I tried a more tactical peacemaking approach,
> creating a group called LISTEN. Through Facebook I
> invited forty-plus people who I thought might be inclined
> toward thoughtful conversation. The list included
> believers and those who were hostile toward Christianity.
> The point was simply to reclaim the practice of hearing
> "the other guy" out. There would be no "yeah-buts"
> and no snark. We had a core group of six to eight for

almost six months. All who committed to attending were Christians (telling, I thought) but were divided on the political spectrum.

We would typically open in prayer, read a verse or a psalm, sing a chant refrain, and have a time of silence, then ask a specific question, e.g., "What is your greatest concern about our current state of division?" or "Is there a position on a cultural or social issue you simply cannot imagine another side to?" And then we would listen. We faced the same challenge most small groups do—scheduling conflicts—and the larger challenge of listening to people say things we don't agree with. But those hours together were charged with the Spirit, and we left every group feeling that somehow our small willingness to consider another point of view was a step in the direction of civility and healing.

Heather's experience shows us that often listening to others is just as important as speaking truth. If we listen with loving ears, we will often be given an opportunity to speak lovingly as well.

Winsome love, then, not only rejects disgust in favor of empathy, it trades pride for humility. It looks to the example of Jesus, does not seek to show others up, is patient in Christ-compelled forbearance, and aims to make disciples of Jesus. Addressing our prideful arrogance is critical if we are to express empathetic, humble love. And that love is winsome. And not only is it winsome, it also honors the image of God in every person.

Image Bearing: Loving Dignity More than Despising Depravity

My office is filled with various gifts and mementos that I've received from former students or old friends. Many of them are odd, such as the five-foot Pez dispenser with my head on top (the kids at Moody Church's vacation Bible school made that). But the item that elicits the most reactions from visitors is the nameplate sitting on the edge of my desk. That's because instead of Dr. Stetzer, the plate reads, "Lying Whore False Prophet"–Westboro Baptist Church.

Located in Topeka, Kansas, Westboro Baptist Church became infamous for their controversial protests and demonstrations, such as their "celebration" of 9/11 as God's judgment. In 2014 I had the pleasure of interviewing Mark Phelps, a former member of Westboro whose late father, Fred Phelps Sr., was the founding pastor. Mark recounted that his father had been filled with hatred, anger, and violence for as long as he could remember. Through his future wife and her parents, Mark was introduced to the real love of Christ and left the church in 1973. Mark ended his interview with me by making an insightful comparison, asking Christians to contrast the ministry of Christ with the behavior of Fred Phelps. Because Mark wants to model the love he sees in Christ, his overwhelming desire is to introduce his family members still at Westboro to the Lord's saving love.[17]

Years before my interview with Mark, this "church" had picketed my church and called me a "lying whore false prophet" because I believe that God loves all people, including homosexuals. As you can tell, they disagree. One of my staff was so amused that she had it made into that nameplate. I keep it on my desk to remind myself and anyone entering my office of one simple truth: You cannot hate a people and reach a people at the same time.

Sadly, many people in the evangelical church believe what Westboro is willing to say out loud. Remember the young gay man profiled by Martha Nussbaum in her book? He was dehumanized by fellow Christians whose message to him was that he was "not suited to the full dignity of a human being." Christians who look at others in this way have forgotten that everyone is made in the image of God. When we exhibit unloving outrage toward others and don't respect the dignity of every human being but equate people's worth with their set of values, we become the church at its worst.

Few ideas have shaped Christian mission more profoundly than the biblical truth that God created man in his image (the theological term is *imago Dei*, Latin for "image of God"). The opening chapters of Genesis contain the record of God's most important creative act: the making of humanity. Once he formed Adam and breathed life into him, God took the unprecedented step of declaring that humanity was created *in his own image* (Genesis 1:26-27; 5:1-2). In Genesis 9:6, as God confirmed his covenant with Noah, he explicitly outlawed murder because it defaces the image of God in man.

While theologians have debated what Scripture means by saying that man is made in the image of God, all agree that it speaks to the inherent value of humanity as God's creation. Christopher Wright perfectly captures the implications of the truth that all humans bear the image of God:

> This forms the basis of the radical equality of all human beings, regardless of gender, ethnicity, religion or any form of social, economic, or political status. . . .
> Christian mission must therefore treat all human beings with dignity, equality and respect. When we look at any other person, we do not see the label . . . but the image of God. We see someone created by God, addressed by God, accountable to God, loved by God, valued and evaluated by God.[18]

The ending of Wright's statement is particularly powerful because it illustrates why an *imago Dei*–shaped love for the lost world is so winsome: Our Creator's value for humanity is intensely relational. God engages with us, desires to be reconciled to us, and ultimately holds each of us accountable to himself alone.

While Westboro is an extreme example, we often justify our retreat from or rejection of communities outside the church on the basis of their sin. But it is ultimately God who holds each of us accountable. He is the Judge of all, not us. A love informed by a recognition of both humanity's intrinsic brokenness and its identity as the image bearers of God has the potential to be powerfully winsome to people struggling with their identity and value. When we look at others as beloved creations of God who have intrinsic dignity and are worthy of our energy, effort, love, prayers, and patience, we can express an *imago Dei*-fueled love.

Imago Dei–*fueled love*

In her book *Undaunted*, my friend Christine Caine recounts how she struggled with her adoption. Although her parents had given her up even before naming her, God declared her to be his prized creation. She sensed God reminding and reinforcing this truth to her this way:

> I formed you. Your freedom will be determined by whether you allow what I think and say about you to matter more than what anyone else thinks or says, including your biological mother or workers filling out forms for the Department of Community Services. They have said what you are not. But I say what you are, and you are created in my image, not theirs. You reflect my glory.[19]

When the strong love of God for his image bearers is contrasted against the empty and finite love of this world, we are set free. Christine experienced this when she recognized that her worth rested in *who she was*, not what she did or could do. We are vessels of the glory of God himself, and that is a compelling reality that fuels our love for others.

Jesus offered another compelling vision of God's image-bearing love in action when he approached Zacchaeus (Luke 19:1-10). In setting the stage for the story, Luke gives us two crucial pieces of information about Zacchaeus: (1) He was a chief tax collector and therefore rich, and (2) he wanted to see who Jesus was. As a tax collector, Zacchaeus accumulated his wealth by abusing his neighbors in service to Rome. He would have been despised in his community. Yet Zacchaeus's desire to see Jesus reminds us that, despite this worldly identity, Zacchaeus was still an image bearer who wanted to relate to his Creator. Even if Zacchaeus did not understand where this desire originated, Jesus responded to it.

Jesus looked past Zacchaeus's worldly identity and called out to him. Jesus then *demanded* to stay with him, drawing closer to someone this world rejected. Predictably, those who saw their exchange were angry because they could not see past Zacchaeus's social status and sin. They could not understand why Jesus would spend time with a man who, in their estimation, did not deserve love.

So that we don't make the same mistake when looking at the despised around us, I believe it is critical for us to observe how Christ's *imago Dei*-fueled love radically transformed Zacchaeus. Even as the crowd grumbled, Zacchaeus repented and promised to make restitution for his past sin. In a world that constantly bombards us with accusations of our failures, our lack of worth, our disqualification for their love, God's image-bearing love endures because it is *who we are.* Christ saw Zacchaeus as a reflection of his own glory, buried under the brokenness of sin. Indeed, at the end of the story, Christ restated his mission that he had come "to seek and to save the lost."

What might seeking the lost look like in our setting? Pastor Dave Gipson offers us a modern-day example through what he calls his "coffee cup communion." Gipson regularly heads to a local coffee shop, where he orders a latte and invites anyone interested to sit down with him to discuss personal matters, relationships, careers, or religion. He began this practice while leading a church in Naples, Florida; he now is the pastor at Tower Grove Church in St. Louis.

Gipson believes it is important for Christians to be a present witness in the world. Recognizing that many people are unwilling to go to church, he began stopping at a Naples Starbucks each week to sip coffee and discuss his faith in Christ with strangers several years ago. Although no topic was off-limits, he did not try to recruit people to his church.

Gipson discovered that people felt free to join him in Starbucks's open courtyard. It was a relaxed atmosphere that didn't make people feel trapped and allowed them to leave whenever they wanted. He answered questions on the love of God, why God allows suffering, and many other topics. Some people even waited so they could talk with him privately. Gipson used this as an opportunity to meet people where they were and to engage relationally with those who may or may not have known Christ personally. Ultimately, he wanted to be a witness to Christ's love.[20]

We live in a world of lost, broken, and hurting image bearers. In our current age of outrage, interactions are usually informed by preexisting political, cultural, and religious identities. As a result, we must be intentional about transcending these divisions and treating others with the inherent dignity they deserve. How does a love fueled by the recognition of God's image in all of us contrast to both worldly and religious love?

Imago Dei *love in contrast*

Much of the outrage that defines our world today arises from failed conceptions of love that lead to deeper levels of anger, division, and loneliness. Yet just as the moon's brilliance is accentuated by the surrounding darkness, so the superiority of image-bearing love is evident when we compare it to two of the more common deficient definitions of love.

> *Worldly love (licentiousness)* seeks to endorse or embrace everything. It begins from the false dichotomy that we either accept without question people's beliefs and behavior (unless it is obviously destructive to someone else) or we are unloving. As a result, we cannot address underlying sin or rebellion. Thus, love is set as opposite to judgment.

> *Religious love (legalism)* is based on the merit of others. Our love is conditional on their proper behavior. This

type of love is far more common in Christian circles than worldly love but is equally problematic. We preach judgment and then claim that we have been "loving" because we have confronted others with their sin. We pat ourselves on the back for how our love has perhaps spared them eternity in hell. Thus love is set as opposite to apathy.

In contrast, Christians need to begin from the premise that all people are made in the image of God and thereby entitled to dignity. We are neither blind to sin (in others or ourselves), nor do we set conditions on our love. Calvin summed up this form of love like this:

> Love of neighbor is not dependent upon manner of men but looks to God. . . . The Lord commands all men without exception "to do good." . . . Yet the great part of them are most unworthy if they be judged by their own merit. But here Scripture helps in the best way when it teaches that we are not to consider that men merit of themselves but to look upon the image of God in all men, to which *we owe all honor and love*. . . . Therefore, whatever man you meet who needs your aid, you have no reason to refuse to help him.[21]

Christians do not need to sacrifice a winsome love for the lost in order to maintain an orthodox theology of sin. Even when we recognize the sinfulness of others, our love must be motivated by the truth that all image bearers are worthy of our care. When Christians love others in an age of outrage, we also are loving the God to whom we *do* owe everything. This is radical in a world dominated by worldly or religious love, both of which inevitably lead to outrage.

In his well-known sermon "Charity and Its Fruits," Jonathan Edwards emphasizes that the indwelling of the Holy Spirit should fundamentally change the way a person thinks, acts, and relates to the world. At the center of this theology was Edwards's belief that "he that loves God, will be disposed thankfully to acknowledge his kindness." Furthermore, our love of God and man are intertwined: "A true love to God, tends to love men, who bear the image of God; and a spirit of love and peace toward men, cherishes a spirit of love to God, as love to the image cherishes love to the original."[22] Edwards recognized that we cannot claim to love God and hate those who bear his image just as we cannot claim to love people and fail to recognize the God who made them.

In our age of outrage, love that is not contingent upon someone's community, behavior, or appearance is powerfully attractive. This love, which is rooted in our shared creation, is more potent than the world's permissive love and more liberating than religion's judgmental love.

I want to be known as a Christian who shares the love of Jesus with a hurting, broken, and lost world. That means that I will share the gospel with people who are like me and, more important, with those who are not.

Winsome love shifts from disgust to empathy, from pride to humility, and then from outrage to an *imago Dei* love. Christians are at their best when they acknowledge the world's depravity but never forget the inherent value and dignity of every human, which gives them the ability to make their own decisions. This empathetic, humble, and *imago Dei*-fueled shift leads to the final element of winsome love: sacrifice.

Sacrifice: The Loving Alternative to Silence

In the age of outrage, we must recognize how our past speech and actions have damaged our witness before we can move forward. For that reason, any discussion of winsome Christian love must highlight hostile and selfish behavior.

As believers watch their cultural authority wane, we face two common temptations. The first is to speak with caustic voices that preach hostility and division for the sake of defending a cultural Christianity that, at best, outlived its expiration date a decade ago. This reaction sadly buys into the "go to battle" mentality that became the rallying cry for the children of the nineties' culture wars. The underlying idea was that Christians had to defend their cultural authority or we would lose everything.

While these shrill voices get the most attention, I believe the far more common reaction among Christians facing significant cultural upheaval is simply to fall silent. Unsure of the correct path forward and wary of the ferocity of an Internet mob set loose upon even the most innocent mistakes, Christians hit the disengage button.

Not only does fear tempt many into silence, but the pace at which culture has been changing produces similar impulses to pull back. In some ways, this cultural change is good. Progress in racial reconciliation and gender inequality particularly have made headway in the church and given a voice to previously marginalized communities. Even in areas where there has been sharp disagreement, as with the LGBTQ community, the church has been forced to think deeply about our theology and ministry in ways that we have previously ignored.

We must grasp that love may prove winsome just as equally when we engage as when we refrain from speaking out. We Christians can be just as unloving, if not more so, by our silence and neglect of suffering and injustice as when we react with overt hostility toward those with whom we disagree. And while our active participation in this world's outrage tends to garner the headlines, what we don't do can lead to the most lasting damage to our witness and mission. In fact, the flip side of prideful engagement is the lack of courage to speak out for the gospel.

If we want to show love to those we are trying to reach, we cannot afford to stay silent. In this respect, the early church father Justin Martyr is instructive. In his *Dialogue with Trypho*, Justin warned: "We know full well that whoever can speak out the truth and fails to do so shall be condemned by God."[23] Evangelism and our public witness demand loving interaction, not passive withdrawal.

In this respect, Scripture calls us to speak out in two respects:

Sacrificially: "Open your mouth for the mute, for the rights of all who are destitute. Open your mouth, judge righteously, defend the rights of the poor and needy" (Proverbs 31:8-9). Competing self-interests fuel much of the world's outrage, so sacrificial love is a radical departure from the status quo. Shifting the focus away from *our* rights, *our* wants, *our* desires, and *our* needs, sacrificial love submits our platform and credibility to the needs of others as we follow up to our claims to love with real action.

Lovingly: "Speaking the truth in love, we are to grow up in every way into him who is the head, into Christ. . . . Having put away falsehood, let each one of you speak the truth with his neighbor, for we are members one of another" (Ephesians 4:15, 25). Scripture supplies the *why* and *how* in the way we are to speak to others. Speaking the truth in love requires that we speak out rather than being silent. Yet our speech is *always to be informed* by kindness and charity, recognizing that the endgame as ambassadors of the gospel is the reconciliation of people with God.

In this respect, winsome love is sacrificial in its actions and intents. It stands up to injustice, unrighteousness, and oppression regardless of the personal or professional costs to us. I would argue that sacrifice is the most difficult facet of winsome love. Silence is often a tempting alternative to engagement in this age, when the slightest misstep can unleash a disproportionate quality and quantity of outrage. But when we choose sacrificial love, we move from nice words to concrete actions. Sometimes, as we will see, such love requires that we pay a heavy price.

The outrage of silence and fear

On February 1, 1933 (just two days after Hitler came to power), a twenty-six-year-old German pastor delivered what was one of the first open criticisms of the Nazi leader. In "The Younger Generation's Altered View of the Concept of the Führer," the intellectual and spiritual giant Dietrich Bonhoeffer warned against the dangers he saw both in Hitler and his followers. In a dark foreboding of what was to come, Bonhoeffer's feed was cut midway through the broadcast, resulting in dead air over the radio. Undeterred, Bonhoeffer expanded the initial address into a lecture he gave at the Technical University of Berlin.[24]

Not yet known for his theological work on discipleship, Bonhoeffer's addresses were merely the opening salvos in a life dedicated to courageously speaking theological truth to the violent and oppressive powers. It was ultimately this steadfast commitment to translate his love into words that led him to be fired from his seminary, imprisoned, and ultimately executed. During his ministry, Bonhoeffer's theology gradually shifted from a view that the church was "against the world" to one that emphasized the church's "responsibility" to the world. Responsibility in Bonhoeffer's writing therefore means "I *simultaneously* represent Christ before human beings, and represent human beings before Christ."[25] According to Bonhoeffer, it is the responsibility of the believer to bring Jesus Christ to the world: "In Christ, we are offered the possibility of partaking in the reality of God and in the reality of the world, but not in the one without the other."[26]

Bonhoeffer reminds us that we cannot cloister ourselves away from the outrage of this world and believe that we are still living out the mission and purpose of the church. The mentality of "just me and Jesus" or even "just me and the church" profoundly misunderstands the Christian faith. If we try to engage God without dealing with the reality of injustice and sin of this world, we will quickly find our faith is half-baked.

Sacrifice means loving when it is not easy

Perhaps the most revered nonpresidential speech in American history is Martin Luther King Jr.'s "I Have a Dream." At a crucial crossroads in the civil rights movement, King delivered an address that masterfully criticized the perpetuation of an unjust status quo and cast a compelling vision of a future where these wrongs had been corrected. In a style that is often emulated but never replicated, King wedded his prophetic dissatisfaction to his spiritual and eschatological hope. Its legacy continues, not because we have achieved King's vision, but because it remains a perpetual calling to what King saw as possible.

It's intriguing to compare King's popularity in American culture and consciousness today with public opinion during his lifetime. A series of polls tracking King's favorability in the final years of his life showed his popularity steadily declining. In the final poll, conducted in 1966, King's total favorability had shrunk to merely 33 percent with only 12 percent holding a highly favorable view. When Pew reissued the poll in 2011, King's total favorability reached the nearly unheard of 94 percent, with 69 percent professing a highly favorable view of him.[27] Indeed, King ranks alongside Washington and Lincoln as one of the most popular figures in American history.

Historians and theologians debate what King's popularity means about race reconciliation in American culture, but I find it interesting in relation to the church. The disparity between his favorability ratings is instructive to us as we consider sacrificial love. Imagine a frustrated King, planning speeches in hotel rooms as he traveled across the country, warding off death threats, and all the while becoming less popular in America. Imagine how reassuring it would have been if he'd had the current levels of admiration and support when he delivered "I Have a Dream" in 1963. Or earlier that same year when he penned his "Letter from

Birmingham Jail." Undoubtedly, King would have appreciated a 94 percent approval rating when he lobbied on behalf of the 1964 Civil Rights Act.

The reality is that a winsome, sacrificial love not only demands that Christians speak up, but by definition, that we do so when it costs us something, even everything. Even when it is unpopular. Quoting Dr. King in 2018 is good, helpful, and insightful, yet it is hardly the same thing as standing with him in 1963. His principles have not changed, but the climate in which we quote him has. We look back on those who publicly stood up for the civil rights movement during this period with respect and admiration, precisely because of their sacrifice. If we want to emulate that kind of love, it goes beyond merely quoting them in the safety of historical retrospect but to speaking out on the same issues, which often remain unpopular today.

In this sense, we are to be watchmen like Ezekiel.[28] The prophet's listeners knew that the watchman signified a lookout or guard on sentry duty who was placed strategically on the walls of the city. Other prophets used this image as well. Isaiah 56:10 refers to sentries who had fallen asleep or gone blind to explain why Israel had fallen into moral failure. Jeremiah 6:17 talks about how God had set up sentries to warn Israel, but the people had fallen asleep and ignored their alarms.

Although the term most frequently applies to religious leaders, the connotation was that all of God's people were to sound the alarm against sin encroaching into the camp. Certainly, pastors today hold a burden of responsibility over the flock to protect them from sin (Acts 20:18-31; James 3:1). However, this does not absolve the congregation from keeping watch over their homes, churches, and communities to prevent sin from infiltrating their thinking. Dr. King was this kind of watchman for the American people, and we are called to follow his example. We have a spiritual obligation to speak truth in love, regardless of the cost and especially when it requires sacrifice.

Back to Bonhoeffer. Writing from jail, the German theologian and pastor cautioned against the temptation to stay silent, even when the forces of outrage and violence were great. He wrote,

> We have been silent witnesses of evil deeds. We have become cunning and learned the arts of obfuscation and equivocal speech. Experience rendered us suspicious of human beings, and often we have failed to speak to them a true and open word. Unbearable conflicts have worn us down or even made us cynical. Are we still of any use?[29]

How are we loving when we are silent on injustice? What good are our claims to love when we shrink back when the voices get too loud or caustic or personal? There will always be good excuses and proof texts to justify a shrug of the shoulders, but we must fight passivity and look to the God who took action on our behalf.

Winsome love moves away from disgust, pride, and outrage to empathy, humility, and *imago Dei* love. These shifts then inform a sacrificial love that is not silent in the face of conflict or struggle. Instead, we engage our culture with compassion for our fellow man and a self-aware acknowledgment of our own need for mercy and grace.

When our love is like this, we will find that the Beatles were right. All we need is love.

CHAPTER 10

Online Activity Aligned with Gospel Mission

- Evangelicals largely reflect culture in the choice of social media platforms they use, with the top four being Facebook (77 percent), YouTube (46 percent), Instagram (28 percent), and Twitter (22 percent).

- Evangelicals cite a higher willingness than non-evangelicals to engage on social or political issues on social media on a *daily basis* (24 percent to 15 percent). Over a third of evangelicals (38 percent) engage on social and political issues through social media at least several times a week.

HIGH SCHOOL ENGLISH, I've decided, is just an exercise in reading classic books that you won't fully understand until you're older. *The Catcher in the Rye, 1984, Lord of the Flies . . .*

I remember reading each of them and thinking, *What in the world is this guy talking about?* (Don't even get me started on Shakespeare.) For those who were born before the advent of Google, the greatest challenge of English class was trying to sound as if you had some clue what was going on. Over time I circled back to a few like *To Kill a Mockingbird* and appreciated their insights, but even now if someone mentions *Catch-22*, I feel as if I might begin to have a panic attack.

One book I do remember clearly, however, is Mary Shelley's *Frankenstein.* The book is a fascinating glimpse into human nature, the relationship between creator and creature, and questions about what it means to fit into society. For teenagers confronted with these issues in their own lives, Shelley's work is essential reading.

Although Frankenstein is an intelligent and articulate creature, he is never accepted, so he lives a tormented life. In the closing scene of the famous 1931 film adaptation, the story concludes in the small town where Frankenstein lived. After the monster murders a professor and a young girl, the villagers form into a mob and finally hunt down and surround him in a windmill. Armed with torches and pitchforks, they eventually set fire to the windmill and kill the monster.

While we may not arm ourselves with pitchforks and torches, I believe that technology has increased our propensity to adopt a mob mentality. At nearly the speed of light and across unthinkable distance, we can connect with others who are similarly outraged. Our offense stokes people's indignation and echoes their anger and outrage, drawing more and more heat. Those who are likewise offended unleash their anger, and those who are unsure or wary often go along with the crowd, either because they are fearful of having it turn on them or simply because they're drawn to the excitement. (After all, who doesn't like a good mob?)

Congressmen, Fortune 500 companies, professors, and pastors have learned the power of the Internet mob. Smart leaders never underestimate the power of a small spark to ignite an army of torches and take great pains to stay on the right side of one when it catches fire. As destructive and self-defeating as this reaction is, we often feel powerless to stop it.

As Martin Marty argues in *The Protestant Voice in American Pluralism,* "We are a society in which everything is permitted, and nothing is forgiven."[1] In other words, our world constantly preaches that you can do or be anything you want until it is offended at what you are doing or what you are. Then a switch flips, a mob forms, and the pitchforks are unleashed. Holiness is replaced by autonomy and justice by rage.

In the midst of this environment, Scripture calls us to be people of the towel rather than people of the pitchfork. Jesus modeled this for us when he washed his disciples' feet (John 13:1-17) without exception or expectation. This was not a simple object lesson but an example of perfect service that reflected Jesus' humility when he came to earth (Philippians 2:1-11). Jesus then asked his disciples to imitate him in washing one another's feet. People of the towel grasp that Jesus wants us to humbly and lovingly serve others in every human interaction. Perhaps there is no place that is more important in our day than in digital conversations.

With that in mind, this chapter explores how Christians can engage online and through technology in the age of outrage without provoking pitchforks. First, I want to highlight common ways the world tries to solve the problem, all of which prove ineffectual or, worse yet, actually exacerbate the problem. Second, I will address the technological discipleship gap by offering a few concrete principles for online behavior that all Christians should consider. Third, I will focus on leadership principles that ministry and church leaders need to consider as their organizations use technology and build an online presence. Finally, I will outline a few characteristics Christians should look for in leaders and influencers they follow on social media.

Just as our worldview, mission, and love all need to be oriented to a posture of humility and service, it is time that we submit our digital behavior to the same standard.

Digital Don'ts

Hollow advocacy

In April 2017, *Saturday Night Live* aired a sketch featuring a mock music video that celebrated the armchair activism of a man. Entitled "Thank You Scott," the song detailed all of the problems in the world and then thanked Scott for making a great contribution by sharing an article on Facebook. The song mockingly states that after sharing the post, "Everything changed." There was peace, prosperity, and reconciliation for all the world because of his social media activism.[2]

The sketch perfectly skewered the way people today often confuse participating in an event with contributing to a solution.

In previous eras, people showed up at rallies, protests, and conferences. They were actively contributing to a cause or a movement. Today we often think our posts, tweets, or comments are changing things, but despite our perception that we are offering our service and support, we are doing so without the sacrifice. Have you ever noticed that after every major disaster, we tweet, we change our profile picture, and we post blogs or open letters? This leaves us with the sense that we are helping, that we are participating by increasing awareness of a need. We are content with the perception of service, support, and activism without the sacrifice.

Showing up digitally may signal our agreement with a cause or support for a group of people, but it simply does not have the same force as getting involved.

Let's imagine how Jesus' parable of the Good Samaritan, recorded in Luke 10, might play out in this culture.

A Christian comes upon a severely injured man on the side of the road. Shocked at the man's condition, he knows he needs to do something to help, so he reaches for his phone. He snaps a quick selfie of himself with a very serious expression; the other man lies in the background. Posting the photo to his Facebook page, the Christian comments: "I can't believe people would do this. Prayers and thoughts." He clicks Send and then walks along, leaving the man on the side of the road.

I am not demeaning the importance of prayer. Often this is all we can do about major events far away. However, let's not confuse posturing with actually doing something. This is not what it means to be a neighbor; a neighbor serves sacrificially. Notice that the Samaritan spent his time (he got into the ditch with the man), spent his energy (he bound up his wounds), and spent his resources (he poured oil and wine on the man's injuries and spent two denarii at the inn) to ensure the man would receive the help he needed. Contrasting this man's generosity to the religious leaders who passed by the injured man with barely a glance, Jesus said, "You go, and do likewise" (Luke 10:37).

Set this kind of serving against the example of Ananias and Sapphira in Acts 5:1-11. After selling a piece of property, they gave some of the proceeds to the apostles. The problem was, Ananias told them he was contributing the full amount from the sale. He and Sapphira wanted the appearance of generous giving without the sacrifice. Peter said that such actions were attempts to "test the Spirit of the Lord" (verse 9). In his sermon on the passage, the church father John Chrysostom reflected on why God responded so harshly to their deception. He wrote, "The matter was not one to be simply passed over: like a gangrene, it must be cut out, that it might not infect the rest of the body."[3] Hollow service begets hollow service. When the world praises fake service, it engenders more by providing the benefits of giving without the actual gift! Such giving reveals that what we are *really* after is the praise. It is about us. Not so in the Kingdom of God.

Although what has popularly been termed *hashtag activism* can be a powerful tool in bringing injustices to light or in uniting people around a cause, it most often stops at the water's edge of actual engagement. Why? Because it is quick, easy, and costs little. It embraces the distance between us and the people we are trying to serve rather than closing the gap.

More important, while these causes burn brightly at first, they tend to burn out. They feed the outrage because, even when begun for a good cause, it's a guessing game as to whether each wave of online activism will lead to change or simply flame out. For every #MeToo movement, there are hundreds of campaigns like Kony 2012 that generate a lot of "awareness" but don't address the problem. Don't get me wrong; raising awareness is good. The fight against human trafficking fails to get the attention it deserves. The trouble is that when every cause vies for awareness, other causes must ratchet up the volume of their own campaigns so they will be heard above the din.

Christians need to recognize that online activism is not true service. It is not Kingdom building.

Anonymous trolling

In general, my response to anonymous commenters is fairly simple: If you have something you need to say on social media; if the Holy Spirit will not allow your conscience to have peace until you have confronted some injustice or sin; if you are convinced it is time to speak truth to power–then I believe as a Christian, you have an obligation to sign your name.

The Christian life is filled with demanding sacrifice, and church history is replete with believers who have lost more than their reputation or job to speak out on injustice and evil. There is no mechanism in Scripture for those who want the fruit of discipline without the hard work of relationally engaging one another. If you believe your elders, your pastors, your employers, or your colleagues are sinning, then the answer is not an anonymous blog or Twitter account. I get that anonymity may be needed in rare instances, but in general, God does not deal in anonymous sniping on social media.

The model for conflict in Scripture is to engage with openness, humility, grace, and directness. When we hide behind faceless avatars or create anonymous blogs by which we lob projectiles at church leaders or those on the other side of social issues, we forfeit any righteousness in our criticism. We have used the tools of the world to try to bring about holiness. Scripture is not fond of that. In Isaiah 31, the prophet condemns those in Israel who sought help from Egypt rather than relying on God's provision.

At its core, anonymity wants the benefits of engagement without the responsibility.

Overplaying Matthew 18

On the flip side of anonymous trolls who try to challenge authority and confront wrongs anonymously are Christians who think that no one should say anything remotely negative. Ever. Whenever I publish an article that criticizes someone's behavior or theology, one of the first responses I receive always seems to come from a well-intentioned Christian asking if I followed Matthew 18 before making my criticisms public. While I am sure some make this comment from a good place, more often than not, this is the response from conflict-averse Christians using a flawed understanding of Scripture to avoid conflict. In more devious instances, Christians use it to silence criticisms they can't adequately address.

In an editorial for *Themelios*, D. A. Carson explained how the accusation of violating Matthew 18 usually plays out:

> This sort of charge is becoming more common. It is regularly linked to the "Gotcha!" mentality that many bloggers and their respondents seem to foster. Person A writes a book criticizing some element or other of historic Christian confessionalism. A few bloggers respond with more heat than light. Person B writes a blog with some substance, responding to Person A. The blogosphere lights up with attacks on Person B, many of them asking Person B rather accusingly, "Did you communicate with Person A in private first? If not, aren't you guilty of violating what Jesus taught us in Matthew 18?" This pattern of counter-attack, with minor variations, is flourishing.[4]

Carson wrote these words in 2011, but I think this problem has deepened as social media use has become more prevalent. Suddenly it's not just bloggers and theologians debating; everyone is getting in on the "gotcha" mentality.

In this article, Carson outlined several reasons why this is a problematic reading of Matthew 18. I think the most crucial is that Jesus was providing direction on how a local community of believers should deal with private sin that has the potential to spill over and hurt other people. This may initially seem like an unimportant distinction, but think about all that comes with being in a local body together. The elders and pastors have authority to mediate a problem within their church.

More important, if we treat all criticism in the same way, we ignore the history of careful theological criticism and debate in the church. Christians have long recognized the importance of Scripture's exhortation to confront and refute those who teach false doctrine or those whose lives contradict and defame the gospel (Titus 1:9). If such a person is in the local body where I am a leader, I will always approach him or her first and try to disciple the individual toward better theology and practice.

Principles of Digital Discipleship

Today's digital technology and the networks it has created present the church with considerable opportunity for advancing the gospel. Instant communication, previously only dreamed of in bad science fiction, is now commonplace. Churches often unwittingly feed the addiction as they rush to adopt technological innovations they hope will draw in new members, effectively engage those currently attending, and expand gospel ministry. Even when technological innovations are necessary, they are rarely, if ever, coupled with accompanying discipleship on proper use.

Every week I am able to equip ministry leaders through my online leadership seminars, collaborate with others on writing projects, and send out massive amounts of content to every corner of the globe where once the challenge of ministering to remote communities was their intense isolation. In addition, the freedom and accessibility of these digital platforms have elevated voices within the church that had been marginalized or ignored in previous generations.

While we often like to point out the flaws of the Internet, we cannot lose sight of the fact that we live in a golden age for producing and sharing ministry information. The key point is that technology is neither good nor bad inherently. It is a tool that God has provided, and one that is becoming more powerful with each generation. It can facilitate the work of the gospel: aiding church plants, getting help to the needy, encouraging the downtrodden, and equipping the saints for ministry. It can also, as the story of the tower of Babel illustrates, be a source of pride that tempts us to place our trust in human ingenuity.[5]

Remember that everyone is watching

The odd thing about an online presence is that communication can feel quite intimate though it is a historically public act. Even when only two people are engaging, on some platforms their conversation is broadcast to anyone who wants to look online. So what feels like two people chatting in a secluded corner of a room can actually be more like a conversation in which multiple people have pulled up chairs to listen. They may not say anything, but they are watching.

Using digital platforms to hash out disagreements is sometimes a good thing. I've had such disagreements with Christian leaders on social media before. This happened recently with Shane Claiborne when I challenged him to be more vocal advocating for life in light of the recent defeat of a bill designed to protect babies after twenty weeks. Claiborne reached out to me on Twitter to give some context on his position, and we had a short but respectful engagement. In the end, we had a better understanding of each other's positions and demonstrated grace for each other.

Something else struck me about that conversation, however. When I looked at the comments, likes, and retweets, I saw just how many people were watching our exchange. In this case, Christians saw two leaders with different positions engage in conflict respectfully.

This is my point: Even when we think we're having a private conversation or posting random thoughts, we need to understand that others are watching our online actions and holding them up against our claims to be Christ followers. We need to see how this is connected to our witness. This also explains

why our never-ending political rants might be the reason our neighbors are a little reticent to grab that cup of coffee;

>   why complaining about the pastor's sermon to friends might
>   be the reason our sister won't come to church with us;
>   why our passive-aggressive subtweeting about our coworkers
>   might be the reason others are guarded around us.

As Christians, we need to see our online lives as very much the public faces we are showing the world. It is often the first glimpse unbelievers have into our lives, and it is an ongoing window into how well we are living out the gospel. The goal isn't to be fake, to keep our messiness off the Internet to fool others into thinking we have it all figured out. The goal is to be sure our online behavior demonstrates the same spiritual maturity with which we live out other areas of our lives.

Choose investment over consumption

One helpful way to frame our social media engagement is by discerning whether we are investing or consuming. In many cases, we are spending too much time following others unwisely. We follow old friends, celebrities, and media platforms because we don't want to be left out or because we crave mindless entertainment. If we were honest, nothing they have done or said has proven useful to our spiritual development. In such cases, we are not investing but consuming.

Challenge yourself to consider what you are getting out of each person who influences you through social media. Are you following people with whom you engage regularly or family and friends who live far away but with whom you want to stay connected? In these cases, you are investing in meaningful real-world connections. Are you tracking leaders who teach you about God, his Word, or how to engage with world events from a gospel worldview? In these cases, you are investing in your walk with Christ by seeking out wisdom. Are you following people from outside your tradition or community who challenge you to consider your blind spots? In these cases, you are investing in your ability to understand and engage others.

See people, not avatars

In *Alone Together*, Massachusetts Institute of Technology professor Sherry Turkle warns, "We build technologies that leave us vulnerable in new ways." She notes that for social media there is a disconnect between us and the people we engage with that often leads to dangerous behavior. While social media often leads to positive interactions, it also opens us up to cruelty: "By detaching words from the person uttering them, it can encourage a coarsening of response. Ever since e-mail first became popular, people have complained about online 'flaming.' People say outrageous things, even when they are not anonymous."[6]

We have already touched on the importance of seeing others as lost image bearers to whom God has called us to show and share the love of Jesus without reservation or fear. We cannot allow the distance and isolation of the digital world to obscure the fact that the person on the other side of those comments is real. When the physical person is not in front of us and when we are able to disengage at the click of a button, we can be tempted not to see others as fellow human beings. They are names on a page, pictures in the corner of a profile page, or sparring partners in a disembodied debate. We don't see them as fellow human beings. Technology is even shaping how we interact with real people in real time.

And this is dangerous for Christians because we represent Christ to the world. When we engage others online, there is a real temptation to no longer see people but only their online avatars. We don't see Marcus or Cassandra, we see "Pro-Choice Advocate X" or "Religious Liberty Defender Y." We see the debate rather than the person. This is dehumanizing, and dehumanization is the work of the enemy of God, not of the lover of Jesus.

I recently spoke at a March for Life event, where I called on Christians to care for the unborn and the born, for those with whom we agree and those with whom we disagree. After speaking, I walked around the crowd. It was filled with young and old people, all of whom were enthusiastic about standing in the fifteen-degree

Chicago cold. But then I walked over to the counter protesters and saw something different.

On one side of the street, pro-choice protesters screamed against those on the other side, waving signs saying that pro-lifers just want women to be breeders. And they had no room to think that pro-life people might simply want our society to value life from conception to natural death.

But it wasn't just the pro-choicers who were angry. Right across the street, on the edge of the crowd I had just spoken to, was a man with a loudspeaker I wished was not there. He yelled. His voice was filled with hate as he said that the pro-choice group were all going to hell unless they repented—"and I tell you this because I love you." I imagine that he would have little to say to the pro-choice crowd that did not involve a megaphone.

Don't get me wrong. I fully believe there's a hell, and I agree that refraining from testifying to it is possibly one of the most unloving things a Christian can do. But there is a difference between preaching, teaching, or engaging others over the reality of hell and yelling about it into a megaphone at a group of strangers across the street.

Yet too much of our engagement as believers looks exactly like that. We scream correct doctrine at others across gaps in digital or real space, believing we are loving. We have to grasp that this tactic inherently prioritizes the debate over the person. Any nuance as to why or how we hold our position is lost, and our overall mission of proclaiming the gospel is transformed into a high school debate forum. It reduces the objective of all disagreement to winning, preventing any listening and engendering a spirit of win-at-all-costs as if the future of the gospel depended upon it.

In reality, most disagreements do not, and should not be expected to, change minds. Rather, expressing differences of opinion broadens our understanding of the issues, drawing our attention to perspectives that we had not, or could not have, considered on our own.

Make grace the default mode

So somebody made a comment that strikes you as offensive. Maybe they voiced an opinion that seemed ignorant or they supported a political candidate you find repulsive if not outright un-Christian. Your first instinct is to tell them that their words were hurtful, that they have hurt their witness, or that they've messed up. There are certainly times when people say outright wrong, offensive, and even blasphemous things that need to be called out. In the last chapter I touched on how even our silence can sometimes produce outrage when we are unwilling to stand up for those who have been hurt. The problem is, many times people don't have the nefarious and sinful motivations that we ascribe to them. Yet when we crank up the outrage right from the start, others tend to get their backs up and entrench themselves even deeper.

In these circumstances, remember that in Christ *we* have received grace upon grace (John 1:16). That even "if we are faithless, he remains faithful" (2 Timothy 2:13). In other words, grace needs to be the starting point for how we engage others.

In December 2017, comedian Sarah Silverman was the victim of an awful verbal attack on social media. Famous for her own often-offensive jokes, Silverman unexpectedly encountered a Twitter user's profanity, which was directed at her. Now I have received some awful comments on social media, but nothing compared to Silverman's experience. Even so, when I come across a hateful comment, my instinct is to either immediately block or ignore it. Other social media users will lash back, sometimes equaling the vitriol and outrage with their own. Silverman, on the other hand, responded with astonishing grace and compassion, asking the man why he had lashed out. She was able to build a bridge that culminated in her encouraging the man to find therapy and even asking her followers to help fund it. Faced with this grace, the man apologized for his profanity and agreed to go for help.[7]

Silverman's response demonstrates the countercultural power of graciousness to break through people's fury. While Silverman doesn't call herself a believer, the graciousness of her response puts to shame the multitude of believers who have experienced the "grace upon grace" of Christ. Though I would never endorse Silverman's worldview or comedy, it is important to recognize the power in her response to even the vilest of attacks.

Resist the urge to fight every battle

Connected with the willingness to extend grace in every situation is the importance of recognizing the need to pick your battles. When we're confronted with outrage, walking away is sometimes the right response, while at other times we have to be ready to engage.

Confused? I bet. But Scripture holds this tension and therefore so do we. Proverbs 26:4-5 says,

> Answer not a fool according to his folly,
> lest you be like him yourself.
> Answer a fool according to his folly,
> lest he be wise in his own eyes.

This is perhaps the best way to sum up the way Christians should approach the Internet. Sometimes we need to engage, and at other times we need to walk away or be silent. A mature Christian recognizes that correcting every wrong on the Internet would take more hours than a full-time job. If you snap every time your great-aunt's friend's cousin thrice-removed makes a snarky comment about "all the contradictions in the Bible," it will consume you and your joy. Consider 1 Corinthians 10:23-24 (NLT): "You say, 'I am allowed to do anything'–but not everything is good for you. You say, 'I am allowed to do anything'–but not everything is beneficial. Don't be concerned for your own good but for the good of others."

We can think about our social media comments the way Paul outlines it. We may have the freedom to engage, but before doing so, we should ask whether it is truly for the good of the church and for those to whom we are witnessing.

Sometimes the hardest thing is knowing when to walk away

from a fight. In these times, my mind starts playing that great American poet Kenny Rogers: "You got to know when to hold 'em. Know when to fold 'em. Know when to walk away. Know when to run."[8] While folksy, the song is on target in the sense that the true test of a poker player is knowing when to stop. Likewise, as social media users, once we've started interacting with other users, it becomes increasingly difficult to simply walk away in love. This is what is often termed *the sunk cost effect*. This is the idea that we are far more likely to keep doing something once we've invested time, energy, or money into it. Christians need to be able to pick their fights wisely and then have the wisdom to recognize when the results aren't going in the right direction. If someone is just looking to pick fights and hurl insults rather than engaging with us, we need to learn to say "God bless you" and walk away.

Here's the thing about social media. Getting into a fight with argumentative people online is like wrestling a pig. You both get dirty, but only pigs like mud.

Value authority over freedom

One thing I love about social media and the Internet is how they have given a voice to people who have been left behind or shut out in the past. But the freedom and liberty preached by the digital world can sometimes make it seem as if it is okay to subvert and disrespect the authorities God has placed in our lives. The danger is that this emphasis upon freedom can blind Christians to their responsibility to respect and honor those whom God has placed in authority over them. Just as Paul exhorts the Thessalonians to "appreciate those who diligently labor among you, and have charge over you in the Lord" (1 Thessalonians 5:12, NASB), Christians need to be sure their online behavior honors their leaders.

Just because we *can* say something doesn't mean we *should*. There are ways of confronting abuses of power, and I am certainly not condoning a mindless obedience. But Christians need to understand that the best place for difficult conversations is usually not online.

Developing Digital Leadership

Over the last decade, we have seen the Internet and technology go from being a curiosity to almost a necessity for churches and ministries. As the Internet has become the first point of contact for so many people, a church without a website is like a church with no sign in front of it. At the same time, leaders have begun to wake up to the importance of social media as a way to engage their people as well as their surrounding communities. People gather on social media to debate, discuss, and share ideas. Social media is the new "town square"–the public space where our local community gathers for social and commercial purposes. Just as the apostle Paul would preach in the town squares, so today we should use our social media "town squares" to engage our community and share the gospel.

It is important that Christians have a voice in the social conversation. According to Pew's Social Media Update 2014, of all adults who are online, 87 percent of those who are eighteen to twenty-nine are on Facebook, as are 73 percent of those who are thirty to forty-nine, 63 percent of those aged fifty to sixty-four, and 56 percent of adults who are sixty-five and older.[9] This is clearly a significant percentage of our population, and we ought to utilize Facebook and other sites to share the gospel. However, it is essential to remember that we must use social media to build real relationships and then embody what we claim on social media with our actions in real life.[10]

We should affirm pastors and church leaders who use social media to connect with others constructively. The space pastors and church leaders occupy is a little different from the space most people occupy on social media, because we often use Facebook, Twitter, and other social media to connect with other pastors whom we're trying to equip and help, as well as church leaders whom we're trying to serve. If you are the pastor of a local church, it is good for you to be known as caring about the community, and social media is one way you can show that. If you are a member of a church congregation, it is good for you to show that members of your Christian community care about the larger community as well.

Now that the majority of people use social media, there is not much point in resisting or avoiding it altogether, especially since it is a well-established and useful tool. However, many people tend to reduce their interpersonal relationships as social media has increased. Just the opposite should be the case. Social media should lead us to *increase* our interpersonal relationships, not decrease them.

As leaders think through how to incorporate technology and an online presence into their ministries, I offer five general principles that I think are a useful starting point.

1. **Don't be afraid to innovate.** Christians have a long history of being innovative in how they engage the world for the gospel. To be sure, many have pulled back from technology, fearful of the way that it might hinder or corrupt the message of the gospel. However, many heroes of the faith accomplished significant work for the Kingdom because they sought out innovative ways to bring the gospel to people. From the printing press to newspapers, radio, and TV, Christians have been some of the earliest adopters of new technology, leveraging its power for Kingdom purposes. To compete with other voices in the world, Christians need to think proactively about technology rather than merely react to it.

   I love hearing stories about churches using technology for the work of the Kingdom of God. There are youth pastors who host video chats with students the night before major exams to pray and encourage them and then again afterward to exhort them not to define their worth by grades. There are churches in neighborhoods with high immigration and little ESL training that have used online material to teach English. When small groups first gained popularity in the nineties, there was little available curriculum, and much of what did exist was bad. Today powerful material is available online that is reaping gospel fruit across denominations, cultures, and demographics. All of these examples started with churches seeing technology as a way to enhance the drive to show and share the love of Jesus. Rather than becoming slaves to technology, Kingdom-minded creative thinkers have found ways to harness technology for the advancement of the gospel.

2. **In everything, remember the mission.** New technology and digital platforms have a way of tempting pastors and ministry leaders to lose sight of their mission. We can become intensely focused on "building the brand" of ourselves or our ministries, justifying it by saying that our success is Kingdom success.

   The line between self-promotion and leveraging technology in creative and innovative ways can be blurry at times. Rather than setting a list of dos and don'ts, I think leaders need to consider critically how each new digital strategy or platform serves Kingdom purposes. Leaders need to be relentless in asking themselves and each other this question: *How does this new technology advance the mission of our church, ministry, or organization?*

   If the answer cannot be articulated with clarity and honesty, then any innovation needs to be rethought and reformulated. While new technology and online strategies may be exciting and generate buzz, if they are not aligned with the theological and organizational mission of the church or ministry, they will eventually muddy the waters.

3. **Think about building community, not simply outputting material.** A mistake I see leaders fall into far too easily is the emphasis upon putting out content, such as podcasts, online sermons, and curriculum videos. I can understand the reason: Content attracts followers. It makes us believe

we are contributing to the growth of our people and even those outside our churches or organizations who make use of the content.

There is always the temptation to produce videos, upload them to the Internet, and sit back and let others digest the content whenever they want. While this is easy and can create the illusion of Kingdom building, I realized early on that it's not actually Kingdom building. Through our online community and private Facebook group, I take opportunities to engage with those in the program, thinking together through some of the ideas raised and how they can apply them to their specific situations. I field questions and try to spark intercommunication. Why? Because I'm trying to cultivate a community of leaders who work through material together rather than consuming it by themselves.

Local church pastors and leaders need to be particularly wary of the temptation to simply produce and post content that they hope will stick. The ultimate goal is to edify and build up the church, not merely pour out content. If something isn't producing greater godliness and fellowship within your community, you need to reconsider whether that project or platform is really serving the purpose of the church. In a society where Netflix and YouTube have trained us to be consumers first, we need to be wary of promoting a similar mentality within the church. Pastors need to be vigilant in ensuring that their content is provoking engagement and commitment from their people rather than enabling them to check out.

4. **Be intentional.** Just as in all areas of the church, leaders need to have a strategy and a vision for what they are hoping to accomplish. Few things can be as destructive as aimlessly adopting some new project with little thought as to the why or the how. Church leaders can no longer afford to delegate

the church's technology with little thought about what it says about their leadership and vision.

Some churches still have a website that the senior pastor asked an intern to build back in 1998. If you go to their websites, the church name still takes up three-quarters of the screen in Comic Sans font. Scroll down and you'll find a flash of Jesus as the running man that the intern believed was a nice touch. If you think I'm lying or have forgotten what was considered hip over twenty years ago, consider this: Bob Dole's presidential campaign website for the 1996 election is still running.[11] (I won't throw any churches under the bus, but I have no problem leaving Bob out to dry.)

My point is that this kind of apathy results from a lack of intentionality. When leaders are confused by or scared of new technology, they tend to convince themselves and others that it's not important. At its core, this mentality is similar to missionaries who go to a new country and don't bother to learn anything about the culture and habits of the people. Jesus condemns this attitude in Luke 14:28-30, asking what kind of builder does not first sit down and count the cost to see if he has enough to complete a project.

We live in a technological world where more and more of our interactions are moving online. Leaders who want to lead effectively must think intentionally about how they need to compete in the religious marketplace of a post-Christian world. If they don't, they risk being ineffectual in Kingdom work. In other words, they risk being like the man who starts building without counting the cost.

5. **Frame caution around winsome love.** There is a tendency to dismiss people who are cautious or hesitant, particularly in regard to technology, as being stubborn or relics. They resist change because "that's not how we do it." Trust me when I say that the phrase "institutional memory" is enough to put me in a bad mood.

At the same time, while I am a huge proponent of integrating technology into our ministries, I think pastors and ministry leaders need to be careful about how far they are willing to go and to be aware of the potential drawbacks.

Caution that is framed around pastoral love always considers what a shift will do for and to one's people. Leaders need to think through what they are giving up to pursue an opportunity, who will be affected, and what this means for them. When churches embrace new technology, they risk ostracizing members unfamiliar with or anxious about the platform. Without proper care and education, these members may believe that they no longer have a place in the community.

I recommend that ministry leaders ask themselves these five questions when thinking through technology and their online presence:

- Are we innovative?
- Are we intentional?
- Are we missional?
- Are we community building?
- Are we loving?

Find and Follow a Faithful (Online) Presence

While I have outlined many of the destructive effects uncritical online engagement can have on our worldview, I believe there is a powerful opportunity for this tool to be used for effective discipleship. It is not a matter of whether to follow Christian, cultural, or political leaders online, but to be discerning about following and listening to the right ones. Just as we think critically about those whom we let mentor and disciple us in real life, we need to be critical about the voices we allow to speak into our lives online.

Often the most difficult challenge is finding the right voices to follow. As with discipleship, no one size fits all. The body is composed

CHRISTIANS IN THE AGE OF OUTRAGE

of many parts. There is no one list of people that everyone should follow, but everyone should follow those who consistently use their social media to improve others' spiritual walks. In so doing, they are building the Kingdom of God. Let me outline some characteristics I look for when I follow people online.

1. Encouraging and edifying

Encourage one another and build one another up.
1 THESSALONIANS 5:11

Encouragement and edification lie at the heart of a faithful online presence. I'm not referring to people with insanely positive dispositions that ignore injustice and evil in the world, but voices that seek to be constructive rather than wallow in outrage and apathy. They may point out the shortcomings, mistakes, or blind spots of others, but they never leave Christians to sort through the mess alone.

Watch for leaders who leave you with important practical truth you can incorporate into your life. You should be able to point to specific godly habits and patterns of thinking that you have gleaned from their articles and videos, not merely curiosities or interesting information but content that has had real benefits to your spiritual walk.

2. Loving and kind

A new commandment I give to you, that you love one another: just as I have loved you, you also are to love one another. By this all people will know that you are my disciples, if you have love for one another.
JOHN 13:34-35

In addition to signing your name, my other rule for the Internet is, don't be a jackwagon. Just as in real life, there is never a justification to withhold love. The ability of Christians to love others through their online presence is one of the most practical ways to distinguish them from the world; in turn, the absence of such love is one of the most destructive impediments to our witness. Showing grace doesn't mean that Christians must be doormats; it doesn't mean we don't call out injustice and sin, and it doesn't mean we slap on a veneer of fake positivity. It begins from the premise that Christ died for us while we were still sinners because of his great love for us (Ephesians 2:4-7). We must demonstrate that same love to others, even if they get on our nerves or hold views with which we disagree.

3. Missional and engaging

> Jesus said to them, "Peace be with you. As the Father has sent me, so I am sending you."
> JOHN 20:21

Christianity is not an insular religion, no matter how much we may want it to be. Being encouraging and loving is essential, but it cannot be the entirety of our digital presence. Look for Christian leaders whose articles, blogs, and social media are not afraid to engage the world with the gospel. The answer to outrage cannot be to run away and hide, but to learn how to bring the gospel with patience and love to every person and situation we encounter in life and online. Find leaders who are able to engage others and evaluate situations with the gospel in mind.

4. Charitable and forbearing

> Put on then, as God's chosen ones, holy and beloved, compassionate hearts, kindness, humility, meekness, and patience, bearing with one another and, if one has a complaint against another, forgiving each other; as the Lord has forgiven you, so you also must forgive.
> COLOSSIANS 3:12-13

The ability of Christian leaders to demonstrate charity and forbearance speaks to their overall generosity to others. Are they respectful and civil? Do they rely on empty rhetoric to dismiss whole groups of people, or do they demonstrate a thoughtful engagement with other communities? An important contrast between effective Christian leaders and those who feed outrage are the way the former demonstrate grace and respect, even for those with whom they disagree. These leaders help you better understand why other groups act or think the way they do while clearly and convincingly explaining why they disagree with that other worldview or theology.

5. Challenging and humble

Not many of you should become teachers, my brothers, for you know that we who teach will be judged with greater strictness.
JAMES 3:1

Humble yourselves before the Lord, and he will exalt you.
JAMES 4:10

I list this category last because it is easily the riskiest category to navigate. However, I believe it is essential for Christians who wish to cultivate an effective online community that influences others toward a gospel worldview. It is risky because it is the most likely characteristic to abuse. We have already seen that many people claim to challenge Christians or be prophetic when in reality they are just controversy hunters.

At the same time, if Christians want to escape their online bubbles, they need to find thinkers outside their traditions and communities who can point out their blind spots. In today's polarized world, Christians need to find leaders who will challenge them culturally, economically, and even theologically. We need to listen with discerning minds and hearts, not readily believing everything but being open to hear criticism about our perspectives when we've been blinded by staying in our own bubbles. Perhaps nowhere is this more needed than in the matter of race.

Social media offers Christians a powerful means of listening to and engaging voices that may be absent from their communities.

Given the verses above, I will offer this important caveat about finding people who challenge you: Seek challenging voices who also exude humility. Look for people who are not afraid or reluctant to admit where they've overstepped, who are willing to admit fault in their own camp or political leanings, and who confess when they need to repent and point to Jesus as the only Savior. Being a teacher and leader is difficult work, and the judgment is going to be strict. Find leaders who grasp the severity of this burden and are willing to model humility, not merely in private but in public as well. Challenging voices who are ready to publicly criticize and rebuke others but are not willing to apply the same standards to themselves (and admit when they fail to live up to them) are not worthy of the mantle of Christian leadership.

I get it. Publicly admitting mistakes in the age of outrage can be one of the hardest things to do. Too often, apologies are seized on by others as justification to dismiss everything someone has done or said. It is little wonder that leaders struggle to admit mistakes, worrying that even the smallest error will destroy their credibility. In this environment, those Christian leaders who nevertheless live out their faith in humbling themselves to admit mistakes are examples of courage worth following.

Why It Matters

Ten years ago, I would never have guessed that I'd spend so much time in social media. I remember making fun of bloggers and thinking Twitter must be the height of narcissism, with people posting what they had for lunch.

Well, it doesn't seem that way now. Grandmothers post on Facebook and use Snapchat, pastors share via Twitter, and Russia uses it to try to influence elections.

And if it's that important, it's important to use it well. It's essential that we use it Christian-ly. Yet so few believers realize that the digital world is a place for discipleship. After all, this is where we choose and follow leaders, craft and participate in community, and reveal our political and theological opinions.

That is why we need online lives that are submitted to the real King of the universe.

CHAPTER 11

Neighborly Engagement

- 46 percent of those who have friendship(s) with an evangelical Christian describe evangelicals with one or more of these positive descriptors: compassionate, principled, charitable, and/or ethical.

- 14 percent of those with no friendships with evangelical Christians describe evangelicals with one or more of these same positive descriptors: compassionate, principled, charitable, and/or ethical.

ON FEBRUARY 19, 1968, a television program debuted that transformed the way the world understood children's programming. Emphasizing compassion, thoughtful questions, and intentional listening, *Mister Rogers' Neighborhood* extended respect to its young viewers. Fred Rogers began every episode by walking through his front door, putting on a cardigan sweater and tennis shoes, and singing a familiar line that quickly became synonymous with him: "Won't you be my neighbor?"

Rogers's simple question obscured its transformative punch. He did not ask if someone *was* his neighbor, but extended an invitation to every person to *be* his neighbor. Just by asking the question, Rogers was demonstrating his neighborliness. Reflecting on the line years later, Rogers said he had always thought of it as "an invitation to be close."[1]

While it might be easy to dismiss the question as a gimmick of a show that played on the set of a neighborhood, this assumption overlooks how intimately connected the question was to Rogers's worldview and faith. An ordained Presbyterian minister, Rogers was famously hesitant to seek the spotlight for himself and rarely gave interviews. One close friend noted that Rogers went "into interviews with all the enthusiasm of a child learning to swim: nose held, head down, head up, cough, cough, can I go home now?"[2] In an age when the media spotlight shines on controversy and celebrity, Rogers feels more like an ancient relic, a holdover from a long-dead civilization that is both foreign and comforting.

In those rare instances when he opened up, Rogers quietly explained that his philosophy of neighborly love flowed from his faith in Christ. In much the same way that Billy Graham transcended outrage by his singular devotion to proclaiming the simple gospel, Fred Rogers engendered an abiding love from everyone he touched through his unique devotion to demonstrating the love of Jesus in a way a child could understand.

In this, Rogers was following the example of Christ, who confirmed the importance of seeing everyone as our neighbor:

> One day an expert in religious law stood up to test Jesus by asking him this question: "Teacher, what should I do to inherit eternal life?"
>
> Jesus replied, "What does the law of Moses say? How do you read it?"
>
> The man answered, "'You must love the LORD your God with all your heart, all your soul, all your strength, and all your mind.' And, 'Love your neighbor as yourself.'"
>
> "Right!" Jesus told him. "Do this and you will live!"
>
> The man wanted to justify his actions, so he asked Jesus, "And who is my neighbor?"
>
> LUKE 10:25-29, NLT

Ironically, the religious leader wanted to know to whom he *had* to be kind and whom he could ignore. Jesus underscored the failure in this thinking by sharing the parable of the Good Samaritan. In this story, some religious Jews overlooked a man in dire need, beaten and left for dead on the side of the road. And then the unexpected happened: A vilified and maligned Samaritan man came on the scene and acted with compassion. He did not know the man but met all his needs with no hesitation. He was not simply in close proximity to the man; he also neighbored him: serving him, meeting his needs, and binding his wounds.

In our day, Rogers not only forced the public to consider the question first answered by Jesus, but he also steadfastly gave Jesus' response. This is what made him a light, opening doors into communities and traditions that today seem barred shut to even the slightest hint of the gospel. His viewers believed Rogers when he said they were his neighbors. He wasn't a great theologian; he was a children's television show host. But Rogers used his God-given gifts and opportunities to advance the Kingdom of God. He helped us understand what it means to engage with others face-to-face.

Moving from Neighbor to Neighboring

The subtle power behind *Mister Rogers' Neighborhood* and its unique question is that it moved *neighbor* from being a designative noun to an action-oriented verb. Mister Rogers was not simply a neighbor; he was neighboring. He answered his question "Won't you be my neighbor?" by playing out what it looked like "to neighbor" in a way that was distilled and broken down for children to understand. Moving from noun to verb makes all the difference when we begin seeing "neighbor" not as a label but as an action.

We have already covered much ground in this book about culture and engaging the online world, but little will truly change without real-life, face-to-face compassion and direct engagement with other people. This is not Ed's idea; it is rooted in the person of Jesus. He did not come during a time in history when he could send letters, upload to Vimeo, post to Facebook, or even tweet (free information: Those Jesus accounts on Twitter are fake). Jesus came as God in the flesh. He stood in the presence of others and modeled community and radical intimacy in a way that informs our own engagement with the world.

Often bolstered by the unwitting contributions of evangelicals, the age of outrage is all around us. It is easy to feel powerless, discouraged, and hopeless as we struggle to connect with the world. This feeling often translates into thinking we cannot effect change. But that is simply a lie meant to keep us paralyzed with inaction and fear.

In chapter 8, I outlined the mentality with which we need to engage our post-Christian world. We need to understand our identity as Scripture lays it out for us: We are ambassadors with a specific purpose and calling to advance God's Kingdom. As a reconciled people, we have been sent to offer this same message of redemption to all. In this chapter, I want to focus on how this can happen only when we take Jesus' exhortation to love our neighbor seriously by engaging face-to-face with others, serving in and through a local church. Finally, I will focus on some simple, practical tools that both churches and individuals can use to boldly engage with our neighbors.

We do not engage in a vacuum or alone. Scripture never views believers as unconnected, isolated, or autonomous in their mission. Rather, the biblical writers always refer to us as parts of a body, a community of believers, an interconnected and interdependent delegation of Kingdom ambassadors. This is God's strategy to reach a broad range of people with the same simple message of the gospel.

Each of us is a member of God's global church. We are also called to be part of a local expression of that church. God has given the local church as a sort of regional outpost to support, encourage, and equip us to neighbor others in a way that winsomely draws them to a God who loves them infinitely. Without a local church, a Christian cannot withstand the age of outrage. But with the support of a church, we can truly change the world.

Engaging as Communities of Grace

God has given us the local church as the primary means through which we can be neighbors who neighbor. God's desire is that the local church impact its community to the glory of God.

Sadly, many churches and Christian leaders love the way they do church more than the people our churches have been called to reach.[3]

Instead of the church being the hope of the world, in many places, we've become a reproach to others, the cause of outrage and sometimes even disgust. Earlier, I shared my personal experience with a church that struggled because of a terrible reputation in their community. Eventually, however, they overcame it through gospel renewal and heartfelt redirection toward mission in their community. No church is beyond redemption if its people are willing to be bold in their gospel proclamation and humble in their demonstration of love.

The local church represents the sovereign reign of God over a world that seems increasingly out of control and chaotic. More than a refuge against the raging storm of a hostile world, the church is the supporting community that unites and sends its people out into the world to engage their communities. The church also helps its members translate the gospel message of reconciliation into the language and culture of their specific neighborhoods.

In a 2010 publication of the Lausanne Movement, Michael Herbst states,

> A church should be a community on the move, crossing boundaries and making inclusion possible. In theological language, I could say it like this: There is no mission without incarnation–at least, when this is about God's mission. As the word became flesh and dwelt among us (John 1:14), so the mission of the church of Jesus must become "flesh" and go where people are, overcoming social and cultural boundaries and immigrating into every social environment.[4]

God's strategy to reach a broad range of people with the simple message of the gospel centers on the church of Jesus Christ. In fact, when God promised that the gates of hell would not prevail against us (Matthew 16:17-19), he was speaking to the church as a whole, not to us as individuals. The church is a sign, a foretaste, and an instrument of the Kingdom reign of God. For now, God equips churches to be the places from which Spirit-filled believers live out the gospel confidently and faithfully in every context.

In today's atmosphere of hyperpartisanship, the world needs to see a countercultural way of life that shows what it means to follow Jesus in our post-everything world. Ephesians 3:10 says God has chosen the church to make known his manifold wisdom. It's the tool, the instrument, the vessel for declaring godly wisdom. And while our gospel message is the same, churches use many forms of communication, styles, and different methodologies to effectively deliver the Good News of Jesus to unique cultures in our world. So if you're currently not in an active relationship with a local congregation, you are missing out on participating with God's ordained means of spreading his Kingdom to the world that so desperately needs it. You simply can't be a good neighbor who engages the world without the support of a local church.

Now I'm not saying the church is always perfect. She's supposed to be the beautiful bride of Christ, but sometimes she looks more like Shrek than Fiona. In fact, this is what makes the failure of churches to stand as heavenly outposts against the tide of cultural outrage all the more destructive to the mission of God.

But God still uses broken people in broken churches to bring his unbroken truth to a broken world. And even more amazing is that when the church neighbors its neighbors, it thrives. The church that equips its people to engage well expands God's Kingdom, taking more ground and starting more outposts for more ambassadors to carry Christ's message of reconciliation into new places. God has been doing a work in and through his churches for thousands of years, and here's the great part: We have eternity to get it right. Although there have always been problems in churches, the solution is always more of Jesus, and we can't screw that up.

Gospel-Translating Communities

Lesslie Newbigin was in his midtwenties in 1936, when he and his wife, Helen, sailed to India, where they would spend forty years as missionaries. He quickly noticed that his fellow workers seemed as concerned about converting people to British culture as to Christianity, something that troubled him. Newbigin began to adapt himself to Indian culture, adopting the people's style of dress and transportation. More significantly, he worked to empower local churches and their leaders. He even received permission to remove himself from the authority of his mission and place himself under the authority of the Indian church. Eventually, he helped the Indian church leaders unite several denominations into the Church of South India,[5] which remains one of the largest Christian bodies in the country.

Long before most mission organizations recognized the problems created when Christians try to impose their own cultural values on others, Newbigin actively championed the local church. After retiring from the mission field, he continued to write and speak about the importance of the local church. In *The Gospel in a Pluralist Society*, he expressed his belief about the central importance of the church community.

> I have come to feel that the primary reality of which we
> have to take account in seeking for a Christian impact
> on public life is the Christian congregation. How is it
> possible that the gospel should be credible, that people
> should come to believe that the power which has the last
> word in human affairs is represented by a man hanging
> on a cross? I am suggesting that the only answer, the
> only hermeneutic of the gospel, is a congregation of men
> and women who believe it and live by it. I am, of course,
> not denying the importance of the many activities by
> which we seek to challenge public life with the gospel—
> evangelistic campaigns, distribution of Bibles and

Christian literature, conferences, and even books such
as this one. But I am saying that these are all secondary,
and that they have power to accomplish their purpose
only as they are rooted in and lead back to a believing
community.[6]

So what does it mean for a local church to be a gospel-translating
community for the Kingdom of God? As the primary means for
engaging our neighbors and friends, the local church is responsible for translating the gospel into the foreign language of the culture around us. Fortunately, the gospel is inherently transferable.
Neighboring can be done in every culture, for every people, anywhere, anytime.

Newbigin went on to say,

If the gospel is to challenge the public life of our society
. . . it will only be by movements that begin with the local
congregation in which the reality of the new creation is
present, known, and experienced, and from which men
and women will go into every sector of public life to
claim it for Christ, to unmask the illusions which have
remained hidden and to expose all areas of public life to
the illumination of the gospel.[7]

This is a compelling vision of the local church as the central
hub through which we engage the world. Building on Newbigin, I
see five ways the local church lives out this translating, missional
posture.

1. **The church is a community of truth.** What defines Chris-
    tian community is truth. A community built on anything
    other than truth will crumble. Our culture of outrage has
    reinforced this lesson time and again. At a time when
    people are encouraged to "find your truth," the church is
    called to hold fast to the enduring truth of the Christian

faith. At the core of our community is not a shared hobby, political view, or culture. It is a shared commitment to and belief in the truth of the Christian faith. A bound set of doctrines that we as Christians confess and submit to as authoritative for our lives. In fact, Jesus reminds us that he is the way, truth, and life. *We* do not define truth but find it in the person and work of Christ. As a community of truth, the church shapes our thinking and worldview that help to deepen and enliven our faith, but also make us more effective translators of the gospel to the culture where truth is perpetually being sought.

Of course, central to the church's identity as a community of truth is its imperative to speak this truth in love (Ephesians 4:15-16). That truth is not a bludgeon by which we can crush our ideological or cultural enemies; rather, it is the light for our path. We speak the truth in love because ultimately, as communities of grace, we want to see that truth take root in each other's lives and produce spiritual fruit. This is why Paul says that it is *only* when we speak truth in love that the church can "grow up in every way into him who is the head, into Christ."

2. **The church is an embedded community.** The community of truth lives within a specific context, embedded in the local community. It takes root and shape in every culture precisely because the gospel is inherently translatable. Newbigin stated, "A Christian congregation is defined by this twofold relation: it is God's embassy in a specific place."[8]

   Either of these vital relationships can be neglected. The congregation may be so concerned about its members' relationship to God that it turns its back on the neighborhood and is perceived as irrelevant to neighborhood concerns. On the other hand, a local church can also be so ingrained in a community that it merely becomes another neighborhood social program. It ceases to translate the gospel to those around it, instead fading into the background as just one more group. Our churches are not above culture, nor are they beyond culture.

We are to be countercultural agents of change—in the world, yet not of it. Together we are called to ask, *What does it mean to be followers of Christ in our local community? In what ways do our values and beliefs shape how we live out the gospel and its implications in our cultural context? How can we best communicate the hope and truth in Jesus' Kingdom to our friends, neighbors, coworkers, and family?*

3. **The church is a community of equipping.** This idea of equipping the saints to carry out our Kingdom mission is based on Ephesians 4:11: "These are the gifts Christ gave to the church: the apostles, the prophets, the evangelists, and the pastors and teachers" (NLT). God has called certain people to build up and train the body so that churches can create new outposts to carry the gospel to new places. Multiplication can only come from equipping. The apostle Paul frames this brilliantly in 2 Timothy 2:1-2: "You, therefore, my son, be strong in the grace that is in Christ Jesus. The things which you have heard from me in the presence of many witnesses, entrust these to faithful men who will be able to teach others also" (NASB).

   This goes beyond Sunday morning, small groups, and spiritual-gift pop quizzes. Equipping refers to the responsibility of churches to facilitate and exhort their people to serve within the local community.

4. **The church is a community of accountability and responsibility.** Someone asked me once, "What are your blind spots, Ed?" I responded (with, I confess, a smirk), "I have no idea. That's what blind spots are, so I don't know what mine are." However, I assure you, my small group knows my blind spots. My coworkers know my blind spots. When I'm in community

with friends and family, they can say, "Ed, you need to grow in this area."

Being ambassadors of truth, founded on the reliable words of Scripture, we are to live out our lives transparently and with greater accountability. In chapter 10, we considered how churches can bridge one discipleship gap by helping people understand how to navigate their digital interactions well. The church should also call us to greater accountability when it comes to our face-to-face engagements. In this respect, churches are to be places where we bear with one another just as Christ first bore our sins and even now continues to bear with us in our failures; where we recognize our behavior as individuals and reflect upon our collective mission as ambassadors.

When the foreign land that surrounds us seems to idolize autonomous individuals who yell on Facebook, saying, "I can say and do whatever I want," it is radically countercultural to live in communities in which we voluntarily give one another deference and accountability. Grace-filled interdependence also points others to the beauty of our King and his Kingdom, giving them a holy image of what it's like to be reconciled to God.

5. **The church is a community of hope.** Churches unashamedly proclaim the glorious hope that Jesus' Good News offers in the age of outrage. Our transformation around this hope happens in genuine community with others. As we pray together and serve one another, we enable the watching world to see this hope.

   I'm a better ambassador and a better Christian because I know some people very well and those people know me very well. For example, a family in our church has a child who has left the faith. And because I know the family, I hurt with them. When my family goes through struggles, this family hurts with me. Every family experiences pain, but when we walk that journey together, we can extend empathy to one another. This generates a hope that is not rooted in us, but in what unifies and unites us: Jesus.

In the movie *As Good as It Gets,* Jack Nicholson says to Helen Hunt, "You make me want to be a better man."[9] One reason I love being married to Donna is that she makes me want to be a better man. And in the same way, being in community with believers provides us with the support, vision, and hope to love our neighbors.

You and I cannot engage the age of outrage alone. The shouting and rage around us will drown out our message, damaging us in the process. This is precisely why God does not send us out as lone-ranger Christians. Jesus called twelve disciples. He sent out the seventy-two believers two by two. And he has given his church to be a gospel-translating community that supports its people as they live on mission, with grace, face-to-face for the glory of God.

Living as Missionaries of Grace

Now that we have looked at the importance of the church as missionaries of grace, we can turn to our unique roles as individual missionaries of grace living with our neighbors, coworkers, and friends. The work of a missionary takes time and skill, and here is where theory meets praxis. We can take practical steps to translate the gospel to others with skill and care.

Here are a few ways to do that:

Missionaries of grace accept correction and training

Part of being a missionary of grace is developing a reputation within your community (online and in real life) as one willing to accept correction and training. Believers who acknowledge areas where God is still growing them toward maturity evidence a godly winsomeness that draws people in.

I was encouraged recently to see such humble maturity in

Joshua Harris. If you were a Christian teenager in the late 90s and early 2000s, you likely read or knew someone who read Harris's wildly popular *I Kissed Dating Goodbye*. In his book, Harris explained why he believed the casual nature of dating tended to make it a "training ground for divorce."[10] He called for Christians to return to the standard of courtship, in which two individuals intentionally moved toward marriage, preferably with the active involvement of their parents. His book inspired years of debate, with many readers hailing it as a guide to navigating past the treacherous waters of dating, while others reviled its premise.

Fast-forward twenty years, and Harris launched a major project to study the impact of his book and engage the criticism head-on. In a 2016 interview with *Slate*, Harris acknowledged that, even though he had considered criticism of the book over the years, it was not until recently that he was able to internalize that critique and effectively respond. Because he was uncertain how to engage in a debate that proved far greater than he had imagined, Harris chose to listen first. In fact, this is what struck me most: No matter the context or platform, he continually emphasizes his willingness and genuine desire to listen to the stories of those who were affected.

His website includes a page titled "Revisiting *I Kissed Dating Goodbye*" that includes a short explanation for his revisitation of this topic and a form for readers to share their experiences, whether "good, bad or a mix of both."[11] Harris admits, "Part of the reason [reevaluating *I Kissed Dating Goodbye*] has been so hard for me is that I have so much of my identity tied up in these books. It's what I'm known for."[12] Yet he has still pushed forward on this difficult path, learning to listen and live differently. He is an example of how Christians can look with humility at their past decisions and take steps to learn to live differently.

This is so countercultural to a world that values a "stick-to-your-guns" mentality. The foreign land we live in celebrates and values bullies who get their way, not the humble person who is willing to change. The ability to accept correction and training is a key testimony in the age of outrage and is a practical skill a missionary of grace needs in order to come face-to-face with their neighbors on mission for King Jesus.

Missionaries of grace lay down their rights and privileges

Effective missionaries of grace who come face-to-face with outrage often need to voluntarily lay down their rights and privileges. Part of neighboring is modeling the Kingdom, and nothing models the upside-down Kingdom of Heaven more than denying ourselves something we have a right to for the betterment of another. This is what Jesus modeled for us in his incarnation and death, and this is the level of sacrifice to which he calls us as well.

Retribution is the normal human response when someone encroaches on our rights. We see evidence of this in Exodus 21:22-25, which teaches *lex talionis*, which is Latin for "the law of revenge." This sounds ominous, but most scholars agree God incorporated it into the law as a way to protect his people by keeping feuds from escalating.

Without *lex talionis*, when you egg my house, I can throw a brick through your window, which leads you to douse my house in gasoline and set it on fire, which leads me to shoot you. In the end, I commit murder because you threw eggs on my house. But with *lex talionis*, justice stops the escalation of violence by demanding a proportionate penalty. At the core of the law is the recognition that the human heart is wicked. It doesn't want to stop at justice; it wants to inflict pain. It wants to escalate.

Jesus calls us, as his missionaries of grace, to go further than even *lex talionis* requires. In the Sermon on the Mount, he calls us to turn the other cheek rather than demand an eye for an eye (Matthew 5:38-42). But why does he go even further, saying, "I say to you, Do not resist the one who is evil"? Before considering this, we need to avoid the temptation to interpret this as Jesus saying we should never stand up to evil, injustice, or oppression. The rest of Scripture contains not only several exhortations to speak out against sin but also examples of God's people doing this (Proverbs 25:26;

Acts 22). Second, it does not mean wrongdoers should have to face no legal consequences. You can turn the other cheek, but someone may still need to go to jail. It does not mean we do not confront evil when we see women trafficked as sex slaves. The Scriptures are very clear that we are to advocate for those who are in need. Christians are to speak up when injustice affects others.

In truth, following Christ does not subvert the laws of justice but calls us to demonstrate a radical degree of sacrifice and humility in how we engage a hostile world. While God has established a system of justice, Jesus reveals how the Kingdom of God obliges us to a greater righteousness. Some claim Jesus' exhortation to forgive seventy times seven sets a limit of forgiveness at 490, but the purpose of this teaching is not to create a specific law but rather a posture of grace by which we engage the world.

A phenomenal example of Christians demonstrating such radical forgiveness is revealed in the statements from family members of people shot and killed in 2015 while attending a Bible study at Emanuel AME Church, the oldest black church in the South, sometimes referred to as "Mother Emanuel."

To the astonishment of many, when the relatives of those killed addressed the defendant at a bond hearing, they did not rage at the man. Though the defendant, accused of murdering nine, showed no remorse, the victims' family members told him they forgave him and were praying for him. They didn't, however, gloss over their grief.

"I forgive you," said Nadine Collier, her voice breaking. The daughter of seventy-year-old Ethel Vance, Collier told the defendant, "You took something very precious from me. I will never talk to her again. I will never, ever hold her again. But I forgive you. And have mercy on your soul."[13]

Believers at Mother Emanuel showed us what it looks like to respond as Jesus would have us.[14] So let me ask: Is this weakness? Were they letting people walk all over them? Not at all. I think this is one of the best demonstrations of strength in American public life in the past decade. When believers live out their faith like this, it shows the grace of Christ to a watching world. It demonstrates what it means to lay down our rights for the gospel.

And as we seek to represent the grand narrative of God's Kingdom to a watching world, giving up our personal rights seems a worthwhile price to pay. As the apostle Paul said, "Why not rather suffer wrong? Why not rather be defrauded?" (1 Corinthians 6:7). This is how Jesus lived too. He did not resist the evil done against him. He did not seek vengeance against his oppressors. Instead, he committed himself to his Father, and his followers took note:

> To this you have been called, because Christ also suffered
> for you, leaving you an example, so that you might follow
> in his steps. He committed no sin, neither was deceit
> found in his mouth. When he was reviled, he did not
> revile in return; when he suffered, he did not threaten,
> but continued entrusting himself to him who judges justly.
> 1 PETER 2:21-23

You have the same power of Jesus residing in you to help you be a missionary neighbor of grace. The Holy Spirit is available to anyone who confesses that Jesus is Lord. You, fellow Christian, have been shown grace to the very extent that you are now equipped to show the same grace to others.

Missionaries of grace are prepared to serve when crisis comes

Missionaries of grace in this age of outrage not only model humility and deference, they are prepared to act when needed. Neighboring doesn't just happen with crotchety neighbors or scheming coworkers. It requires being present in crises, emergencies, and tragedies.

We live in a world constantly and consistently outraged, and too many Christians are joining the outrage, which kills their empathy and compassion for those in need. Missionaries of grace should be known for laying their lives down for the poor and marginalized, not for showing aggression and outrage or for rejecting those who need our compassion the most. When we live in this way, the world will notice—and be drawn to Christ's love. Dr. Stephen Foster is a good example. Foster is a missionary surgeon in his late sixties who has lived in Angola for forty years. Angola has the highest child mortality rate of any country in the world and was headed by a Marxist regime hostile to Christianity for most of the years Foster served there.

Yet something remarkable happened. "We were granted visas," he said, "by the very people who would tell us publicly, 'your churches are going to disappear in 20 years,' but privately, 'you are the only ones we know willing to serve in the midst of the fire.'"[15]

Foster served in the war-torn country and raised his children there. One son contracted polio, a daughter survived cerebral malaria, and during a particularly bad period of famine, his family nearly starved when they shared their rations with over one hundred villagers.

Nicholas Kristof, the journalist who profiled Dr. Foster, is a *New York Times* columnist who admits that he has little in common with people of faith. But the article ends with a short paragraph I want to highlight: "The next time you hear someone at a cocktail party mock evangelicals, think of Dr. Foster and those like him. These are folks who don't so much proclaim the gospel as live it. They deserve better."[16]

What a privilege and lesson Dr. Foster's faithfulness gives us. When Christians serve in the midst of crisis, people's perception of Jesus and his followers changes. Dr. Foster proves that problems are better solved through engagement and radical neighboring than through isolation and distant critique.

The Roman emperor Julian, otherwise known as Julian the Apostate (who attempted to bring back pagan religion to Rome), complained about the actions of Christians during and after the plagues and widespread poverty that existed during his reign. He wrote that "the impious Galileans support not only their own poor but ours as well, all men see that our people lack aid from us."[17] Ultimately, he could not turn back the forward movement of

Christianity. (The label "the apostate" is a reminder that Christians would later write the history of his reign.)

Those early Christians—and people like Dr. Foster whose faith shines brightly in desperate communities—show that living as missionaries of grace can have reverberations throughout the world and throughout history. Your obedience today as a missionary who engages face-to-face with others could influence the gospel hundreds or thousands of years from now, just like those "impious Galileans." We don't need to move to Angola or jump in a time machine back to the third century; we simply need to be prepared with open arms to offer what we have in moments of crisis. God does not use extraordinary striving. He uses extraordinary availability to reach the world with the message of his Kingdom.

But how do we make this practical? Let me share with you the most effective tools I have found for being a missionary of grace and neighboring our neighbors. Let's start with a story about one of the most contemporary means of connecting with strangers these days: Uber.

Learning Everyday Mission in an Uber

Over the past few years, I have become an Uber connoisseur. I live and work in the western suburbs of Chicago but have been serving for a time as interim pastor at Moody Church in downtown Chicago. The constant back-and-forth plus a crazy travel schedule means I have had every Uber experience one can hope for in a lifetime.

Overly chatty? Check.

Screaming metal music? Check.

Awkwardly emotional phone conversation? Check.

Sales pitch for a pyramid scheme? Check.

One evening I arranged for a ride through Uber after speaking at Moody Bible Institute's annual missions conference. My schedule that day had been insane, and I had capped it off by spending the night talking with college students. That had left me both encouraged and drained. As I stood at the curb waiting for the

Uber, I silently prayed for a quiet ride home. In a moment of brilliance, I realized Uber needs an "introverted driver" button. (If anyone from Uber reads this and implements it, you can send the royalty check as a donation to Wheaton College.)

The moment I got in the car, I realized God had other ideas about what was best for my ride home. My driver was many things, but introverted was not one of them. The door was barely closed before he started an unending wave of questions:

"What is Moody Bible Institute?"

"What's a missions conference?"

"What do Christians believe?"

I had planned to rest on my hour-long ride home, but the driver was asking some specific questions about God, Jesus, and the Bible. As I tried to answer him by outlining how someone becomes a Christian through faith and repentance, he suddenly asked a question that broke through my tiredness and rang my theological bell: "So that's kind of like soteriology, right?"

Ding. That's an oddly specific and technical word for the doctrine of salvation. I know many lifelong Christians who wouldn't know that word, let alone an Uber driver who had just been asking me who Jesus was a few minutes ago. When I asked how he knew that word, a big smile spread across his face. He told me he was a seminary student at Trinity Evangelical Divinity School, just north of Chicago. Needless to say, he was amused with himself at picking on the tired professor in his car. I was less amused!

Reflecting on the experience, however, I recognize how disengaged I can get. I hold a chair of evangelism and missiology, speak at missions conferences, and lead an organization dedicated to gospel proclamation and discipleship. Yet faced with a real person expressing an interest in hearing more about Christ, I had done my best to check out. Even as I tried answering his questions, my mind had started to drift as I looked at what was on social media and thought through upcoming meetings and ideas for future articles.

During that ride with my Uber driver, what was driven home (no pun intended) was that the first step to engaging and serving in the age of outrage is living out the gospel within our physical location. That may include the neighbors who live next door, the coworkers we see every day at work, or even the Uber driver who takes us home after a long day.

Remember that I mentioned how Mister Rogers helped Americans understand that neighboring is not a designative noun but an action verb? Now I'd like to move from nouns to verbs and introduce you to three action words that answer the question: How do we neighbor well? I have been living and exploring this idea of neighboring for years, and the following process has helped me start communities, lead others to Jesus, and plant churches. It involves three activities: mapping, listing, and engaging my neighbors.

Map your neighbors

There is no better place to serve as a missionary of grace than with the people who live next door, on your street, in your building, or in your subdivision. And it starts with a period of discovery. The first step in moving mission from the theoretical to the practical is physically mapping your neighborhood. By introducing yourself to your neighbors, creating a map, and placing it in a prominent location in your house, you will be reminded to look for mission opportunities in your everyday life. Making such a map is not new with me. Nor is a list. They are just reminders to be intentional.

We do this with the knowledge that where we live is no accident, something the apostle Paul told the believers at Athens:

> He made from one man every nation of mankind to live on all the face of the earth, having determined allotted periods and the boundaries of their dwelling place, that they should seek God, and perhaps feel their way toward him and find him. Yet he is actually not far from each one of us.
> ACTS 17:26-27

Paul said God determined the "boundaries of [your] dwelling place" long before the world began. And he placed you there to be his ambassador so your neighbors could seek God and find him. God is not far from anyone, and he makes himself known to the world through his people. This theological truth has dramatic significance to how you and I live in our communities.

A few years ago, Donna and I became convicted that we were not reaching our neighbors the way we wanted, so we created a map of our neighborhood. We drew a diagram of the streets and cross streets, and began to fill it in with everything we knew about each neighbor. Our intention was to be mindful of all the people in the immediate proximity of our house.

We wrote down the names of eight of our nearest neighbors who didn't know Christ. We started to find excuses for our kids to play together. We hosted cookouts and Super Bowl parties, and then we started a Bible study. With every trial, success, and crisis came the opportunity to preach the gospel. Avoiding the "Christianese" that can obscure the gospel, we would emphasize that only in Jesus can we find fulfillment for those most common desires of the human heart–to be known, loved, and valued. Several people attended, and over a year, we saw a key couple in the neighborhood trust Christ, be baptized, and start leading a Bible study in their home.

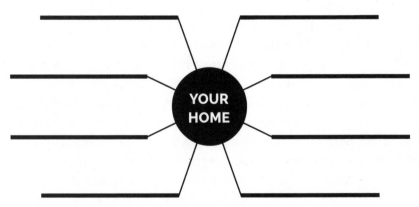

Our efforts to reach out to our neighbors began with this map, giving us a reason to discover who our neighbors actually were. It became fun! The key was that we sought to intentionally neighbor our neighbors. We oriented our lives, our actions, and the rhythms of our household and personal relationships around getting to know them, and the map kept that goal at the forefront of our minds. It represented not just some things we did, but the people we became: missionary neighbors.

We intentionally built community by keeping our neighborhood map in our minds and in our prayers throughout an entire year. Not all our neighbors made it easy to get to know them; in fact, one couple didn't like us (well, probably me). But we continued to be faithful and prayed for them. I even had the opportunity to pray for another couple who seemed opposed to the gospel message until they were in crisis.

It takes intentionality and time to meet and map out where our neighbors live and then to pray over them and know where they are physically and spiritually. Doing so makes us more like Jesus and shows that we are his disciples. The first step in engaging others face-to-face in this age of outrage is mapping your neighbors.

List your connections

The second step in moving mission from the theoretical to the practical is keeping and updating a list of the connections you have. This moves beyond simply mapping those in close physical proximity to listing the names of the people who are in relational and professional proximity to you and your family, including your coworkers, friends, acquaintances, and family, both near and far. You might see some of these people only once or twice a year, and you might see others every day, but having and keeping a list will help you take next steps consistently and regularly to minister to your family and friends. Remembering names and personal details will help you neighbor better. Keep this list in front of you by placing it next to your bed, on a bathroom mirror, or in your Bible, as I do. It reminds me to pray for the people on my list as I read Scripture. I'm more likely to find connections during the day because my heart is attuned to the opportunity.

Why is writing out this list of connections and keeping it up to date worthwhile? A study of college students by the Association for Psychological Science revealed that taking handwritten notes led to deeper processing and memory retention than typing notes on a laptop.[18] Likewise, as students of our neighborhood and culture, we need a way to remember key information about those around us. This process of getting to know someone is crucial as we look for opportunities to take the kernel of the gospel and plant it in the soil of a person's heart. Consistently learning and tracking your broader connections will help you become a better neighbor and friend. It will also keep these relationships at the forefront of your mind (much like mapping the neighbors).

In addition, I use my list as a record of my interactions with each person because I know that whatever we measure in our lives improves. For instance, when I regularly weigh myself and track my food intake, I lose weight. I don't even have to be on a specific diet; simply measuring and focusing on the right metric keeps this objective at the front of my mind. My volition follows my focus. This is why it is so important to make a list of people in your life with whom you are intentionally building relationships.

The point of keeping this list of connections is to continue learning about them. Write down the names of their family members and their personal needs. Then remember to pray for them. Check in regularly with the key people on your list because following up with the small things in other people's lives is essential to building their trust. As you gain more information, add it to the list. It might feel disingenuous at first to keep such notes, but it's not. It is, in fact, placing your focus squarely on people in a good, healthy way to be a better missionary, ambassador, and neighbor.

When speaking at Moody Church and Saddleback Church in California about engaging with our neighbors, I created cards and asked the congregants to insert them in their Bibles. These cards looked something like this:

Kathy Jones—employer	☐ Pray	☐ Engage	☐ Invite
Tim & Mary Chung—PTA	☐ Pray	☐ Engage	☐ Invite
Lamar Shields—coworker	☐ Pray	☐ Engage	☐ Invite
Alex Fredricks—Amy's soccer coach	☐ Pray	☐ Engage	☐ Invite
Omar & Yasma Khan—new neighbors	☐ Pray	☐ Engage	☐ Invite

Engaging with others is not a onetime event. Pray consistently for each person on your list. Reach out to them in relationship, love, and service. Learn their stories, hopes, fears, and dreams. Keep praying. Keep reaching. Keep learning. And as you do, you will raise the evangelistic temperature within your heart and your household.

Engage your community

The third step toward moving mission from the theoretical to the practical is engaging your neighbors, coworkers, friends, and family in practical service to your wider community. You are inviting them to act like Jesus, even if they do not yet know him personally. In John 20:21, Jesus tells us, "As the Father has sent me, even so I am sending you." We are, literally, joining Jesus on his mission to the world, and we can engage with our community and invite them along for the ride.

There are almost as many causes to be involved in as there are people. You see, Christians can serve and invite others to serve with them.

One example of such a Christian at her best is Rhonda Edmunds, one of the founders and the director of nursing at Lily's Place in Huntington, West Virginia. Lily's Place cares for babies born addicted to opiates because their mothers used them during pregnancy. After birth, these babies may experience a variety of symptoms, including stomach cramping, pain, excessive sucking, tremors, and inconsolable crying. This period of withdrawal is known as neonatal abstinence syndrome (NAS).

The staff at Lily's Place do their best to assist families with infants suffering from NAS by providing much-needed medical care to the infants, as well as support, education, and counseling designed to help families end the cycle of addiction. Such services are desperately needed in areas where the opiate crisis has hit hardest, as hospitals are overwhelmed and overflowing with babies in need of additional care.

Before her time at Lily's Place, Edmunds was instrumental in the creation of the Neonatal Therapeutic Unit (NTU) at Cabell Huntington Hospital.[19] She is also a member of Antioch Missionary Baptist Church in Ona, West Virginia, where she recruits volunteers for Lily's Place. One of her pastors, Jacob Paul Marshall, told me they are "blessed to have such a gift" in their church. Rhonda Edmunds is a wonderful example of a woman of God living out her higher calling by spreading his love to her neighbors, and she involves others as volunteers.

Local churches and nonprofits minister to the homeless, prisoners, hospital and nursing home patients, military families, women in crisis pregnancies, and underserved children who need help with their homework. The list of possibilities is almost endless, but the important point is inviting your neighbors and connections to join in a larger cause together.

Not only does this engage people who might not know Jesus, but it also models a holy imagination to help them explore what it might look like if they choose to follow Jesus. They will see that Christianity is not about aiming to float on clouds and listen to angels on harps, but it's real, practical, present, sacrificial, consistent service of other people done because and out of the love of Jesus.

This means that during times of service *with* your community and *in* your community, you can be operating as a missionary of grace to two groups. Engaging in community service gives us an entrée with our neighbors, an opportunity to join their community. (And remember, you can join in a cause they initiate as well. Serving the hurting in the name of Christ is not something we always have to organize.) It is good for people to be involved with something beyond themselves that they can invite their neighbors to. As ambassadors who neighbor the Kingdom of God, serving enables us to help make the world more as it should be.

It is not necessarily about the type of engagement and service in and of itself; it's about what working together *for* a cause does to build community, rapport, and intimacy among people serving together. Even people who are not open to the gospel know that doing something to help others is a good thing.

When we map, list, and engage our neighbors, we are moving from the theoretical to the practical in ways that are simple and reproducible for ourselves and for others. We train ourselves to move beyond apathy to engagement, beyond distraction to focus, and beyond dysfunction to health. And it begins with the simplicity of intention that dares to believe that Jesus' model of "follow me" discipleship actually works.

The key to the effectiveness of these tools is faithfulness to the task out of the proper motivation. Discovering and praying for your neighbors through mapping, following their joys and sorrows with a list, and faithfully engaging them toward a service and a cause take discipline. The only way you will be faithful is to be motivated by the fact that Jesus is already faithful on your behalf. Jesus lived as an exiled missionary-ambassador and labored for your soul so you can joyfully join him in his mission for the world.

The Gospel Truth

We are living in an age of outrage. The world is not as it should be, and it is clear that we are in a unique season of antagonism toward the principles that make the gospel the "Good News." Worse yet, we contribute to this outrage by sometimes responding poorly to the world around us. But all is not lost. In fact, there is incredible hope for the Christian. Jesus calls us to join our lives with him, follow his lead, repent of our failures, and respond to outrage with radical grace, winsome love, generous compassion, and prayerful hearts that break with the brokenness of the world.

And here is the gospel truth: We were once under God's wrath. In fact, the only response from a perfect and holy God was outrage to our sin and sinfulness. But God did not leave us. He drew near to us. He engaged us and saved us by sending Jesus to become the very outrage we could not overcome. Jesus took the full and unmeasured wrath of God so that, through faith, we can now have the peace that passes all understanding. While we were still enemies of God, Jesus reconciled us to himself, offering peace and forgiveness. We are now not simply forgiven but welcomed back into God's family. He adopts us as his children and gives us an inheritance with his obedient Son. As if that were not enough, we are now invited to join Jesus in his mission to bring others back to himself and to set everything right again. He gives us divine jobs as ambassadors of his reconciliation, and he sends his Spirit to empower us to live as missionaries of grace and neighbors who neighbor. And this is just the beginning!

This is the Good News that changes us from outraged spectators to grace-filled participants in God's redemptive plan for the world. If we honestly and truthfully believe this, it changes everything.

Now put down this book and go out into the age of outrage. Leave behind angry nationalism. Leave behind political excuses. Leave behind unloving tribalism. Leave behind prideful Facebook posts and endless arguments.

Embrace the disciplines and influences that will shape and mold your thinking according to the gospel. Embrace your identity as an ambassador of the Kingdom of God, sent with a message of reconciliation to a lost people. Embrace a winsome love rooted in the love Christ first modeled to us, counteracting the hostility of our world. Embrace your online relationships as an opportunity to learn, engage, and innovate for the advancement of the Kingdom. Embrace your responsibility as a missionary of grace to those around you, seeing your local community as a mission field to which God calls his church.

You have the Holy Spirit inside you, empowering you and enabling you to live on mission. In a world at its worst, live out your calling to be a Christian at your best in the age of outrage.

Key Findings from the Billy Graham Center Institute

Chapter 1: Outrage Cause #1: A Cultural Forking

- Of evangelicals with an opinion, 82 percent believe that since the 2016 presidential election, groups within the Christian church have become increasingly polarized on issues of politics.

  Q: "Since the 2016 presidential election, groups within the Christian church have become increasingly polarized on issues of politics."

  A: Evangelical by belief: 82 percent agree (strongly agree, 35 percent; somewhat agree, 47 percent)

- Of evangelicals with an opinion, 73 percent believe the 2016 presidential election revealed political divides within the Christian church that have existed for a long time.

  Q: "The 2016 presidential election revealed political divides within the Christian church that have existed for a long time."

  A: Evangelical by belief: 73 percent agree (strongly agree, 30 percent; somewhat agree, 43 percent)

Chapter 2: Outrage Cause #2: The Technology Discipleship Gap

- Evangelicals are more likely than non-evangelicals (49 percent to 38 percent) to connect with people like themselves on social media, leading to the formation of possible echo chambers.

  Q: "I prefer to follow or befriend people on social media who have the same or similar thoughts on social and political issues as mine."

  A: 49 percent of evangelicals by belief and 48 percent of self-identified evangelicals follow or befriend people with similar thoughts, compared to 38 percent of non-evangelicals.

- Evangelicals (73 percent) and non-evangelicals (67 percent) overwhelmingly agree that interactions on social media have increased the divisive political climate in America.

  Q: "Interactions on social media have increased the divisive political climate in America."

  A: Over two-thirds (73 percent of evangelicals by belief; 71 percent of self-identified evangelicals; 67 percent of non-evangelicals) agree that interactions on social media have increased the divisive political climate in America.

Chapter 3: Lie #1: "Christians Are the Worst!"

- Of non-evangelicals who changed their opinion about evangelicals since the 2016 election, six said their opinion worsened for every one who said it improved.

  Q: "Since the 2016 presidential election, my perceptions of evangelical Christians have . . . (select one)"

A. - Improved: 5 percent
   - Stayed about the same: 64 percent
   - Worsened: 31 percent

Chapter 4: Lie #2: "My Outrage Is Righteous Anger"

- Evangelicals (78 percent) and non-evangelicals (74 percent) express high levels of concern about the lack of civility in the public discussion of social issues.

   Q: "I am very concerned about the lack of civility in today's public discussions of important social issues."

   A: Three-fourths (78 percent of evangelicals by belief; 74 percent of self-identified evangelicals; and 74 percent of non-evangelicals) are very concerned about the lack of civility in today's public discussions of social issues.

Chapter 5: Lie #3: "_____ Will Save Me from the Outrage!"

- When asked to describe their feelings when each party held the presidency, evangelicals' top responses for how they felt during a Republican administration were protected (34 percent) and safe (33 percent). During a Democratic presidency, they said they felt fearful of the future (34 percent) and frustrated (29 percent). This difference suggests that evangelicals, along with the rest of society, associate political control with the safety and stability of their community.

   Q: "Typically, when the US has a Republican president, I feel . . . (select all that apply)"

   A: Evangelical by belief: protected, 34 percent; safe, 33 percent; respected, 25 percent

Q: "Typically, when the US has a Democratic president, I feel . . . (select all that apply)"

A: Evangelical by belief: fearful of the future, 34 percent; frustrated, 29 percent; threatened, 21 percent

Chapter 6: Lie #4: Mission Is Optional

- 42 percent of evangelicals agree that the divisive political climate in America makes it harder for them to share their faith. Only a small percentage said it was easier.

  Q: "The divisive political climate in America today makes it harder for me to share my Christian faith."

  A: - Evangelical by belief: strongly agree, 18 percent; somewhat agree, 24 percent
     - Self-identified evangelicals: strongly agree, 15 percent; somewhat agree, 29 percent

- 41 percent of evangelicals agree that the divisive political climate in America makes it harder for them to build relationships with neighbors, coworkers, or acquaintances.

  Q: "The divisive political climate in America today makes it harder for me to build relationships with neighbors, coworkers, or acquaintances."

  A: - Evangelical by belief: strongly agree, 17 percent; somewhat agree, 24 percent
     - Self-identified evangelicals: strongly agree, 15 percent; somewhat agree, 28 percent

Chapter 7: A Worldview Shaped by the Gospel

- 62 percent of evangelicals attend a religious service at least once a week compared to only 15 percent of non-evangelicals.

Q: "How often do you attend religious services at a Christian church? (select one)"

A: - More than once a week: evangelicals by belief, 29 percent; self-identified evangelicals, 21 percent; non-evangelicals, 3 percent
   - Once a week: evangelicals by belief, 33 percent; self-identified evangelicals, 31 percent; non-evangelicals, 12 percent

- 39 percent of evangelicals by belief say their pastor uses Scripture to address political topics at least once a month, perhaps showing that such topics are not often addressed.

Q: "How often does your pastor use Scripture to address topics that politicians are debating? (select one)"

A: - More than once a week: evangelicals by belief, 17 percent; self-identified evangelicals, 14 percent; non-evangelicals, 10 percent
   - 2 or 3 times a month: evangelicals by belief, 13 percent; self-identified evangelicals, 16 percent; non-evangelicals, 15 percent
   - Once a month: evangelicals by belief, 9 percent; self-identified evangelicals, 12 percent; non-evangelicals, 8 percent

- Only 43 percent of evangelicals agree that their pastor should address issues currently being debated by politicians, with the largest share of respondents (31 percent) *strongly* disagreeing, perhaps showing that many people adamantly oppose their pastors weighing in on political issues.

Q: "I desire advice from my pastor on how to think about issues debated by politicians."

A: - Evangelicals by belief: strongly agree, 17 percent;
   somewhat agree, 26 percent; somewhat disagree,
   17 percent; strongly disagree, 31 percent; not sure,
   10 percent
  - Self-identified evangelicals: strongly agree, 14 percent;
   somewhat agree, 26 percent; somewhat disagree,
   17 percent; strongly disagree, 32 percent; not sure,
   8 percent

Chapter 8: Kingdom Ambassadors in a Foreign Land

• Politics were identified as *extremely important* to a greater
  percentage of evangelicals than to non-evangelicals
  (30 percent to 18 percent).

Q: "How important is politics to you?"

A: 13 percent of evangelicals by belief, 15 percent of
   self-identified evangelicals, and 22 percent of non-
   evangelicals say politics is not important, whereas
   30 percent of evangelicals by belief, 23 percent of
   self-identified evangelicals, and 18 percent of non-
   evangelicals say politics is extremely important to them.

• A significant majority of evangelicals (67 percent) agreed
  that a Christian can benefit from a political leader even if
  that leader's personal life does not line up with Christian
  teaching.

Q: "Committed Christians can benefit from a political
   leader even if that leader's personal life does not line up
   with Christian teaching."

A: - Evangelicals by belief: strongly agree, 33 percent;
   somewhat agree, 34 percent; somewhat disagree,
   12 percent; strongly disagree, 12 percent; not sure,
   9 percent

- Self-identified evangelicals: strongly agree, 27 percent; somewhat agree, 39 percent; somewhat disagree, 15 percent; strongly disagree, 10 percent; not sure, 9 percent

Chapter 9: Winsome Love

- Over a third of evangelicals (35 percent) say they disagree with their friends and family up to half of the time. Evangelicals disagree with their *friends and family* often. We have to learn how to disagree effectively and winsomely, or we are going to be lonely.

  Q: "How often do your friends and family agree with your political views?"

  A: - Evangelicals by belief: always, 9 percent; most of the time, 42 percent; half the time, 23 percent; less than half the time, 9 percent; never, 3 percent; not sure, 13 percent
  - Self-identified evangelicals: always, 7 percent; most of the time, 40 percent; half the time, 25 percent; less than half the time, 10 percent; never, 3 percent; not sure, 14 percent

Chapter 10: Online Activity Aligned with Gospel Mission

- Evangelicals largely reflect culture in the choice of social media platforms they use, with the top four being Facebook (77 percent), YouTube (46 percent), Instagram (28 percent), and Twitter (22 percent). The question is how they use it.

  Q: "Which, if any, of the following types of social media do you use regularly? (select all that apply)"

  A: - Facebook—evangelicals by belief, 77 percent; self-identified evangelicals, 74 percent; non-evangelicals, 71 percent

- YouTube—evangelicals by belief, 46 percent; self-identified evangelicals, 46 percent; non-evangelicals, 44 percent
- Instagram—evangelicals by belief, 28 percent; self-identified evangelicals, 29 percent; non-evangelicals, 33 percent
- Twitter—evangelicals by belief, 22 percent; self-identified evangelicals, 22 percent; non-evangelicals, 23 percent

- Evangelicals cite a higher willingness than non-evangelicals to engage with social or political issues on social media on a *daily basis* (24 percent to 15 percent). Over a third of evangelicals (38 percent) engage on social and political issues through social media at least several times a week.

Q: "How often do you engage others on social or political issues on social media?"

A: - Every day: 24 percent
   - Several times a week: 14 percent
   - Several times a month: 9 percent

Chapter 11: Neighborly Engagement

- 46 percent of those who have friendship(s) with an evangelical Christian describe evangelicals with one or more of these positive descriptors: compassionate, principled, charitable, and/or ethical.
- 14 percent of those with no friendships with evangelical Christians describe evangelicals with one or more of these same positive descriptors: compassionate, principled, charitable, and/or ethical.

See page 291 for the related question and a summary of the responses.

Which, if any, of the following traits describe evangelical Christians?

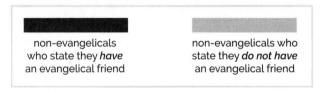

non-evangelicals
who state they *have*
an evangelical friend

non-evangelicals who
state they *do not have*
an evangelical friend

Negative Traits

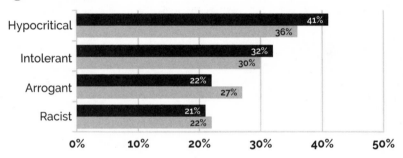

Hypocritical — 41% / 36%

Intolerant — 32% / 30%

Arrogant — 22% / 27%

Racist — 21% / 22%

0% 10% 20% 30% 40% 50%

Positive Traits

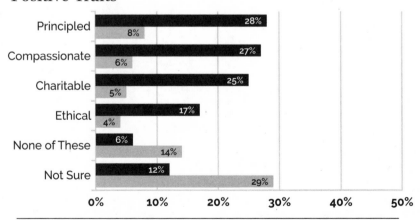

Principled — 28% / 8%

Compassionate — 27% / 6%

Charitable — 25% / 5%

Ethical — 17% / 4%

None of These — 6% / 14%

Not Sure — 12% / 29%

0% 10% 20% 30% 40% 50%

This research study was conducted in 2018 by the Billy Graham Center Institute, in partnership with LifeWay Research. The completed sample includes three thousand surveys, with a margin of error that does not exceed ± 3.2 percent for non-evangelicals; ± 3.1 percent for those with evangelical beliefs; and ± 2.4 percent for self-identified evangelicals.

Acknowledgments

I'M THANKFUL for the help from our team that helped make this book a reality. Andrew MacDonald was the key researcher and editor who made this all happen. The book would not exist without his tenacity, brilliance, and partnership. I am thankful also to others on my research team, including Josh Young, Selena Safiol, Jason Sampler, Bethany Faulds, and Desmond Henry.

Thanks to the team at Tyndale, particularly Jon Farrar and Kim Miller. Through their persistence in forcing me to strive for clarity and application, they helped shape the manuscript for the betterment of the church.

My agent, Mark Sweeney, actually suggested this topic and helped me focus on what matters most in its writing.

Thanks to the people of Moody Church, who heard parts of this book preached in sermons from Matthew about how to relate to a hostile world in the spirit of Jesus. Their encouragement and feedback were instrumental but not as important as watching the church faithfully live out this teaching throughout the week.

Thanks to my colleagues at the Billy Graham Center and Wheaton College who stepped into the gap while I worked on this book. That extra work fell to John Richards, Colleen Cooper, Laurie Nichols, Maureen Romero, and many others. I am blessed to serve alongside and lead a team of faithful Kingdom ambassadors who tirelessly show and share the love of Jesus to the lost.

Donna, my wife, and my three daughters were patient while I was up late far too many nights. My girls are growing up in a day when Christians no longer have the home field advantage. My hope is that this book and emphasis will serve them and other believers long after I am gone.

Finally, thank you to the Christians who faithfully and lovingly engage this outraged world every day. Some made it into the book as inspiring examples, but many others are simply and quietly living out the implications of the gospel in their homes, churches, and communities.

Notes

INTRODUCTION: WELCOME TO THE AGE OF OUTRAGE

1. This term was coined by Mark Godwin, an attorney and early Internet user, way back in 1990. Today it rings true more than ever.
2. Joshua Feuerstein, "Starbucks REMOVED CHRISTMAS," Facebook, November 5, 2015, https://www.facebook.com/joshua.feuerstein.5/videos/689569711145714/.
3. Alex Abad-Santos, "Starbucks's Red Cup Controversy, Explained," *Vox*, November 10, 2016, https://www.vox.com/2015/11/10/9707034/starbucks-red-cup-controversy.
4. Ibid.
5. Marc Hogan, "Coachella Co-Owner's Latest Charitable Filing Shows Deep Anti-LGBTQ Ties," *Pitchfork*, January 31, 2018, https://pitchfork.com/news/coachella-co-owners -latest-charitable-filing-shows-deep-anti-lgbtq-ties/.
6. Ibid.
7. Non-evangelicals included mainline, Catholic, and Orthodox Christians, as well as people of other faiths or no faith.
8. Todd Starnes, "Costco–The Bible Is Fiction," Fox News Opinion, November 18, 2013, http://www.foxnews.com/opinion/2013/11/18/costco-bible-is-fiction.html.
9. Ed Stetzer, "Another Day, Another Faux Christian Outrage: Costco's Fiction Bible," *The Exchange* (blog), *Christianity Today*, November 22, 2013, https://www .christianitytoday.com/edstetzer/2013/november/another-day-another-faux-christian -outrage-costcos-fiction-.html.
10. Ibid.

PART 1: WHY THE AGE OF OUTRAGE?

1. Jeff Hawkes, "Literacy Teacher Actually Employed by a Church," *U.S. News & World Report*, March 31, 2018, https://www.usnews.com/news/best-states/pennsylvania/articles /2018-03-31/literacy-teacher-actually-employed-by-a-church.
2. Ibid.

CHAPTER 1: OUTRAGE CAUSE #1: A CULTURAL FORKING

1. Frank Newport, "In the News: Billy Graham on 'Most Admired' List 61 Times," Gallup, February 21, 2018, http://news.gallup.com/poll/228089/news-billy-graham-admired -list-times.aspx.
2. BGC Pastor Entrepreneurial Evangelism Report, 33–36 (unpublished).

3. "America's Changing Religious Landscape," Pew Research Center, May 12, 2015, http://www.pewforum.org/2015/05/12/americas-changing-religious-landscape/.
4. Ibid.
5. The General Social Survey (GSS), which monitors societal change in the United States, was created and is conducted by the National Opinion Research Center at the University of Chicago.
6. Ed Stetzer, "Christianity Isn't Dying," *USA Today*, October 18, 2012, https://www.usatoday.com/story/opinion/2012/10/18/christianity-christians-pew-research/1642315/.
7. Ed Stetzer, "Nominal Christians Are Becoming More Secular, and That's Creating a Startling Change for the U.S.," *Washington Post*, November 4, 2015, https://www.washingtonpost.com/news/acts-of-faith/wp/2015/11/04/nominal-christians-becoming-more-secular-and-thats-creating-a-startling-change-for-the-u-s/?utm_term=.c4391ab3f390.
8. Lauren Markoe, "Pew Study: More Americans Reject Religion, but Believers Firm in Faith," Religion News Service, November 3, 2015, https://religionnews.com/2015/11/03/pew-americans-religion-believers-faith/.
9. Sarah Eekoff Zylstra, "Pew: Evangelicals Stay Strong as Christianity Crumbles in America," *Christianity Today*, May 11, 2015, http://www.christianitytoday.com/news/2015/may/pew-evangelicals-stay-strong-us-religious-landscape-study.html.
10. Not all people who self-identify as Christian hold genuine Christian beliefs, so this categorization is actually about self-identification and practices, not orthodoxy.
11. Harold R. Isaacs, *Idols of the Tribe: Group Identity and Political Change* (New York: Harper & Row, 1975).
12. Stephen D. Reicher et al., "Core Disgust Is Attenuated by Ingroup Relations," *Proceedings of the National Academy of Sciences* 13, no. 10 (March 8, 2016), 2631–35, http://www.pnas.org/content/113/10/2631.
13. "The Partisan Divide on Political Views Grows Even Wider," Pew Research Center, October 5, 2017, http://www.people-press.org/2017/10/05/the-partisan-divide-on-political-values-grows-even-wider/.
14. John Gramlich, "Far More Americans Say There Are Strong Conflicts between Partisans Than between Other Groups in Society," Pew Research Center, December 19, 2017, http://www.pewresearch.org/fact-tank/2017/12/19/far-more-americans-say-there-are-strong-conflicts-between-partisans-than-between-other-groups-in-society/.
15. Amy Chua, *Political Tribes: Group Instinct and the Fate of Nations* (New York: Penguin, 2018), 9.
16. Todd Spangler, "The Rust Belt Gave Trump Victory, Now They Want Jobs in Return," *Detroit Free Press*, January 18, 2017, https://www.usatoday.com/story/news/politics/2017/01/18/rust-belt-voters-donald-trump/96670922/.
17. "Changing Attitudes on Gay Marriage," Pew Research Center, June 26, 2017, http://www.pewforum.org/fact-sheet/changing-attitudes-on-gay-marriage/.
18. Clarence Page, "Why We Find Comfort in Our Tribes," *Chicago Tribune*, September 2, 2014, http://www.chicagotribune.com/news/opinion/page/ct-american-diversity-information-bubbles-page-ope-20140902-column.html.
19. Brian Uzzi, "Why Echo Chambers Are Becoming Louder–and More Polarizing," *Thrive Global*, May 10, 2017, https://medium.com/thrive-global.com/why-echo-chambers-are-becoming-louder-and-more-polarizing-44aba2a231e7.
20. Melody Green, *No Compromise: The Life Story of Keith Green* (Nashville: Thomas Nelson, 2008), 239.

21. Daniel Marans, "How Democrats Got Mired in a Nasty Internal Battle over Abortion," *HuffPost*, April 29, 2017, https://www.huffingtonpost.com/entry/bernie-sanders-heath -mello-abortion-debate_us_59036cd0e4b02655f83ce695; Ben Kamisar, "Women's Rights Groups Slam DNC for Event with Anti-Abortion Mayoral Candidate," *The Hill*, April 20, 2017, http://thehill.com/homenews/campaign/329753-womens-rights-groups -slams-dnc-for-event-with-anti-abortion-mayoral.

22. David Brooks, "The Abortion Memo," *New York Times*, February 1, 2018, https://www.nytimes.com/2018/02/01/opinion/abortion-democrats-compromise.html.

23. Thomas M. Nichols, *The Death of Expertise: The Campaign against Established Knowledge and Why It Matters* (New York: Oxford University Press, 2017), 5.

24. Mark A. Noll, *The Scandal of the Evangelical Mind* (Grand Rapids, MI: Eerdmans, 1994), 3.

25. "The World's 50 Greatest Leaders," *Fortune*, April 19, 2018, http://fortune.com/longform /worlds-greatest-leaders-2018/.

26. Tish Harrison Warren, "The Wrong Kind of Christian," *Christianity Today*, August 27, 2014, http://www.christianitytoday.com/ct/2014/september/wrong-kind-of-christian -vanderbilt-university.html.

27. Jeff Chu, "Princeton Seminarians Were Outraged over Tim Keller. Here's Keller's Point I Wanted My Peers to Hear," *Washington Post*, April 12, 2017, https://www.washingtonpost .com/news/acts-of-faith/wp/2017/04/12/princeton-seminarians-were-outraged -over-tim-keller-heres-kellers-point-i-wanted-my-peers-to-hear/?utm_term =.8a9703a5d975.

CHAPTER 2: OUTRAGE CAUSE #2: THE TECHNOLOGY DISCIPLESHIP GAP

1. Sarah Hulett, "High Lead Levels in Michigan Kids after City Switches Water Source," *NPR*, September 29, 2015, https://www.npr.org/2015/09/29/444497051/high-lead-levels -in-michigan-kids-after-city-switches-water-source; "Flint Water Crisis Fast Facts," CNN.com, April 8, 2018, https://www.cnn.com/2016/03/04/us/flint-water-crisis-fast -facts/index.html.

2. Ralph Vartabedian, "Pros and Cons of Getting Lead Out," *Los Angeles Times*, May 9, 1985.

3. Philip J. Landrigan, "The Worldwide Problem of Lead in Petrol," *Bulletin of the World Health Organization* 80, no. 10 (2002): 768, http://www.who.int/bulletin/archives /80(10)768.pdf.

4. Claudia Dreifus, "Why We Can't Look Away from Our Screens," *New York Times*, March 6, 2017, https://www.nytimes.com/2017/03/06/science/technology-addiction -irresistible-by-adam-alter.html.

5. Adam Alter, *Irresistible: The Rise of Addictive Technology and the Business of Keeping Us Hooked* (New York: Penguin, 2017), 3.

6. Jean M. Twenge et al., "Decreases in Psychological Well-Being among American Adolescents after 2012 and Links to Screen Time during the Rise of Smartphone Technology," *Emotion*, January 22, 2018, https://www.ncbi.nlm.nih.gov/pubmed /29355336.

7. Ibid.

8. Awr Hawkins, "Christian Speaker Beth Moore Stands in the Gap for Hillary Clinton," *Breitbart*, October 12, 2016, http://www.breitbart.com/big-government/2016/10/12 /christian-speaker-beth-moore-stands-gap-hillary-clinton/.

9. Beth Moore (@BethMooreLPM), Twitter, October 9, 2016, 7:07 a.m., https://twitter.com/bethmoorelpm/status/785119502769852418?lang=en.

10. Beth Moore (@BethMooreLPM), Twitter, October 9, 2016, 7:22 a.m., https://twitter.com/bethmoorelpm/status/785123300636667905?lang=en.

11. Beth Moore (@BethMooreLPM), Twitter, October 9, 2016, 7:34 a.m., https://twitter.com/bethmoorelpm/status/785126388776873985?lang=en.

12. Beth Moore (@BethMooreLPM), Twitter, October 9, 2016, 8:32 a.m., https://twitter.com/bethmoorelpm/status/785141013085949952?lang=en.

13. Jack Murtha, "What It's Like to Get Paid for Clicks," *Columbia Journalism Review*, July 13, 2015, https://www.cjr.org/analysis/the_mission_sounds_simple_pay.php.

14. John Suler, "The Online Disinhibition Effect," *CyberPsychology & Behavior* 7, no. 3 (June 2004): 321–26, https://www.ncbi.nlm.nih.gov/pubmed/15257832.

15. Ibid., 325.

16. *Collins Dictionary*, s.v. "fake news." See https://www.collinsdictionary.com/woty.

17. Jamie Ducharme, "U.S. Ambassador to Netherlands Apologizes after Bizarre 'Fake News' Exchange," *Time*, December 23, 2017, http://time.com/5078452/pete-hoekstra-fake-news/.

18. Kate Shellnutt, "Russia's Fake Facebook Ads Targeted Christians," *Christianity Today*, November 3, 2017, http://www.christianitytoday.com/news/2017/november/russia-fake-facebook-election-ads-targeted-christian-voters.html.

19. Ed Stetzer, "Some Christians Hate Joel Osteen More Than They Love the Truth. And That's Wrong," *Christianity Today*, August 29, 2017, http://www.christianitytoday.com/edstetzer/2017/august/some-people-hate-joel-osteen-more-than-they-love-truth-hous.html.

20. Ben Ward (@pixelatedboat), June 12, 2016, 1:07 a.m., https://twitter.com/pixelatedboat/status/741904787361300481.

21. After Ken Bone, who was wearing an unforgettable red sweater, was hailed for asking a question on energy policies during a townhall debate, he agreed to allow anyone to access his Reddit account. He was quickly skewered for some of his posts. Gary Alan Coe, aka Gary from Chicago, unknowingly joined a tour bus that received a private audience with many actors and actresses prior to the Academy Awards. His likable persona was tarnished when people discovered he'd been released from prison just a few days earlier after serving a twenty-year sentence. See Abby Ohlheiser, "Ken Bone Was a 'Hero.' Now Ken Bone Is 'Bad.' It Was His Destiny as a Human Meme," *Washington Post*, October 14, 2016, https://www.washingtonpost.com/news/the-intersect/wp/2016/10/14/ken-bone-was-a-hero-now-ken-bone-is-bad-it-was-his-destiny-as-a-human-meme/?utm_term=.0300994666ed; see also Christie D'Zurilla, "Oscars' 'Gary from Chicago' Finished a 20-Year Stint in Prison Just before Meeting Hollywood's A List," *Los Angeles Times*, February 28, 2017, http://www.latimes.com/entertainment/gossip/la-et-mg-oscars-gary-from-chicago-prison-20170228-htmlstory.html.

22. Eliott C. McLaughlin, "How Keaton Jones' Bullying Plea Brought Him More Bullying," CNN.com, December 13, 2017, https://www.cnn.com/2017/12/12/us/keaton-jones-bullying-video-reaction/index.html.

23. "All Roads Lead to Rome—Milliarium Aureum," CreatingHistory.com, http://www.creatinghistory.com/all-roads-lead-to-rome-milliarium-aureum/.

PART 2: OUTRAGEOUS LIES AND ENDURING TRUTHS

1. The e-mail has been edited slightly for readability.

NOTES

CHAPTER 3: LIE #1: "CHRISTIANS ARE THE WORST!"

1. Sarah Pulliam Bailey, "Study: Conservative Protestants' Divorce Rates Spread to Their Red State Neighbors," *Washington Post*, January 21, 2014, https://www.washingtonpost.com/national/religion/study-conservative-protestants-divorce-rates-spread-to-their-red-state-neighbors/2014/01/21/cfbd5534-82ef-11e3-a273-6ffd9cf9f4ba_story.html.
2. Jennifer Glass and Philip Levchak, "Red States, Blue States, and Divorce: Understanding the Impact of Conservative Protestantism on Regional Variation in Divorce Rates," *American Journal of Sociology* 119, no. 4 (January 2014): 1002–46, https://www.ncbi.nlm.nih.gov/pubmed/25032268.
3. Ibid.
4. Michelle Goldberg, "Is Conservative Christianity Bad for Marriage?" *The Nation*, July 22, 2014, https://www.thenation.com/article/conservative-christianity-bad-marriage/.
5. "Marriage Rates by State: 1990, 1995, and 1990–2016," CDC/NCHS, National Vital Statistics System, https://www.cdc.gov/nchs/data/dvs/state_marriage_rates_90_95_99-16.pdf.
6. C'Vera Cohn, "The States of Marriage and Divorce," Pew Research Center, October 15, 2009, http://www.pewresearch.org/2009/10/15/the-states-of-marriage-and-divorce/.
7. Charles E. Stokes, "Findings on Red and Blue Divorce Are Not Exactly Black and White," Institute for Family Studies, January 22, 2014, https://ifstudies.org/blog/findings-on-red-and-blue-divorce-are-not-exactly-black-and-white/.
8. Casey E. Copen et al, "First Marriages in the United States: Data from the 2006–2010 National Survey of Family Growth," *National Health Statistics Reports* 29 (March 22, 2012), https://www.cdc.gov/nchs/data/nhsr/nhsr049.pdf.
9. Ibid.
10. Bailey, "Study: Conservative Protestants' Divorce Rates Spread to Their Red State Neighbors."
11. Michael Lipka, "A Closer Look at America's Rapidly Growing Religious 'Nones,'" Pew Research Center, May 13, 2015, http://www.pewresearch.org/fact-tank/2015/05/13/a-closer-look-at-americas-rapidly-growing-religious-nones/.
12. "U.S. Public Becoming Less Religious," Pew Research Center, November 3, 2015, http://www.pewforum.org/2015/11/03/u-s-public-becoming-less-religious/.
13. Robert D. Putnam and David E. Campbell, *American Grace: How Religion Divides and Unites Us* (New York: Simon & Schuster, 2010), 124–26.
14. Ed Stetzer, "Defining Evangelicals in Research," *National Association of Evangelicals*, Winter 2017/18, https://www.nae.net/defining-evangelicals-research/.
15. Gregory A. Smith and Jessica Martínez, "How the Faithful Voted: A Preliminary 2016 Analysis," Fact Tank, Pew Research Center, November 9, 2016, http://www.pewresearch.org/fact-tank/2016/11/09/how-the-faithful-voted-a-preliminary-2016-analysis/.
16. Rebecca Savransky, "Poll: 37 Percent of Alabama Evangelicals More Likely to Vote for Moore after Allegations," *The Hill*, November 12, 2017, http://thehill.com/homenews/senate/360010-poll-37-percent-of-alabama-evangelicals-more-likely-to-vote-for-moore-after.
17. Bob Smietana, "Many Who Call Themselves Evangelical Don't Actually Hold Evangelical Beliefs," LifeWay Research, December 6, 2017, http://lifewayresearch.com/2017/12/06/many-evangelicals-dont-hold-evangelical-beliefs/.
18. Thomas S. Kidd, "Roy Moore and the Confused Identity of Today's 'Evangelical' Voter," *Vox*, December 13, 2017, https://www.vox.com/first-person/2017/11/22/16686614/roy-moore-evangelical-voter.

19. Bradley R. E. Wright, *Christians Are Hate-Filled Hypocrites . . . and Other Lies You've Been Told* (Bloomington, MN: Bethany House, 2010), 133.
20. Ibid.
21. Ibid., 136.
22. Ibid.
23. Jonathan Edwards, *The Sermons of Jonathan Edwards: A Reader*, ed. Wilson H. Kimnach, Kenneth P. Minkema, and Douglas A. Sweeney (New Haven, CT: Yale University Press, 1999), 92.
24. Ross Douthat, "The Christian Penumbra," *New York Times*, March 29, 2014, https://www.nytimes.com/2014/03/30/opinion/sunday/douthat-the-christian-penumbra.html.
25. John Stott, *The Living Church: Convictions of the Lifelong Pastor* (Downers Grove, IL: InterVarsity Press, 2007), 19.
26. Antony Flew, *How to Think Straight: An Introduction to Critical Reasoning*, 2nd ed. (Amherst, NY: Prometheus Books, 1998), 49.

CHAPTER 4: LIE #2: "MY OUTRAGE IS RIGHTEOUS ANGER"

1. J. I. Packer, *Knowing God*, 2nd ed. (London: Hodder & Stoughton, 1993), 168.
2. John Murray, *Epistle to the Romans* (Grand Rapids: Eerdmans, 1997), 35.
3. Reportedly declared on May 31, 1911, at the launch of the *Titanic*, https://www.archives.gov/exhibits/american_originals/titanic.html.
4. See Matthew 5:17.
5. See Matthew 5:21-48. Verse 31 actually reads, "It was also said . . . But I say to you . . ."
6. Jonathan T. Pennington, *The Sermon on the Mount and Human Flourishing: A Theological Commentary* (Grand Rapids, MI: Baker Academic, 2017), 183.
7. See for instance Daniel Kahneman's *Thinking, Fast and Slow* (New York: Farrar, Straus, and Giroux, 2011) or Alan Jacobs's *How to Think* (New York: Currency, 2017) as recent popular examples.
8. Evan Low and Barry H. Corey, "We First Battled over LGBT and Religious Rights. Here's How We Became Unlikely Friends," *Washington Post*, March 3, 2017, https://www.washingtonpost.com/news/acts-of-faith/wp/2017/03/03/we-first-battled-over-lgbt-and-religious-rights-heres-how-we-became-unlikely-friends/?utm_term=.7652fd0142a7.

CHAPTER 5: LIE #3: "_____ WILL SAVE ME FROM THE OUTRAGE!"

1. Cornelius Plantinga Jr., *Not the Way It's Supposed to Be* (Grand Rapids, MI: Eerdmans, 1995), 10.
2. Ibid., 14.
3. John Calvin, *Institutes of the Christian Religion* I.11.8, Christian Classics Ethereal Library, https://www.ccel.org/ccel/calvin/institutes.iii.xii.html.
4. Tim Keller, *Counterfeit Gods: The Empty Promises of Money, Sex, and Power, and the Only Hope That Matters* (New York: Penguin, 2009), 98–99.
5. Ed Stetzer, "On Christians Unable to Critique President Trump: Loyalty and the Rorschach Test," *Christianity Today*, August 14, 2017, http://www.christianitytoday.com/edstetzer/2017/august/exposing-loyalty-rorschach-test-of-charlottesville-for-evan.html.
6. Marguerite Michaels, "Billy Graham: America Is Not God's Only Kingdom," *Parade* magazine, February 1, 1981.
7. Benjamin Watson, *Under Our Skin: Getting Real about Race. Getting Free from the Fears and Frustrations That Divide Us* (Carol Stream, IL: Tyndale House, 2016), 145–48.

8. Philippians 3:8; see also 2 Corinthians 4:7.
9. Augustine, *The Confessions of St. Augustine, Modern English Version* (Grand Rapids, MI: Baker, 2005), 16–17.
10. Gal Tziperman Lotan, "FBI Expert on Noor Salman: 'I Realized . . . that She Knew' about Pulse Attack,'" *Orlando Sentinel*, May 1, 2018, http://www.orlandosentinel.com /news/pulse-orlando-nightclub-shooting/os-noor-salman-evidence-motion-hearing -20171221-story.html.
11. "As Orlando Mass Shooting Unfolded, Son Texted Mom: 'I'm Gonna Die,'" *CBS News*, June 12, 2016, https://www.cbsnews.com/news/as-orlando-mass-shooting-unfolded -son-texted-mother-im-gonna-die/.
12. Ross Douthat, "The Terms of Our Surrender," *New York Times*, March 1, 2014, https:// www.nytimes.com/2014/03/02/opinion/sunday/the-terms-of-our-surrender.html.
13. Plantinga, *Not the Way It's Supposed to Be*, 199.

CHAPTER 6: LIE #4: MISSION IS OPTIONAL

1. Ed Stetzer, "The State of Evangelism," *The Exchange* (blog), *Christianity Today*, May 12, 2014, http://www.christianitytoday.com/edstetzer/2014/may/state-of-evangelism.html.
2. N. T. Wright, *Surprised by Hope: Rethinking Heaven, the Resurrection, and the Mission of the Church* (New York: HarperCollins, 2008), 30.
3. Charles H. Spurgeon, Sermon #472: "Believers–Lights in the World," (sermon, Metropolitan Tabernacle, Newington, London, September 28, 1862), http://www .spurgeongems.org/vols7-9/chs472.pdf.
4. John Stott, *For the Lord We Love: Your Study Guide to the Lausanne Covenant* (n.p.: The Didasko Files, 2009).
5. Graham Hill, *Salt, Light, and a City* (Eugene, OR: Wipf & Stock, 2012), 6.
6. Ed Stetzer, "Kaepernick, Speech, and a Job: The Cleat May Soon Be on the Other Foot," *The Exchange* (blog), *Christianity Today*, September 24, 2017, http://www .christianitytoday.com/edstetzer/2017/september/kaepernick-speech-job.html.
7. Ed Stetzer, "Why Can't We Disagree Well? Reflections on Colin Kaepernick, VP Mike Pence, and Listening Well," *The Exchange* (blog), *Christianity Today*, October 10, 2017, http://www.christianitytoday.com/edstetzer/2017/october/kaepernick-protest -pence.html.
8. John C. Richards Jr., "The Helpful History of Minority Demonstrations," *The Exchange* (blog), *Christianity Today*, September 26, 2017, http://www.christianitytoday.com /edstetzer/2017/september/helpful-history-of-minority-demonstrations.html.
9. Michael Hamkin Lee, "Understanding Worldview and the Flag," *The Exchange*, October 3, 2017, http://www.christianitytoday.com/edstetzer/2017/september /understanding-worldview-and-flag.html.
10. Rod Dreher, *The Benedict Option* (New York: Sentinel, 2017), 12.
11. Responding to critics who said he seemed to suggest that Christians should isolate themselves from the world, Dreher wrote, "The Benedictines of the Cluny monastery ended up having a lot to do with the Christianization of Europe because they first built their monastery and nurtured the internal spiritual lives of its monks, and sent them out across Europe to spread the faith by establishing other monasteries" (Rod Dreher, "Critics of the Benedict Option," *The American Conservative*, July 8, 2015). Yet to avoid confusing my point with Dreher's, I make the contrast using Columba because Columba is known for his external-facing mission and Benedict for his internal-facing "rule." (It was called the "Rule of Saint Benedict," a way of preserving the faith.) Put

another way (and too simply), when you Google Columba, you get mission; when you Google Benedict, you get preservation.

12. Ian Bradley, *Columba: Pilgrim and Penitent* (Glasgow: Wild Goose Publications, 1998), 28.

13. Ibid., 29–35.

14. Alexander Ewing, *The Cathedral or Abbey Church of Iona, and the Early Celtic Church and Mission of St. Columba* (Edinburgh: R. Grant & Son, 1872), 10.

15. E. M. Bounds, *E. M. Bounds on Prayer* (Peabody, MA: Hendrickson, 2006), 103.

16. *Sun-Times* Staff, "Illinois '200 for 200': Every Nomination from Our Panel of Experts," *Chicago Sun-Times*, December 1, 2017, https://chicago.suntimes.com/illinois-200 /illinois-bicentennial-history-200-every-nomination-from-our-panel-of-experts-lincoln -obama/.

17. It was commonplace in the eighteenth and nineteenth centuries for churches to charge a yearly fee to rent or own a pew seat. One of the reasons Free Methodists broke away from the Methodist Episcopal Church in 1860 was over doctrine, but in their breakaway, they made sure their pews were never available for rent or purchase, precisely so the poor could have the same access to gospel preaching that the financially affluent had.

18. Lyle W. Dorsett, *A Passion for Souls: The Life of D. L. Moody* (Chicago: Moody, 2003), 398.

19. David W. Bebbington, *The Dominance of Evangelicalism: The Age of Spurgeon and Moody* (Downers Grove, IL: InterVarsity, 2005), 47.

20. Associated Press, "Quotes from the Life of the Late Hugh Hefner," *Chicago Tribune*, September 28, 2017, http://www.chicagotribune.com/news/sns-bc-us--hugh-hefner -quotebox-20170928-story.html.

21. David French, "Hugh Hefner's Legacy of Despair," *National Review*, September 28, 2017, https://www.nationalreview.com/2017/09/hugh-hefner-playboy-legacy-despair -pornography-marriage-family/.

22. Kevin Ezell, "Every Church on a Mission: The North American Mission Board in the Twenty-First Century" in *The SBC and the 21st Century: Reflection, Renewal, and Recommitment*, ed. Jason K. Allen (Nashville: B&H Publishing, 2016), 183–84.

23. Quoted in: L. B. Cowman, *Streams in the Desert*, ed. James Reimann (Grand Rapids, MI: Zondervan, 1997), 437.

24. Ezell, "Every Church on Mission," 185. Italics in the original.

CHAPTER 7: A WORLDVIEW SHAPED BY THE GOSPEL

1. William Paul McKay and Ken Abraham, *Billy: The Untold Story of a Young Billy Graham and the Test of Faith That Almost Changed Everything* (Nashville: Thomas Nelson, 2008), 257.

2. William Martin, *A Prophet with Honor: The Billy Graham Story* (Grand Rapids, MI: Zondervan, 1991), 113.

3. Billy Graham, *Just As I Am* (New York: HarperCollins, 1997), 139.

4. Ibid., italics in the original.

5. Sage Lazzaro, "'The Dress' Is 1 Year Old Today—You Won't Believe the Impact It's Had on Science," *Observer*, February 25, 2016, http://observer.com/2016/02/the-dress-is -1-year-old-today-you-wont-believe-the-impact-its-had-on-science/.

6. N. T. Wright, *Jesus and the Victory of God: Christian Origins and the Question of God*, vol. 2 (Minneapolis: Fortress Press, 1996), 138.

7. Charles Colson, *How Now Shall We Live?* (Carol Stream, IL: Tyndale House, 1999), 14.

8. Philip Graham Ryken, *Christian Worldview: A Student's Guide* (Wheaton, IL: Crossway, 2013), 18. Italics in the original.

9. Quoted by Jordan Ballor in "Bavinck on Good, Enduring Reformation," *The Calvinist International*, October 31, 2013, https://calvinistinternational.com/2013/10/31/bavinck-good-enduring-reformation/.

10. Emil Steiner, "Binge-Watching in Practice: The Rituals, Motives and Feelings of Streaming Video Viewers" in *The Age of Netflix*, ed. Cory Barker and Myc Wiatrowski (Jefferson, NC: McFarland & Co., 2017), 147.

11. Alice G. Walton, "Binge-Watching TV Is Linked to Poorer Sleep and Insomnia," *Forbes*, August 18, 2017, https://www.forbes.com/sites/alicegwalton/2017/08/18/binge-watching-tv-linked-to-poorer-sleep-quality-and-insomnia/#72c945625ee0.

12. "Social Media Fact Sheet," Pew Research Center, February 5, 2018, http://www.pewinternet.org/fact-sheet/social-media/.

13. Sean Casey, "2016 Nielsen Social Media Report," Nielsen, January 17, 2017, http://www.nielsen.com/us/en/insights/reports/2017/2016-nielsen-social-media-report.html.

14. Eugene Peterson, *A Long Obedience in the Same Direction: Discipleship in an Instant Society* (Downers Grove, IL: InterVarsity Press, 1980).

15. Philip Nation, *Habits for Our Holiness: How the Spiritual Disciplines Grow Us Up, Draw Us Together, and Send Us Out* (Chicago: Moody Publishers, 2016), 13, italics in the original.

16. James K. A. Smith, *You Are What You Love: The Spiritual Power of Habit* (Grand Rapids: Brazos Press, 2016), 19. Italics in the original.

17. Walter Brueggemann, *A Commentary on Jeremiah: Exile and Homecoming* (Grand Rapids: Eerdmans, 2003), 73.

18. Ed Stetzer, "The Epidemic of Bible Illiteracy in Our Churches," *The Exchange* (blog), *Christianity Today*, July 6, 2015, http://www.christianitytoday.com/edstetzer/2015/july/epidemic-of-bible-illiteracy-in-our-churches.html.

19. Bob Smietana, "Young Bible Readers More Likely to Be Faithful Adults, Study Finds," LifeWay Research, October 17, 2017, https://lifewayresearch.com/2017/10/17/young-bible-readers-more-likely-to-be-faithful-adults-study-finds/.

20. The quotes from this passage are taken from the New Living Translation.

21. "American Protestants Deviate from Biblical Discipleship Standards," LifeWay Research, May 29, 2009, http://lifewayresearch.com/2009/05/28/american-protestants-deviate-from-biblical-discipleship-standards/.

22. Philip Schaff, *History of the Christian Church: Vol. 1, Apostolic Christianity* (New York: Charles Scribner's Sons, 1910), 5.

23. Ibid., vii.

CHAPTER 8: KINGDOM AMBASSADORS IN A FOREIGN LAND

1. Bob Allen, "Grand Ole Opry Moving to Baptist Church," *Word & Way*, 2010 Archives, https://wordandway.org/item/1290-grand-ole-opry-moving-to-baptist-church.

2. Martyn Percy, *Power and the Church: Ecclesiology in an Age of Transition* (London: Cassell, 1998), 47.

3. Anthony Bash, *Ambassadors for Christ: An Exploration of Ambassadorial Language in the New Testament* (Tübingen, Germany: Mohr Siebeck, 1997), 4.

4. David J. Bosch, *Transforming Mission: Paradigm Shifts in Theology of Mission* (New York: Orbis, 1991, 2002), 390.

5. Brian Warth, e-mail interview with author, May 5, 2018.

6. Ibid.

7. Blaise Pascal, *Pensées* (New York: Penguin Group, 1995), 45.

8. Kevin McSpadden, "You Now Have a Shorter Attention Span than a Goldfish," *Time*, May 14, 2015, http://time.com/3858309/attention-spans-goldfish/.

9. Ibid.

10. *Ennui* is the "feeling of listlessness and dissatisfaction arising from a lack of occupation or excitement" (https://en.oxforddictionaries.com/definition/us/ennui).

11. Arthur Schopenhauer, *The World as Will and Representation*; vol. I, trans. E. F. J. Payne (New York: Dover Publications, 1969), 260.

12. Melissa Healy, "British Government Targets a Modern Public Health Scourge: Loneliness," *Los Angeles Times*, January 17, 2018, http://www.latimes.com/science /sciencenow/la-sci-sn-minister-of-loneliness-20180118-story.html.

13. John T. Cacioppo and William Patrick, *Loneliness: Human Nature and the Need for Social Connection* (New York: W. W. Norton & Co., 2008), 7.

14. David Brooks, "Building Better Secularists," *New York Times*, February 3, 2015, https:// www.nytimes.com/2015/02/03/opinion/david-brooks-building-better-secularists.html.

15. Jennifer Taw and John Peters, *Operations Other than War* (Santa Monica, CA: RAND, 1995), 22.

16. Steve Beirn and George W. Murray, *Well Sent: Reimagining the Church's Missionary- Sending Process* (Fort Washington, PA: CLC Publications, 2015), 63–67.

17. See the Billy Graham Center's web page at https://www.wheaton.edu/academics /academic-centers/billy-graham-center/.

18. "Study: Churchgoers Believe in Sharing Faith, Most Never Do," LifeWay Research, January 2, 2014, https://lifewayresearch.com/2014/01/02/study-churchgoers-believe -in-sharing-faith-most-never-do/; Joe Carter, "Study: Most Churchgoers Never Share the Gospel," *Gospel Coalition*, August 30, 2012, https://www.thegospelcoalition.org /article/study-most-churchgoers-never-share-the-gospel/.

19. Melissa Steffan, "Majority of Churchgoers Never Share Their Faith, LifeWay Study Shows," *Christianity Today*, August 15, 2012, https://www.christianitytoday.com /news/2012/august/majority-of-churchgoers-never-share-their-faith-lifeway.html; Joe Carter, "Study: Most Churchgoers Never Share the Gospel."

20. Ibid.

21. Jonathan Edwards, *The Works of Jonathan Edwards*, vol. II-1, ed. Edward Hickman (London: William Ball, 1840), 75.

22. Bob Smietana, "New Research: Americans Pray for Friends, Family but Rarely for Celebrities or Sports Teams," LifeWay Newsroom, October 1, 2014, https://blog.lifeway .com/newsroom/2014/10/01/new-research-americans-pray-for-friends-family-but -rarely-for-celebrities-or-sports-teams/.

23. Ibid.

24. Ibid.

25. Brian Warth, e-mail interview with author, May 5, 2018.

CHAPTER 9: WINSOME LOVE

1. John Lennon and Paul McCartney, "All You Need Is Love," © 1967 by Sony.

2. Augustine, *Confessions*, 2.2.

3. Cathy Lynn Grossman, "Survey: Non-Attendees Find Faith outside Church," *USA Today*, January 9, 2008, https://usatoday30.usatoday.com/news/religion/2008-01-09 -unchurched-survey_N.htm.

4. Jonathan Pennington, *The Sermon on the Mount and Human Flourishing: A Theological Commentary* (Grand Rapids, MI: Baker Academic, 2017), 79.

5. Roy and Revel Hession, *We Would See Jesus* (Fort Washington, PA: CLC Publications, 1958, 2017), chapter 2.

6. Martha C. Nussbaum, *From Disgust to Humanity: Sexual Orientation and Constitutional Law* (New York: Oxford University Press, 2010), xii.

7. Colin McGinn, *The Meaning of Disgust* (New York: Oxford University Press, 2011), 6–7.

8. Richard Allen, *The Life, Experience, and Gospel Labours of the Rt. Rev. Richard Allen* (Philadelphia: F. Ford and M. A. Ripley, 1880), 47–48.

9. Ibid., 53.

10. Carl F. H. Henry, *The Uneasy Conscience of Modern Fundamentalism* (Grand Rapids, MI: Eerdmans, 1947), 1.

11. Ibid., 39.

12. The Carter-Reagan debate was held on October 28, 1980, in Cleveland; Reagan brought up the "age issue" in his debate with Mondale on October 21, 1984, in Kansas City.

13. Shane L. Windmeyer, "Dan and Me: My Coming Out as a Friend of Dan Cathy and Chick-fil-A," *Huffington Post*, January 28, 2013, https://www.huffingtonpost.com /shane-l-windmeyer/dan-cathy-chick-fil-a_b_2564379.html.

14. Ibid.

15. John Chrysostom, *The Homilies of St. John Chrysostom, Archbishop of Constantinople, on the First Epistle of St. Paul the Apostle*.

16. James Calvin Davis, *Forbearance: A Theological Ethic for a Disagreeable Church* (Grand Rapids, MI: Eerdmans, 2017), 10.

17. Ed Stetzer, "Saved from Hate: An Interview with Mark Phelps, Son of Westboro Founder Fred Phelps Sr.," *The Exchange* (blog), *Christianity Today*, April 16, 2014, https://www .christianitytoday.com/edstetzer/2014/april/my-interview-with-mark-phelps-son-of -former-westboro-leader.html.

18. Christopher J. H. Wright, *The Mission of God: Unlocking the Bible's Grand Narrative* (Downers Grove, IL: InterVarsity Press, 2006), 423.

19. Christine Caine, *Undaunted: Daring to Do What God Calls You to Do* (Grand Rapids, MI: Zondervan, 2012), 53.

20. Robin Demattia, "Pastor Dave Gipson Sips Coffee, Talks Religion," *Naples Daily News*, October 29, 2014, http://archive.naplesnews.com/lifestyle/faith/pastor-dave-gipson -sips-coffee-talks-religion-ep-648584674-336360411.html.

21. *Calvin: Institutes of the Christian Religion*, ed. John T. McNeill, trans. Ford Lewis Battles, 2 vols. (Louisville, KY: Westminster John Knox Press, 1960), 696, emphasis added.

22. Jonathan Edwards, *Charity and Its Fruits: Living in the Light of God's Love*, ed. Kyle Strobel (Wheaton, IL: Crossway, 2012), 241.

23. Justin Martyr, *Dialogue with Trypho*, trans. Thomas B. Falls, rev. Thomas P. Halton (Washington, DC: Catholic University of America Press, 2003), 128.

24. Stephen Plant, *Bonhoeffer* (London: Continuum, 2004), 88.

25. Dietrich Bonhoeffer, *Ethics*, trans. Reinhard Krauss, Charles C. West, and Douglas W. Stott (Minneapolis: Fortress Press, 2015), 176.

26. Ray S. Anderson, *Theological Foundations for Ministry: Selected Readings for a Theology of the Church in Ministry* (Edinburgh: T&T Clark, 1979), 539.

27. Jeffrey M. Jones, "Americans Divided on Whether King's Dream Has Been Realized," Gallup, August 26, 2011, http://news.gallup.com/poll/149201/americans-divided -whether-king-dream-realized.aspx.

28. Ezekiel 3:17-20.

29. Dietrich Bonhoeffer, *Letters and Papers from Prison* (Minneapolis: Fortress, 2015), 19–20.

CHAPTER 10: ONLINE ACTIVITY ALIGNED WITH GOSPEL MISSION

1. Martin E. Marty, *The Protestant Voice in American Pluralism* (Athens, GA: University of Georgia, 2004), 32. Marty is paraphrasing his friend Alan Jones, dean emeritus of Grace Cathedral in San Francisco.

2. Carla Herreria, "'SNL' Introduces 'Thank You Scott' Anthem for Lazy Armchair Advocates," *Huffington Post*, April 9, 2017, https://www.huffingtonpost.com/entry /snl-thank-you-scott_us_58e9c42be4b05413bfe37e16.

3. John Chrysostom, "Homily 12 on the Acts of the Apostles," *Nicene and Post-Nicene Fathers, First Series*, vol 11, ed. Philip Schaff, trans. J. Walker, J. Sheppard, and H. Browne (Buffalo, NY: Christian Literature Publishing Co., 1889), http://www.newadvent.org /fathers/210112.htm.

4. D. A. Carson, "Editorial: On Abusing Matthew 18," in *Themelios* 36, vol. 1 (May 2011): 4–6, http://themelios.thegospelcoalition.org/article/editorial-on-abusing-matthew-18.

5. Genesis 11:1-9.

6. Sherry Turkle, *Alone Together: Why We Expect More from Technology and Less from Each Other* (New York: Basic Books, 2011), 235.

7. Allison Klein, "A Sexist Troll Attacked Sarah Silverman. She Responded by Helping Him with His Problems," *Washington Post*, January 8, 2018, https://www.washingtonpost .com/news/inspired-life/wp/2018/01/08/a-man-trolled-sarah-silverman-on-twitter-she -ended-up-helping-him-with-his-medical-problems/?utm_term=.b7b4024ea1b8.

8. Kenny Rogers, "The Gambler," written by Don Schlitz, United Artists, 1978.

9. "Social Media Update 2014," Pew Research Center, January 9, 2015, http://www .pewinternet.org/files/2015/01/PI_SocialMediaUpdate20144.pdf.

10. Ed Stetzer, "Why Your Church Should Be on Social Media Right Now," *The Exchange* (blog), *Christianity Today*, February 10, 2015, http://www.christianitytoday.com /edstetzer/2015/february/why-your-church-should-be-on-social-media.html.

11. See http://www.dolekemp96.org/main.htm, accessed April 24, 2018.

CHAPTER 11: NEIGHBORLY ENGAGEMENT

1. Fred Rogers, *Dear Mr. Rogers, Does It Ever Rain in Your Neighborhood?: Letters to Mr. Rogers* (New York: Penguin, 1996), xi.

2. Jeanne Marie Laskas, "What Is Essential Is Invisible to the Eye," in *Mister Rogers' Neighborhood: Children, Television, and Fred Rogers*, ed. Mark Collins and Margaret Mary Kimmel (Pittsburgh: University of Pittsburgh Press, 1996), 16.

3. Adapted from Ed Stetzer, "Engaging an Ever-Changing Culture with a Never-Changing Gospel," *The Exchange* (blog), *Christianity Today*, August 1, 2014, http://www.christianitytoday.com/edstetzer/2014/june/avoiding-church-culture -pendulum-swings-engaging-ever-chang.html.

4. Michael Herbst, "Witnessing to Christ in a Secular Culture," Lausanne Movement, 2010, https://www.lausanne.org/content/witnessing-to-christ-in-a-secular-culture.

5. Tim Suttle, "Lesslie Newbigin (1909–1998): A Missional Life" *Patheos*, November 28, 2015, http://www.patheos.com/blogs/paperbacktheology/2015/11/lesslie-newbigin -1909-1998-a-missional-life.html.

6. Lesslie Newbigin, *The Gospel in a Pluralist Society* (Grand Rapids, MI: Eerdmans, 1989), 227.

7. Ibid., 232–33.

8. *Lesslie Newbigin: Missionary Theologian: A Reader*, comp. Paul Weston (Grand Rapids, MI: Eerdmans, 2006), 154.

9. A clip of this scene can be watched here: https://www.youtube.com/watch?v =A75AgrH5eqc.

10. Joshua Harris, *I Kissed Dating Goodbye* (Sisters, OR: Multnomah, 2003), 71.

11. Joshua Harris, "Revisiting I Kissed Dating Goodbye," https://joshharris. com/kissed-dating-goodbye/.

12. Ruth Graham, "Hello Goodbye," *Slate*, August 23, 2016, http://www.slate.com/articles /life/faithbased/2016/08/i_kissed_dating_goodbye_author_is_maybe_kind_of_sorry.html.

13. Mark Berman, "'I Forgive You.' Relatives of Charleston Church Shooting Victims Address Dylann Roof," *Washington Post*, June 19, 2015, https://www.washingtonpost .com/news/post-nation/wp/2015/06/19/i-forgive-you-relatives-of-charleston-church -victims-address-dylann-roof/.

14. Bertram Rantin, "Victims' Families Offer Forgiveness, Not Condemnation, to Suspect in Charleston Church Murders," *The State*, June 19, 2015, http://www.thestate.com /news/local/crime/article25033732.html.

15. Nicholas Kristof, "A Little Respect for Dr. Foster," *New York Times*, March 28, 2015, https://www.nytimes.com/2015/03/29/opinion/sunday/nicholas-kristof-a-little-respect -for-dr-foster.html.

16. Ibid.

17. Wilmer C. Wright, trans., *Julian*, vol. 3 (Cambridge, MA: Harvard University Press, 1923).

18. Pam A. Mueller and Daniel M. Oppenheimer, "The Pen Is Mightier Than the Keyboard: Advantages of Longhand over Laptop Note Taking," *Psychological Science* 25, no. 6 (June 2014), 1159–68, https://cpb-us-west-2-juc1ugur1qwqqqo4.stackpathdns.com /sites.udel.edu/dist/6/132/files/2010/11/Psychological-Science-2014-Mueller -0956797614524581-1u0h0yu.pdf.

19. See https://www.lilysplace.org/about/.

About the Author

ED STETZER, PHD, holds the Billy Graham Distinguished Chair for Church, Mission, and Evangelism at Wheaton College, where he is dean of the School of Ministry, Mission, and Leadership. He also serves as the executive director of the Billy Graham Center at Wheaton. Stetzer is a prolific author and a well-known conference speaker. He has planted, revitalized, and pastored churches; has trained pastors and church planters on six continents; holds two master's degrees and two doctorates; and has written or cowritten more than a dozen books and hundreds of articles.

Stetzer is a contributing editor for *Christianity Today* and a columnist for *Outreach* magazine. He is frequently interviewed for or cited in news outlets such as *USA Today* and CNN. He is also the general editor of The Gospel Project, a Bible study curriculum used by more than one million people each week.

Stetzer cohosts *BreakPoint This Week*, a radio broadcast that airs on more than four hundred media outlets.

He serves as the interim teaching pastor at The Moody Church in Chicago.

Stetzer lives in Wheaton, Illinois, with his wife, Donna, and their three daughters.